In Between

In Between

Memoir of an Integration Baby

Mark Morrison-Reed

SKINNER HOUSE BOOKS
BOSTON

Printed in the United States

Text design by Suzanne Morgan
Cover design by Kathryn Sky-Peck
Author photo by Yvonne Charneskey

ISBN 1-55896-541-6
978-1-55896-541-6

8 7 6 5
13 12 11 10

Library of Congress Cataloging-in-Publication Data

Morrison-Reed, Mark D., 1949-
    In between : memoir of an integration baby / Mark Morrison-Reed.
        p. cm.
    ISBN-13: 978-1-55896-541-6 (pbk. : alk. paper)
    ISBN-10: 1-55896-541-6 (pbk. : alk. paper) 1. Morrison-Reed, Mark D., 1949- 2. African American Unitarian Universalists—Biography. 3. Unitarian Universalist Association—Clergy—Biography. I. Title.
    BX9869.M68A3 2008
    289.1092—dc22
    [B]
                                                            2008018557

"Dear Lovely Death," from *The Collected Poems of Langston Hughes* by Langston Hughes, edited by Arnold Rampersad with David Roessel, associate editor, copyright © 1995 by The Estate of Langston Hughes. Used by permission of Alfred A. Knopf, a division of Random House, Inc.

Yvonne Seon, "Transcending Boundaries," *Been in the Storm So Long*, reprinted with permission of the author.

Kathy Fuson Hurt, untitled poem, *Quest*, reprinted with permission of the author.

To Philip, Carole, Lauren and
all my other sisters and brothers

Contents

Mother's Ancestors

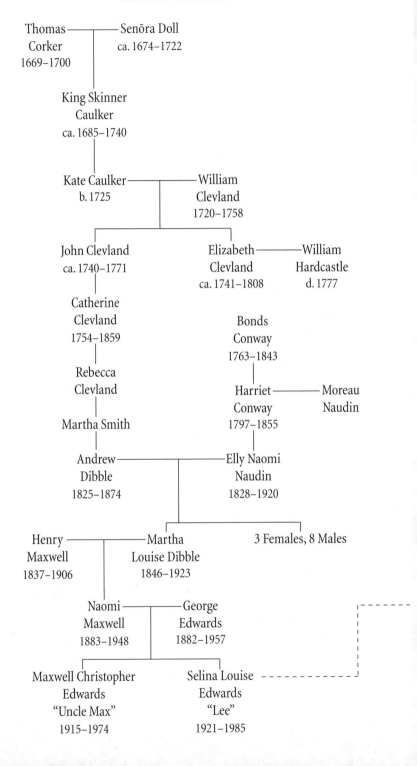

Father's Ancestors

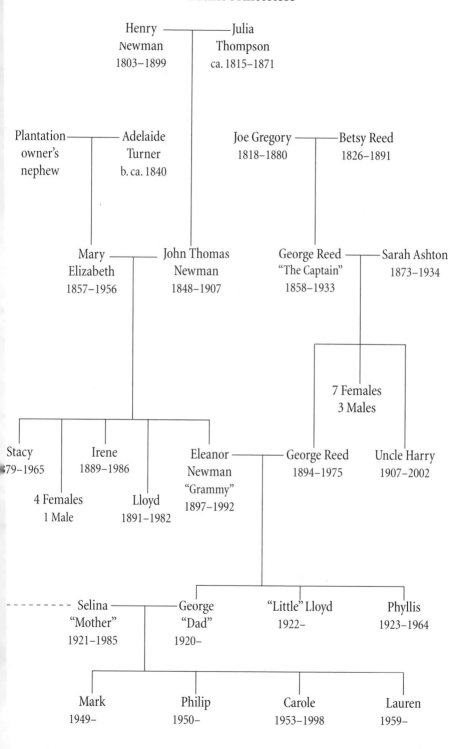

Henry Newman 1803–1899 —— Julia Thompson ca. 1815–1871

Plantation owner's nephew —— Adelaide Turner b. ca. 1840

Joe Gregory 1818–1880 —— Betsy Reed 1826–1891

Mary Elizabeth 1857–1956 —— John Thomas Newman 1848–1907

George Reed "The Captain" 1858–1933 —— Sarah Ashton 1873–1934

7 Females
3 Males

Stacy 1879–1965

4 Females
1 Male

Irene 1889–1986

Lloyd 1891–1982

Eleanor Newman "Grammy" 1897–1992 —— George Reed 1894–1975

Uncle Harry 1907–2002

Selina "Mother" 1921–1985 —— George "Dad" 1920–

"Little" Lloyd 1922–

Phyllis 1923–1964

Mark 1949–

Philip 1950–

Carole 1953–1998

Lauren 1959–

Note to Reader

I use the terms *Negro, colored people, nigger,* and *black* in order to reflect the language of a particular time and context. Otherwise, I use *Afro-American* instead of the current parlance, *African American.* The former term refers to those whose roots in the United States go back to slavery and differentiates them from those who are more recent immigrants of African ancestry.

Additional notes of interest can be found on pages 263–270.

Foreword

Mark Morrison-Reed has been a pioneer of sorts throughout his career—one of the few black ministers in liberal faith traditions that are overwhelmingly "white." I am delighted that he has been willing to share his story because I know how important his presence has been to many ministers of color who came into the ministry after him, myself included. And although I am the first African-American president of the Unitarian Universalist Association, there are many who thought that honor should have been his.

Mark's memoir is at once a personal tale and an analysis of the ways race plays out in our lives and distorts our very perceptions. Despite the attractive fantasy that our world is "color blind," race is always a part of the experience of persons of color. While white persons can forget racial categories and their place in them, people of color attempt to do this at our peril.

Perhaps racial categories in the United States are beginning, just beginning, to blur and their power lessen. That is a "glass is half full" hope. The realities of racial and religious pluralism, interracial marriage, and transracial adoption must begin to have some impact. But the appeal of escape to Europe, part of Mark's story as well, where the operation of the categories is at least different, has long been an aspect of the African-American experience.

The greatest gift of Mark's story is his willingness to expose the fact that real life is not lived in dichotomous categories of identity. Black-White. Gay-Straight. Latina/o-Anglo. Despite the reality of the categories and their impact on our lives, each of us is unique and experiences life from the inside-out. Our interior landscape is always richer and more complicated than the categories can contain.

Our identities become more complex all the time. It is no longer a black-and-white world. Our children know a different truth. How common it is to see interracial couples. African Americans dating Asians. Whites dating Latinas. The 2000 Census for the first time allowed respondents to claim multiple racial identities because there are now so many people unwilling to compromise by naming only one. My son, whose mother is white, refuses to use a simple category to describe his racial identity and insists on telling the whole story of his lineage. These kinds of stories talk about lived experience. So does this book. So many of us live "in between." So many of us have had to become border crossers. So many of us deal with identities which our culture has not even found language to talk about, let alone give their just due.

Mark's story intersects with and is shaped by the broad cultural shifts of the last fifty years—segregation, early attempts at integration, Dr. King and the civil rights struggle, the emergence of Black Power, Vietnam, affirmative action, and more. We live in response to events and shifts that are largely beyond our control. In dealing with those events, we create our own personal narratives.

So many of Mark's stories recall stories from my own life, allowing me to revisit my own responses to the events through which we have both lived. Perhaps that will be the final gift of this book, that it will encourage many people to remember and tell their own stories once again. And we may dare to imagine, dare to hope, that one day our national narrative will make room for the reality of our lived experience, in all its richness and complexity.

The Reverend William G. Sinkford
President, Unitarian Universalist Association

Prologue

The time has come to realize that the interracial drama acted out on the American continent has not only created a new black man, it has created a new white man, too.

—James Baldwin, *Stranger in the Village*

Barging in on the only other black student in my dorm, I was ready to vent. "Man, that good-for-nothin' s.o.b. Mike. You see wha—"

"That was bad, man," Tim blurted out before I could finish the sentence. "No shit, that was baaaaad. That was really, really bad, man . . ." he repeated, drowning me out.

Then I got it. *The brother wants me to evaporate.* Having just seen me tried and crucified by the biggest, baddest black man on campus, Tim was as scared as I was angry.

Martin Luther King Jr. had been shot. The prevailing mood among my fellow black students was boiling with radicalism. Whites were the enemy. Full of misgivings, I had slipped into the meeting of the Black Student Union.

I had gone because I yearned to belong, to be one of them, especially following King's assassination. This was no time to retreat. It was a time for change, for organization, for solidarity, and everybody was supposed to show. That meant me.

And yet, my sense of foreboding was so strong that I spent all afternoon convincing myself to go. I couldn't help feeling that I didn't really belong. How could I? My father was a research chemist at the University of Chicago and my mother was director of social work at its Bobs Roberts Memorial Hospital for Children; I'd been raised in a white liberal Unitarian Sunday School and later educated in a progressive Swiss boarding school. I had more white friends than black and everybody knew it.

Now, at least, I'm ready to admit the truth: I was afraid. Stay away and they'd label me "Tom." So I went—only to be collared and branded.

With the Dreamer dead, passions inflamed, and ghettoes ablaze; with the antiwar message of *Hair* rocking Broadway, Black Panther leader Huey P. Newton in jail, and a hundred thousand war protestors marching on the Pentagon, the nation was in turmoil. I was unprepared for this transition: no more interracial solidarity, civil rights forsaken for Black Power, desegregation supplanted by separatism, nonviolence under attack by those arming for self-defense, naïve notions about love and peace swept aside by brutal realities. The days of singing "Black and white together, we shall not be moved" were over. The bullet that killed King wounded us all. The ricochet tore through my family, fracturing our lives, our relationships, and our faith in integration. Yet my whole life had been an exercise in integration, and as despair-fueled fury enveloped the black community, I didn't know how to respond.

Cultural amalgamation—the melding of cultures and races through conquest and slavery, migration and miscegenation—is older than Moses's marriage to a Cushite bride. It's in our blood. During the fifties and sixties, this process emerged as an unusually self-conscious effort to transform society. This era of racial integration, from the time Jackie Robinson joined the Brooklyn Dodgers in 1947 until King's assassination twenty-one years later, bracketed the formative years of my life. This story describes that life—a life often spent as one among a handful of Afro-Americans in otherwise white communities, sometimes the only one. The day I was born in a Chicago hospital, my father—because of his race—wasn't allowed into the fathers' waiting room; we were living on the cusp of change, and my father's experience belonged to an era that was ending.

Growing up in the fifties, integration was all I knew—kids, white and black and the odd Asian, playing together in nursery school, church, kindergarten, and children's choir. It would continue in Switzerland, where my family spent a sabbatical year and I stayed for two more. From a rustic international boarding school located in a remote mountainside village, I watched the civil rights movement, the Sixteenth Street Baptist Church bombing in Birmingham, Malcolm X's assassination, and James Reeb's murder in Selma.

As the cultural storm mounted, I reluctantly returned home and tried and failed to straddle the divide between black and white. Battered, I set out upon a tortuous search for redemption that eventually led back to the Alps, but did not end there. The urge to stay was strong but the call to the Unitarian Universalist ministry was stronger. Returning to America, I entered seminary. There I married another student, an Anglo-Canadian, and with her raised two multiracial children of dual nationality. For twenty-six years, we served as co-ministers in a religious movement that was, and remains, overwhelmingly Anglo-American. In all this, without realizing it, I was being true to my lineage—four hundred years of interracial relations and miscegenation.

Caught in a twilight zone between the races, my family was part of the interracial drama of which James Baldwin wrote. As slaves and slaveholders; as Union and Confederate soldiers; as a scientist facing government-sanctioned discrimination while working on the atom bomb; as GIs serving in a segregated U.S. Army, defending freedom from Nazi tyranny; as lawyers and laborers; as lovers and rapists, my ancestors played their bit parts. I, like them, was just another extra. But the realities of our lives have led me to this truth: Integration is inevitable. There is no other way. Never was and never will be.

This story, however, is not just about how America's emerging multiracial identity played out in my life and those of my ancestors; it is also about self-integration and as such subsumes and transcends what we call *race*. By self-integration I mean the embracing of one's heritage and ancestors, accepting their struggles as one's own without romanticizing them or claiming the good parts while sloughing off the embarrassments. All their stories are mine and mine theirs—a seamless continuation. And because that is so, my choices were never mine alone. They were framed by my ancestors' lives—an extension of their passions, values, and failings. I am their manifestation in the present and trajectory into the future.

Self-integration and self-acceptance asks still more; ultimately I also have to come to terms with myself. A bundle of human needs, contradictions, and potential, I was born into an upwardly mobile, middle-class Afro-American family, raised in an interracial milieu, and fated to come of age during the either-or era of Black Power. But driven toward wholeness—for I don't know how else to describe surviving bouts of depression, conquering a victim mentality that seems endemic among Afro-Americans, and owning the depth of my smothered rage—I came to celebrate and be empowered by my heritage, to give thanks for my upbringing, to accept my tempestuous feelings, and to acknowledge rather than hide the warring elements of my personality. This spiritual quest for integration, this process of incorporation, is me taking responsibility for my own life. This is the story of my wayward journey toward wholeness.

Slavery Served Us Well

Not to know what happened before we were born is to remain perpetually a child. For what is the worth of a human life unless it is woven into the life of our ancestors by the records of history? . . . The influence and achievements of our ancestors we cannot escape.

—Cicero, *De Oratore*

Having read the history distributed at family reunions, I knew, and steadfastly ignored, that my ancestors had been "traders in ivory, wood, iron, cloth and slaves." Slaves were listed last, as if just another commodity. The facts, however, lead to a different conclusion. Slaves were crucial to the plantations in the British colonies, to Atlantic triangular trade of the eighteenth century, and to my ancestors who were in the business.

In 1684, at age fourteen, Thomas Corker Jr. was sent by the Royal African Company to the Sherbro coast of Sierra Leone. There Corker took an African wife—Senōra Doll, Duchess of Sherbro. A member of the Ya Kumba family of the Bulom tribe, she was probably of mixed blood, since Portuguese traders had arrived in the region and begun intermarrying two centuries earlier. By 1692 the Company had promoted Corker to chief agent of York Island, and Senōra Doll had given birth to three sons. Six years later, Corker became governor of an outpost to the north of Sierra Leone in

1

Gambia, and in 1700 he returned to England laden with ivory, gold, precious timber, and slaves. However, within months, Corker died of congestive heart failure and his eldest brother, a member of Parliament and mayor of Falmouth, wrote in epitaph: "The young man that lies here was a glory to the English and the Africans." Eight degrees north of the equator and scarcely a league from Sierra Leone lie the Banana Islands, and a little further south sits a smaller group called the Plantains, where Skinner Caulker, the eldest son of Senõra Doll and Thomas Corker, ruled as king. (The spelling of Corker had been changed.) The forest-dwelling Mende, my father's matrilineal ancestors and rivals of the Bulom, my mother's ancestors, lived inland from these islands. Warring Bulom factions used the Mende as mercenaries, so it is within the realm of possibility that my mother's people sold my father's foremother into slavery.

Midway through the 1730s, William Clevland of Devonshire, England, arrived in the region as a mate on a slave ship. He remained, became clerk to King Skinner Caulker, and married the king's daughter Kate, who subsequently gave birth to John and Elizabeth. William Clevland, younger brother of the First Secretary of the Admiralty, had done what younger brothers had to do. He set out to make his fortune, and the slave trade became the basis of his livelihood. Returning to England, he was entrusted with a ship and cargo, and once back in the Bananas he built a business trading goods for slaves, who he then conveyed to the West Indies.

John Clevland attended school in England, but when his father died in 1758, the eighteen-year-old returned to the Bananas to succeed him. Like her brother, Elizabeth Clevland was educated in England, but in her youth she also visited South Carolina with their father who had relatives there and, as one letter stressed, "must have possessed great influence." In 1764, John sent his five-year-old daughter, Catherine Clevland, to South Carolina in the company of her aunt Elizabeth. Sailing as passengers on the *Queen of Barra*, which carried three hundred slaves, they landed in Charleston, the hub of the North American slave trade.

During the eighty years between Thomas Corker's arrival in Africa and Catherine Clevland's departure, nearly seventy thousand slaves had been exported from Sierra Leone. Without knowing the details, I knew the truth. But to avoid feelings of confusion and guilt, I had never let myself focus upon this reality until my mind snapped to attention midway through a genealogical presentation at a family reunion. The speaker, my cousin, said that when Elizabeth Clevland Hardcastle died in 1808 she had left Catherine Clevland—my mother's great-great-great-great-grandmother—the 750-acre Raccoon Hill Plantation, along with the interest from twenty-two bank shares, sheep, hogs, two carriage horses, and five slaves: Old Dick, Old Bess, Old Tom, Old Nelly (Dick's wife), and Johnny.

I waited. We were Afro-Americans and slave owners? Certainly my cousin would elaborate. When she didn't, I asked. She equivocated. "These were the oldest slaves," she said. "They were given to Catherine because she would care for them." *Oh, yeah! We take care of our darkies*, the cynic in me snarled, but the Boy Scout within wanted it to be true. Yet how could she manage a 750-acre plantation without slaves? It seemed unlikely that, in an economy built upon slavery, she would be an exception. Conflicted, I remained silent as the presentation wandered elsewhere. Hearing this admission stirred feelings I didn't understand and raised moral implications I had never considered. I could comfortably identify with my forebears who had been slaves, but I was emotionally unprepared to incorporate the fact that I also had ancestors who were slave traders and owners.

Slavery had served us well. One look around that downtown Washington hotel banquet hall was all that was required to see how well. D.C. was my father's hometown and his family had been successful enough; there were farmers, clerks, and teachers, but also two professors and a Mutual of New York vice president. But these were my mother's people—a judge, an ambassador, a brokerage house vice president, a bank manager, the medical director of one insurance company and an assistant vice president of another mingling with physicians, lawyers, dentists, and academics.

Confronted with the reality that some of my advantages were the fruits of slavery, I turned to my sister, Carole. What a blunder. Instead of the sympathetic sibling I sought, I found Carole's other persona, the insurance company assistant VP who had just negotiated a multimillion-dollar surety bond adjustment. "So what? She owned slaves. That's supposed to be a problem?"

Being cross-examined was not what I, her esteemed eldest brother, had expected.

"Come off it," she snapped. "Why should that bug you? It doesn't have anything to do with us."

I winced, sucked my teeth, and retreated into silence. Carole, I suppose, meant *Get over it.* I wondered whether I was the only one troubled by this legacy, whether anyone else felt even a twinge.

Shame struck me, and then this intuition: My family was more indebted to the past than we acknowledged. Once I had made the connection between our social status and our past, seen it reflected in that gathering and realized that our advantages, acquired on the backs of others, would carry into the future, my sense of guilt intensified. I didn't feel at fault; I felt ashamed. I had taken fate's largess for granted—a blindness I recognized as an affliction I shared with white Americans.

Even today, I doubt many of them know that the U.S. Capitol, citadel of democracy, was built with slave labor. Do they see the paradox? The bastion of freedom buttressed by human bondage. I wonder whether white Americans understand the implication of America's central, self-defining myth: If God especially ordained America as the new holy land, and Americans as the new chosen people blessed to inhabit a land of opportunity, how do they reconcile this with the plight of Afro-Americans? How does such a great nation explain why so many black Americans remain poor and so many black men are incarcerated? And I ask why the vaunted American dream has eluded so many of us. Is the Negro race less able, moral, intelligent, and deserving of God's grace? Some white Americans say yes, but many more are simply perplexed. Whites, as passive beneficiaries, look out from the protective cocoon of white prerogative and cumulative advantage, and are mystified. Indeed, many, themselves embattled and feeling victimized, see no difference between blacks and whites.

But there is a difference and as I thought about it my own sense of guilt grew. Similar to white Americans, my prosperity was partly the result of a pernicious evil. How natural to prefer the Disney version of history to the ugly, uncomfortable, messy tragedy that is our true past. And how self-serving to discount the effect of four hundred years of slavery on the Afro-American psyche. Early America was no empty frontier waiting to be settled by Europeans. That myth helps us evade the painful truth that the real "American Wilderness" is a moral one: The genocide of Native Americans—called "black ducks" by the English colonists who hunted them—was a sin compounded by the enslavement of kidnapped Africans—called "niggahs" as they were sold on the auction block. Deemed savages and brutes, neither group possessed any rights a white man was bound to respect, and so aboriginal land and African life-blood fed the infant nation's avarice. Indeed, the Constitution, our country's most sacred document and guarantor of freedom, had slavery written into it. Ironically, this was not incongruent, for the freedom it espoused was meant only for white, land-owning males. But freedom as an ideal was greater than the narrow meaning it held in the Constitution. Once the notion of freedom was in the air it couldn't be contained. The "Emancipation Proclamation" set the slaves free. The "Jim Crow" era that followed and the caste system it perpetuated only delayed real liberation. The unfinished revolution continued and continues still.

A West African proverb says: As a people, we stand on the shoulders of our ancestors. Looking around that air-conditioned Washington ballroom, I saw the influence of the past, and nothing I could do would change it. The present, however, is different. Today's deeds shape tomorrow and in this moment, which resides between indebtedness and hope, it is possible to make a difference.

Andrew Dibble, Catherine Clevland's great-grandson and my mother's great-grandfather, was born in 1825. Family oral history tells us that Andrew's mother, Martha Smith, was half Native American, and it's likely her father was a member of a band that lived in the vicinity of Raccoon Hill Plantation. It's clear from photos that he was mulatto—thin lips, light skin, long wavy hair. In 1843 he married another free Negro of mixed race, Elly Naomi Naudin. Elly's father, Moreau, was the son of John Naudin, a French Huguenot who had become an American citizen in 1803; her mother was Harriet Conway. In 1793 Harriet's father, Bonds Conway, had been the first Negro in Camden, South Carolina, to purchase his own freedom.

Andrew was a tailor and, of necessity, traveled around the South. In the years just prior to the Civil War, white workers, resenting Negro competition, instituted house-to-house searches and Negroes unable to prove their status were enslaved. In 1860, to protect himself, Andrew acquired Freedom Papers that documented his descent from a free person.

Born in 1846, Martha Louisa Dibble was my mother's grandmother and the eldest of Elly and Andrew's twelve children. In 1870 she married Senator Henry Johnson Maxwell. A photograph of Senator Maxwell appears in *A Pictorial History of the Negro in America*. Mother first showed it to me when I was about nine years old. At the bottom of the photo, a legend read "Radical Members of the So. Ca. Legislature." She pointed at a brown, bearded man and said, "That's your great-grandfather, Senator Maxwell. You look just like him." Her words stayed with me, and every once in a while I would pull the book from the shelf, stare at his picture, and wonder what it meant that I looked like him.

Born free in 1837 on Edisto Island, South Carolina, Henry Maxwell was raised in Charleston, but left for the North at the age of nineteen. After the Civil War began, he tried to enlist. Twice rejected because of his health, he became, instead, a recruiter for the Union Army. While not as perilous as battle, it was nonetheless dangerous, and following a series of narrow escapes, he resigned.

Successful on his third attempt to enlist, he was made a first sergeant in Battery A of the 2nd U.S. Colored Light Artillery—one of 180,000 Negroes who fought in the Union Army. Following the Civil War, he was elected to the South Carolina legislature, serving as senator from Marlboro County from 1868 to 1877. While in the legislature he was also elected Marlboro County's first school commissioner, appointed postmaster of Bennettsville, South Carolina—the first Negro postmaster in the United States—and was admitted to the South Carolina bar. Thereafter he practiced law.

Henry and Martha Maxwell had eight offspring. Their sons became a dentist, a physician, a businessman, a barber, and a railroad waiter who also was a labor organizer; their three daughters became schoolteachers. Like many Dibbles and Maxwells before and after, Naomi Theresa, their sixth child and my grandmother, enrolled in Clafin College. Founded in 1869, Clafin was the oldest Negro college in South Carolina, and Naomi graduated in 1902.

The Maxwells lived on the same street in Sumter, South Carolina, as the Edwards family. One of eighteen siblings, my grandfather, George Edwards, was sent North at age eight to be raised by his grandmother and two aunts. During his annual visits south, George came to know Naomi. They were wed in 1908, and Naomi returned with George to Wilkes-Barre, Pennsylvania, a northern Appalachian coal mining town waiting for the Susquehanna to flood yet again.

Mother told us Granddad was well respected by Negro and white alike. She went on to add, "And he should've been postmaster." But he was never promoted beyond supervisor of the special delivery division, even though he trained a steady stream of white employees—including those who were made his boss.

Naomi had been a teacher in South Carolina, but was unable to obtain a teaching position in largely white Wilkes-Barre. She became a social worker, only to be fired during the Great Depression, when a new rule mandated that one family couldn't hold two government jobs. Mother maintained that it was just a way of getting rid of her. Naomi, determined as always, began growing and selling roses and gladioli and taking on piano students. But first and foremost, she focused her energy on her two children: Christopher Maxwell—Uncle Max to me—and Selina Louise, my mother. Normally a child born in January, as Mother was, would have had to wait until the September following her sixth birthday to enroll in school. Naomi wouldn't hear of it. Having already taught Selina to read, she insisted that her daughter begin mid-way through the school year. So on Mother's first day of school she was the youngest in her class and the only Negro, and she was assigned the last seat in the last row.

I shrank away whenever I saw the bitterness in Mother's eyes as she spoke of how her parents had been treated, or heard the bridled rage in her voice as she recalled the humiliation she felt on the first day of school. But when she talked about her brother, I saw pain rather than indignation. Six years older than Mother, Max was captain of the school debating team and salutatorian for his nearly all-white high school class. I can only imagine the expectations Naomi must have laid upon her boy, scion of Senator Maxwell, as he headed off for Bucknell, a white liberal arts college in Lewisburg, Pennsylvania. Max wasn't the school's first Negro graduate—that was Edward McKnight Brawley who graduated in 1875—but he seems to have been the only Negro enrolled in 1933, and that posed a problem. The dean of the university wrote that Max was a "very high type young man . . . who would prove the least objectionable to prejudiced people of any colored man I know." While he admitted that it was "unchristian," he wavered at placing Max in a dormitory. He wrote, "We have men from the South and other sections of the country who . . . have a deep-seated prejudice with respect to rooming or eating with colored people." After a flurry of letters about—but not to—Max, the situation was resolved when he was offered a rent-free room downtown in the basement of the College Inn.

I learned early that Uncle Max was brilliant. If I wasn't careful, he'd trap me as I passed through the living room, and that meant listening to a recitation from the Bible or Shakespeare or his favorite, Ralph Waldo Emerson's essay "Self Reliance." "To believe your own thought," he would begin before I could escape, "to believe that what is true for you in your private heart is true for all men— that is genius. Speak your latent conviction, and it shall be the universal sense."

I also knew something was very wrong with Uncle Max. In his senior year at Bucknell, he had a nervous breakdown and even though he managed to graduate two years later he never really recovered. He came and went and worked, but only sporadically. Sometimes we would drive northwest of Chicago to visit him in a scary mental hospital surrounded by a tall, spiked fence. Once through the gate and past the guardhouse, we marched down pale green, echoey hallways looking for him, but the person we found was never the uncle I knew; they had turned him into a zombie. Fragments of overheard conversations were all I had to go on: When he was a boy a brick had fallen on his head; there had been the stress of attending an all-white college; there was his roommate who was Jewish, which wasn't a problem but (Mother always whispered this part) he was having an affair with a professor's wife. Mother always sought an explanation for the onset of his schizophrenia. Now, whenever I think of Max, I wince and wonder what it was like for this gifted, high-minded young man. In the racially hostile world of the 1930s, how was he supposed to cope not only with his own hope of attending Columbia Law School, but also with his mother's towering expectations? Perhaps his mental health was the price he paid.

When it was time for Mother to attend college, she enrolled in a local school, Bucknell University Junior College. In 1940 she received an associate's degree, and Naomi sent her off to Howard University—the black Harvard. Mother went to continue her education, but also because Naomi must have been certain that no suitable Negro man would be found in Wilkes-Barre. Once on campus, that didn't take long.

The Educational Imperative

It was then that I made my vow—that I would forever fight to keep hope alive because there is always a way . . .

—Percy Julian, "Response"

Westmoreland County, the birthplace of George Washington, stretches along the south bank of the Potomac River, its brackish tidal waters full of salt marshes, the land covered with forest and farms. General Robert E. Lee was born there as well, and a few miles to the southeast of his birthplace is Zacata, a town so small I have yet to find it on a road map. Route 645 runs past Siloam Baptist Church and adjacent to it is a cemetery. There headstones hide behind rangy grass, and many bear my father's family name: Reed. Chiseled into one are Sarah Reed (1873-1934) and George Reed (1858-1933), my great-grandparents. Every time I stand there, I can't help but wonder what they were like.

When George Reed was two his father, Joseph Rodgers Gregory, rode down to Montross to enlist in the Confederate Army. The county seat was crowded with young men; Joe at forty-three would have been among the oldest. Joe was white but he lived with a colored woman, which though unusual was not unheard of, so perhaps the others didn't wonder much about him. I can only imagine that Joe, a private serving in Company C, "Lee's Light Horse" of the Ninth Regiment of the Virginia Cavalry, was just doing what was expected—defending Virginia and the Southern way of life. But I wonder what Betsy Reed, his partner and my great-great-grandmother, thought about his stand. And I wonder what to make of it as well.

Betsy, like her parents, was a free Negro. How they came to be free remains a question; perhaps they always were. They may have been indentured servants who had served out their indentures or slaves who purchased their freedom, or they may have been among the 500 freed by Robert Carter III; I simply don't know. Documents about Negroes are hard to find, incomplete when located, or hidden in lists as numbers under their owners' last names. What I do know is that the 1860 census of Westmoreland County records Betsy and Joe as living in the same household and shows the county populated by 3,700 slaves, 1,200 free Negroes, and 3,400 whites. Great-uncle Harry, one of Joe's grandsons and my grandfather's youngest brother, told me there were "white Reeds galore" whom they "called cousin now and again"—a remnant of relationships hidden in the antebellum past. This past, in which race mixing was more common, began in earnest with the establishment of Jamestown, Virginia, the first English colony, in 1607, and the marriage of John Rolfe to Pocahontas in 1614, and continued with the arrival of the first Africans as indentured servants in 1619. By 1681 enough race mixing had taken place that the Commonwealth of Virginia passed a law forbidding mixed marriages. So while Betsy Reed and Joe Gregory lived together and raised their six children, they couldn't do so within the bonds of marriage.

About a mile and a half beyond the cemetery stands the Reed homestead. "Fact is," said Great-uncle Harry, "when the Captain bought all this farmland around us here he didn't know much about farming." The Captain is what my yarn-spinning great-uncle called his father when expounding to his nieces and nephews. "You know, the Captain signed his name with an X and could read just enough to check the ship's log." It was Sarah, the Captain's wife and Harry's mother, who had an elementary education.

Harry said, "Mama was rail-thin and sour-faced and beat me every day of the week and twice on Sunday." Sarah managed the farm, ran a country store, and ruled the family. Perhaps Sarah looked so severe because the Captain, who Harry said "was a fisherman at heart and hated farming," was absent so often. Maybe he stayed away because he was truly in command only on board his three-masted schooner, *Mary Jane*. A short, big-boned, bowlegged man renowned for his strength, he leased three acres of oyster ground, caught crabs in the brackish Chesapeake Bay, and hauled timber up to Georgetown and Baltimore on his boat and returned with supplies. As a "waterman," he made his living on the bay and like many others he couldn't swim a lick. His boys, however, were left at home. The Captain told them, "Time's a comin' when a man won't make a living on the water." Instead, they worked the farm and went to school.

In Virginia, prior to the Civil War, it was illegal to educate Negroes. Public free schools were not established until 1870. The legislation stated: "The public free schools shall be free to all persons between the ages of five and twenty-one years residing within a school district, provided that white and colored people shall not be taught in the same school, but in separate schools under the same regulations as to management, usefulness and efficiency." Despite this law, no school for colored people existed in Zacata until 1900, when George Warren Reed, the Captain's eldest child and my grandfather, was six years old. "I reckon it was just about there," Great-uncle Harry said, taking the pipe from his mouth and pointing as we drove past. "You know the Captain gave the land and built the one-room school about the time your grandpa was school age. Hewed the benches and desks from logs himself. Once the Captain built that schoolhouse, the State of Virginia had to send a teacher"—his bald head shook as he chuckled—"but some of those teachers couldn't figure out the arithmetic even though the answers were in the back of the book." School in Zacata went up to the ninth grade and then, because secondary education for Negroes in the South was mainly private, the Reed children were sent to residential schools paid for by their picking tomatoes, the cash crop that went to the cannery at Deep Point.

The Captain and Sarah must have been of the same mind about education, because once this illiterate son of an illiterate father built a schoolhouse, his strict wife made sure their children attended. Great-uncle Harry told me that when my grandfather was old enough, "the Captain drove your grandpa down to Northern Neck Industrial Academy in the old horse and buggy, and left him standing by one of the buildings, cryin' his eyes out." In turn, all seven of my grandfather's brothers and sisters were sent away to high school. Most continued their education; three earned bachelor's degrees, one of them adding a master's and another adding a doctorate from the University of Pittsburgh. My grandfather enrolled at Virginia State but when the First World War began, he dropped out and enlisted in the Navy.

I wasn't quite seven when my father's maternal grandmother, Mary Elizabeth Newman, died at the age of ninety-nine. All I remember of her now is her thin, silent silhouette sitting in the front parlor of her home on S Street. I stared from the safety of the next room. A tall snake plant sat on a table beside her, its tapered, turgid, green leaves rising behind her head. To me, she looked like an Indian, but I wasn't sure what she was. We didn't talk. I didn't go near her, yet I was fascinated because she was so old. When I got a little older, her age led me to wonder if she had been a slave and so I asked my grammy. "I don't want to hear any talk about slavery in my house," she ordered, so I shut up and found the truth elsewhere.

On January 1, 1863, the Emancipation Proclamation took effect and among those freed was Mary Elizabeth, then five years old. "Mama was born in Chantilly, Virginia," Great-aunt Irene said, "and for quite a while Mama lived with two white families. You see, she being a little fair child, I guess being one of the boss man's children, evidently, my mother was trained in the white people's house and grew up with this man's daughter. You know, they all came along together and everything that their daughter did, my mother did, too."

Katherine Darne owned Mary Elizabeth; her mother, Adelaide
Turner; and older brother, James; and she gave them all to her sister, Jane Hancock. It seems likely that it was Jane's eldest son who
fathered Mary Elizabeth. This would explain why she was raised
in their home, and why she remained with the Hancocks until she
married at the age of eighteen in 1875. When Great-aunt Irene
showed me her mother's wedding picture, she added: "Child, you
know she had to get married early and move away before some
white man took advantage of her. In those times people lived that
kind of way and people did those kind of things."

Mary Elizabeth married John Thomas Newman. John
Thomas was the seventh of Harry and Julia Newman's ten children. Harry's name appears in the 1837 will of Thomas Pres-
graves and his value was $600; Julia was also a slave but lived on a
different plantation. The story of their lives, already obscured by
the realties of slavery, is made even murkier by our family lore.
The tale was passed down that a Fijian named Henry accepted a
captain's offer to join his crew for the voyage to the United States;
and all who came on this ship were given the last name Newman and told they would be "free slaves." We've never identified
who Henry might be, nor could I understand how one could be
a "free slave," although I think it's a kind of indenture. At times
I've been inclined to dismiss this oral history as a tall tale, a creative attempt to deny our African heritage. But family lore often
reflects historical fact. In the early nineteenth century, American
vessels en route to the Orient traded in the South Pacific islands,
and during these stopovers captains had to recruit new crew
members as sailors died or deserted. Islanders sometimes made
up as much as three-quarters of a crew. Add to this a mysterious family mandate: The Newmans were to pass down the name
Maury in memory of Lieutenant Matthew Fountaine Maury, the
U.S. Navy navigator who sailed to the South Pacific and charted
the waters around Cape Horn. On the one hand, the story doesn't
fit what is known; on the other, it's improbable that it could be
entirely fictitious.

We do know that in the 1880s John Thomas and Mary Elizabeth sold their farm and moved the family to Washington so that, as Mary's obituary noted, "the children could receive an education . . . and all her children fulfilled her wish by graduating from high school." In Mary Elizabeth's house, her wish was law— every time my feisty Great-aunt Irene talked about her mother, she would wag a finger and say, "Mama was a real general."

"It was about 1899 that my grandfather Newman's property was settled up and Papa had to go up in Virginia," Irene said, "and when he came back all he brought with him was a shotgun. Being a hostler and moving about from job to job working with people's horses, Papa didn't have any use for the land. The only thing of value he could see was the gun. Well, Mama was so disgusted she took that gun outside and chopped it up. That's the way Mama was.

"You know if it had not been for Mama, we would never have had any education. Papa believed in putting his children out to work, and you were never too young as far as he was concerned. But there was one place Mama always sent you. Just like she sent you to church, Mama insisted that you go to school."

Education was no less mandatory on the General's side of Dad's family than on the Captain's. When my grandmother Eleanor, the youngest of Mary Elizabeth's children, graduated from Armstrong High School in 1915, her brother Lloyd grilled her about her career plans. "I had no answers" she said, but then the head of the household arts department "pounced" on Grammy while she was visiting Myrtilla Miner Normal School—D.C.'s premier teacher's college. By the time she graduated, she knew she disliked teaching and so enrolled in a school for beauticians.

When she completed beauty school, Grammy's "one and only" came into her life. Great-aunt Irene elaborated on this event in more colorful fashion: "Well. At that time, just about everybody was wearing some kind of uniform and your grandmother met the cutest little trick in a Navy suit. You know, Eleanor had a lot of admirers but when she met George Reed—that was his name— that was it. And she had plenty of competition, too, but she held on tight and got her man. Yes, she did."

Married in 1918, Grammy and Grandpa moved into a brick row house on U Street in Northwest Washington, D.C. Dad was born in 1920 and was named after his father, George Warren Reed. At one point on the day of his birth, Grammy's brother Lloyd snatched up his nephew, carried him to the attic, and hoisted him above his head. "Taking a baby to the highest point in a house is supposed to make him smart," Lloyd said, defending his action when I laughed, "and it worked."

As a young mother, Grammy cut people's hair in her home. In the 1930s, she and Grandpa also spent evenings catering, sometimes at the White House. First Lady Eleanor Roosevelt not only spoke with Grammy—who never let us forget it—but also wrote a letter of recommendation that led to Grammy being hired as a clerk in the U.S. Department of the Interior. My grandparents worked long hours, but Grammy, yet another fierce matriarch preparing her brood for success, forbade her children from delivering newspapers or doing any other outside work. For Dad, his brother "Little" Lloyd, and sister Phyllis, studying came first.

Segregation was such a fact of life that Dad didn't think about it when he passed the white school that was halfway between his house and the Negro school he attended, a school he described as "packed to the rafters." His experience was so unfair and unlike my own that I demanded to know how that could be. But a gruff "That's just the way it was" ended the conversation.

Growing up in Washington, D.C. in the twenties and thirties, the only significant contact my father had with white people was in the Third Church of Christian Science. Third Church, he said, provided him with a unique experience in his otherwise totally colored world. In that setting he had the opportunity to "relate to white people in a different way. Not as them-over-there, but as someone that you had a meaningful relationship with. And this happened in a time when D.C. churches were either black or white and there was nothing in between."

When Dad completed elementary school, there were three high schools to choose from—Armstrong for industrial education, Cardozo for business, and Dunbar for academics. There wasn't any question. Following in his uncle Lloyd's footsteps, Dad enrolled in Dunbar. The school's second principal had, in 1870, been the first Afro-American graduate of Harvard, and Dunbar was known for the quality of its faculty, an ironic benefit of the dearth of academic opportunities available for Negro teachers. With its high standards, Dunbar was "the breeding ground of the old Negro elite," a reputation upheld by the achievements of its graduates. For many decades, more Afro-American PhDs had been graduates of Dunbar than of any other colored high school in the country. In this environment, one of Dad's teachers ignited his interest in chemistry, and by the time Dad was a junior he realized he would need to learn German if he were going to become a scientist. However, that language hadn't been taught at Dunbar since the First World War, when anti-German hysteria had swept the country. Dad and another student approached the principal; he found a teacher and they recruited the students. Graduating in 1938, Dad enrolled at Howard University; and there, in 1940, he met Selina "Lee" Edwards.

"You gotta check this cool chick out," one of Dad's buddies informed him when Mother arrived on campus. Dad did, and promptly asked for a date. He was an Alpha, and she a Delta—the most desirable of the Greek-letter societies at Howard. Old photographs of my parents together show them to be a handsome pair. He was dark; she was fair. He was tall and slender with a widow's peak and wire-rimmed glasses that gave him a scholarly look. She was beautiful, but not in a made-up way. Her warmth, poise, and vivaciousness drew people to her. He called her, "Hon," "Boo," and "Sugar"; she called him "Sweet Heart." But the only other thing I remember being told about their romance—and it always came from Mother when she was exasperated with Dad—was that the one time she ever saw him cry was when she went on a date with someone else.

They both graduated in 1942. Dad remained at Howard to work on an MS in chemistry, Mother worked for a year before enrolling in the MSW program at the University of Pennsylvania. Meanwhile, Dad completed his degree, found a job, and began saving for an engagement ring.

Before Dad received his master's degree, faculty members called him in to discuss his future. The best, and practically only, options were teaching chemistry in a Negro college or following his uncle Lloyd into medicine. Dad, with no interest in medicine and having never taken biology, surprised them when he announced that he planned to become a scientist. "When I decided to become a scientist," he explained, "I was too naïve to appreciate the obstacles and lack of opportunities black men faced. The sort of awareness found among today's youth did not exist, at least not in the all-black community I was exposed to. This may have been fortunate, as one was not turned off before there was a chance to be turned on. My life story would have been very different had not World War II intervened with the need to more fully utilize all the nation's manpower and the continued opening up of opportunities."

Dad graduated and a draft notice arrived, but so did a job offer to be a junior chemist, from the highly classified Special Alloy Metals (SAM) Laboratory at Columbia University in New York City. Dad's brother, Little Lloyd, who had enlisted, wrote home: "The draft board will feel cheated with George having eluded them for three years. I told the fellows here that he was working on the atomic bomb up there at Columbia. For all I know he may have been. He never said what he was doing." His brother guessed the truth, but Dad didn't know what he was working on and couldn't have said if he did. "We were purifying uranium," he said, "but I was totally in the dark. We weren't even supposed to talk to the people in the lab next to us."

SAM was part of the Manhattan Project, which produced the materials needed to make atomic bombs. Professor Leon Shereschefsky, chairman of the chemistry department at Howard, was on leave to the project and it was he, a white man, who helped

Dad secure the position. To Dad's relief, it also meant his exemption from the draft. But when he realized his white colleagues were being sent to the Army for six weeks of basic training, returning with the rank of corporal or private first class, Dad said he "smelled a fish" and went to his "colored" draft board in D.C. "These guys have gotten in the Army through SAM," he told them. "I'm 1-A and I want to go in that way, too." His draft board looked into it and reported back: "We are not allowed to touch you." Dad protested, saying, "They are going to have all the benefits of having been in the Army and I'm not going to have anything," but his draft board proved powerless. As far as he knew, the same held true for the other handful of Negro scientists working on SAM.

Mother and Dad were married on June 30, 1945, and moved into a small apartment in Brooklyn. Japan surrendered on September 2 and soon afterward everyone on the SAM team who wished was transferred to the Oakridge Laboratory in Tennessee—everyone except Dad. He requested a transfer, and when told that Oakridge wasn't ready to take a Negro scientist, he marched into the personnel director's office. "There is something wrong here," Dad said. "I want to go to Tennessee." The response: "I can't do anything about it."

Just before Dad began working at Columbia, another Howard graduate had arranged for him to be interviewed by Argonne National Laboratory, administered by the University of Chicago. Once Dad understood that there was no place for him in Tennessee, he followed up on the interview at Argonne and by November had moved to Chicago. Two months later, Mother joined him.

In 1947 Dad enrolled in a PhD program at the University of Chicago and there developed a close friendship with a white student, Clair Patterson, whom we called Uncle Pud. They studied together and had children of about the same ages, and he introduced my parents to Unitarianism, a faith which would come to play a central role in our lives. Like Dad, Clair Patterson had worked on the A-bomb, and his participation in its creation weighed on him. I was surprised when Uncle Pud confessed this to me in 1981, because Dad had never expressed any guilt. To the contrary, he answered my questions about it with a shrug, saying his role had been peripheral. The conversation with Uncle Pud made me wonder about the difference between these two men, who had so much in common—except the color of their skin. Dad doubted that he would have been employed at all had he not been hired during a moment of national duress. In a country defending democratized racism from racist fascism, he still faced discrimination and finally exclusion once the crisis passed. More telling than his shrug was the ambivalence he expressed on occasion: "Maybe [we feel] this country doesn't belong to us like it does to everyone else."

Becoming a full member of the scientific community remained a challenge. Barred from the military, Dad did not qualify for the GI Bill. He had to find an alternate way to finance his education, and to that end received a Rosenwald Foundation Fellowship, a scholarship that aided many talented Negroes. It helped, but wasn't enough; he would need a full fellowship to remain in graduate school.

The National Research Council (NRC) awarded Atomic Energy Commission Fellowships and, encouraged by the chairman of the chemistry department, Dad applied. But he got the runaround from the secretary of the department until, days before the application was due, the department head had to intervene. Then another obstacle emerged. Traditionally, the NRC relied on recommendations from the chemistry department when awarding fellowships. However, each faculty member had favorite students and Dad, the department's only Negro graduate student, was not among any of them. Dad said he would have been "dead as a doornail" if the old process had prevailed, but that year the NRC decided to require a competitive examination instead. Dad took the exam and was awarded a fellowship.

On the Cusp

When I disobey, when I make too much noise, I am told to
"stop acting like a nigger."
　　　　　　　—Frantz Fanon, *Black Skin, White Masks*

My arrival was almost normal: anxious parents appearing at the hospital too early, a long labor, a midnight delivery. The anomaly went unnoticed until I was twenty-one. I stood, stunned, staring at my own birth certificate at the counter in the Cook County Bureau of Vital Statistics. Then I laughed. Maybe that black s.o.b. Mike, the big man on campus, had been right after all. For there it was on the shiny, officially embossed photostat:

> Mark Douglas Reed – Born: June 16, 1949
> Mother: Selina E. Reed – Race: white
> Father: George W. Reed Jr. – Race: white

Mother, with her fair complexion, hazel eyes, petite nose, and wavy dark hair—a reflection of her mixed heritage—could be mistaken for Caucasian, but not Dad. He was teak brown, all the way to the top of his prematurely bald head. And I was his unmistakably brown-skinned baby. When I asked how this could have happened, Dad said that before their arrival at the University of Chicago Lying-in Hospital, the facility hadn't admitted many, if any, Negro patients. Since my father was barred from the waiting room, the hospital staff didn't see him. They looked at my fair-skinned Mother, and continued with their routine procedures—despite my brown skin, curly hair, and full lips. I was indeed black, but my birth certificate and Mike, my nemesis, said otherwise.

Following my birth, family converged on our small first-floor apartment: both grandfathers, Grammy, and of course, Great-aunt Irene, who had retired from the U.S. Bureau of Engraving and Printing just to remain with us as long as needed. She stayed two months before returning to Washington, D.C., but I would never stop needing her.

Thirteen months and three days after I was born, Dad was allowed into the same hospital waiting room he had been banned from at my birth. Progress had been made, so he got to attend the birth of his second son. Philip cried a lot. "He's colicky," they said—it meant they didn't know why he fretted so. I called him Baba. "Baba cryin', Baba cryin'," I bellowed, while barreling down the hallway, acting as Mama's little helper. I also tried to strangle him, I'm told, so I suppose he had cause to cry and I reason to resent his intrusion. Ours would be a love-hate relationship, fed by him receiving too many hand-me-downs from me, and too many occasions on which I was held accountable for his behavior.

Chicago Lying-in Hospital had begun to accept Negroes, but the University of Chicago neighborhood that surrounded it had not. "Every colored man who moves into the Hyde Park neighborhood knows he is damaging his white neighbor's property" read a local newspaper article in 1920. Earlier the community had adopted restrictive covenants making it illegal to sell homes to Negroes. However, in 1948 the Supreme Court declared the covenants unconstitutional in *Shelley v. Kraemer*. The University, which had fiercely defended restrictive covenants, began developing new strategies to stave off the "Negro invasion" and keep Hyde Park a white enclave on Chicago's South Side.

Dad didn't bother looking for an apartment in Hyde Park. Instead he found one at 410 East 62nd Street in a Negro neighborhood a good mile from campus. Just beyond our building, 62nd Street came to a dead end at the South Park Way. South Park would later be renamed Martin Luther King Jr. Drive, but this was before the world had heard of him. A busy thoroughfare, it carried traffic from one end of South Side Chicago to the other, and until we moved to Switzerland, I fell asleep listening to its hum.

Race doesn't mean much to young children, and I was incapable of grasping what people thought upon seeing my mother's father—a diminutive, fair-skinned, elderly gentleman with straight white hair—in a suit and tie, pushing Philip in a stroller while I scampered along beside. We would walk three blocks east, then three north to the playground in Washington Park. Later I'd explore the lagoon while he watched from a park bench, and sometimes we walked as far as the *Fountain of Time*, a huge monument that stands at one end of the Midway Plaisance. Pointing east toward the ivy-covered limestone buildings with their towers and turrets, Granddad would say, "Your daddy is a very smart man, and that's where he goes to school."

When my father received his PhD in nuclear chemistry in 1952, I was three and Philip two. Grammy and Grandpa came and we all dressed up and went to the graduation. From within the narthex at Rockefeller Chapel, I peered down the long aisle at the ceremony. When they read Dad's name I saw him for an instant as he crossed in front of the aisle, and then was gone, as usual.

Following Dad's graduation, Benjamin Mays, the charismatic president of Morehouse College, personally recruited Dad to his faculty, as did interested parties from a half dozen other Negro colleges. But set on pursuing research, Dad returned to Argonne and accepted a parallel appointment as a research associate at the University of Chicago. He loved research and brought it home by the satchel. But it was his world, not ours. Dinner-table conversation seldom touched on his work, for Dad's explanations were arcane. The location of his laboratory, buried deep in a corner of the subbasement of Ryerson Hall, contributed to the mystique. To reach it I had to walk down a dark stairwell, along dusty corridors where large discarded equipment loomed in the shadows, down another set of steps, and through a double door. Suddenly I would be blinded by the glare of a fluorescent-lit room dominated by a huge box made of lead bricks. The room, with its low ceiling, was little more than a corridor around the enormous contraption. Sometimes as I sat at Dad's desk in that cave, a row of electric typewriters would start to clatter, and numbers would appear, column after column. In the years before computers, it all seemed like science fiction. I didn't know what the numbers meant. I didn't know what lay behind the lead bricks, or that they were keeping cosmic rays out rather than deadly radiation in. And I didn't know what Dad was doing, except that he coveted meteorites.

South Side Chicago was gritty, pulsating, and, after Harlem, the greatest black metropolis in the United States. Bronzeville, as it was called, was home of the *Chicago Defender*, *Jet*, and *Ebony*, and was full of black businesses, blues bars, and houses of worship— big Baptist churches, Black Muslim mosques, and little storefront congregations, whose shouts of praise poured out into the street. Its Negro inhabitants had been streaming in since the First World War. Brought to "the top of the world" from Mississippi, Arkansas, and Louisiana on the Illinois Central Railroad, they immediately headed back south along Michigan Avenue, Cottage Grove, and South Park. They didn't find the South Side any warmer but they found lots of their people. In 1954 the Reed family joined the migration as the black middle-class vanguard surged still farther south into white neighborhoods. There were now five of us. Carole had joined Philip and me in 1953, and we grew to six in 1959 with the birth of our youngest sister, Lauren.

Chatham, our new neighborhood, would come to be known as the Black Bungalow Belt, but my world was simply "the block." Its boundaries were the schoolyard; the house of Eugene Payton, an older kid who lived up Calumet Avenue; and my friend Nipper Nipson's on South Park. From our front window, we saw the gravel expanse of our schoolyard, so near we could rush out the front door upon hearing the school bell and not be late. I usually only left this world to attend church, or for the occasional journey to the Loop.

Downtown Chicago is called the Loop because of the way the El, the elevated train, loops around the downtown business district. Riding the El, my frown would deepen as, with each stop, the neighborhoods grew dirtier and the buildings more dilapidated. We passed soot-covered second-story windows and mortarless walls. We passed windows with cardboard where panes should have been, sagging four-story wooden back porches, and litter-strewn tarred rooftops with chimneys that seemed ready to topple over. Below, grassless yards sparkled with broken glass, and vacant lots accumulated abandoned cars, rusty shopping carts, and crops of ragweed. We passed colored men wearing stocking caps and sweat-stained T-shirts, and rag-headed women with aprons covering ample bellies. As they lounged on back stoops, I could see the nodding of their heads and the gestures of their hands. Wondering about their lives as we rumbled by, I always felt uneasy. But the El was as close as I came.

Mother turned every trip downtown into an etiquette lesson. "Mark, the seats are all taken. Please, offer yours to that woman."

"What?"

"Get up!"

I hated traveling with her, for the nattering never ceased. "Now remember to walk on the curb side of the street when you're escorting a lady."

"Why, Mama?"

"To keep her from getting splashed when the street is wet."

"Huh?"

"Mark!"

Hearing the edge to her voice, I quickly said, "I beg your pardon?" but my anger simmered, my pout grew, and my hands slipped deeper into my pockets. No infraction, however, went unobserved or uncorrected.

"Stop slouching," she would snap. "Hold your head up and pick your lip up off the ground this instant."

"Philip, what did I tell you? Hold the door open, please" "Don't forget to look the man in the eye and give him a firm handshake. No dead fish now."

"Mark, what do you say?" "Yes, sir." "How do you do?" "A pleasure to meet you, madam." "After you, please."

I was compliant, but all the while I noticed that lots of people weren't following her rules. Rather than resist, I whined, "Why?"

"Because that's the way well-mannered children behave," Mother said.

"But I don't care and I don't wanna."

"Well you better care about what people think of you."

"Why should I?"

"Because you're a Negro and you'll never amount to anything if you don't try harder and act better than white folks."

"That's not fair."

"That's life."

"But why?"

"Because that's the way it is."

"Why?"

The next words exploded from her mouth. "Because I won't have you acting like a common Negro!"

That cut off the conversation. Ashamed, I fell silent. I knew what she meant—no sassing or jiving, no cursing or signifying, no strutting down the street or saying "gimme five." God help me if I acted like Little Richard instead of Little Goody Two-Shoes.

The lesson, however, wasn't really about etiquette; it was more urgent. She was passing on the secrets of surviving in a white world to yet another generation, as it had been passed on to her and poor Uncle Max. The training began early and implanted within me a sense of vigilance, a wariness that at times veered toward paranoia.

I spent the entire first day of kindergarten rooted to a bench by the cloakroom, staring at the toys, the bay window, my teacher, and the other colored kids. I was still too young to understand that our arrival guaranteed more white flight. But every year the half dozen of us increased until, in seventh grade, only one white boy remained.

In first grade I made one good friend, Grover. His hair was shaved close to his cocoa-brown skin and a nylon stocking cap hugged his scalp, making his nappy hair lie straight. Grover was ready to take the lead in having fun and, although unfailingly timid, I could be coaxed into following. One day while we swung on the jungle gym in my backyard, Grover taught me my first poem. Dashing into the house I said, "Listen, Mama. Listen."

> Look in my eye.
> What do you see?
> A little black nigger
> Trying to hypnotize me.

The look in Mother's eyes froze me in place. My cheeks began to burn. Hands on her hips, she leaned forward. "Where'd you hear that?" she demanded.

My back stiffened. Eyes fixed on the floor, I clenched my teeth. She couldn't make me tell.

She grabbed my arm and shook me with each word. "Who taught you that?"

I turned my head away. I wasn't going to say.

She dug her fingers into each cheek as she turned my face back toward hers and yelled, "Tell me!"

I went numb. "Grover," I mumbled.

"I won't have that language in my house." And louder. "Do you hear? I won't have you talking like poor white trash. We're not common Negroes. I won't have it." Pushing me toward the door she said, "Go tell that boy you can't play with him anymore." I didn't budge. She shoved harder, sending me stumbling onto the back porch. Behind me the screen door banged shut. I stood there, my hands in my pockets. "Get going," her voice spit through the screen door. Feeling the pressure of her gaze, I reluctantly stepped off the porch.

Grover was swinging away, seeing how high he could go. I looked at him but the words wouldn't come. Eyes fixed upon the patch of dirt beneath the swing, I whispered, "My mama says I can't play with you anymore."

He stopped swinging and stared at me. "What you say?"

"Mama says I can't play with you."

"Huh?" he said.

I couldn't look him in the eyes, not then nor ever again. "Ya gotta go," I mumbled. I heard his feet shuffle toward the alley and the gate slam shut. I didn't even look up. I just slipped into our garage, a dark place with a cinder floor, cobwebs, broken windows, and bogeymen, a place I usually avoided. But that afternoon I squatted there in a corner until Mother called me to dinner for the third time.

Grover and I stopped talking to one another after that, and my feelings at school changed from boredom to shame. Although my parents, like the General and the Captain before them, placed their faith in education, I was at best an indifferent student. At worst I hated school, and I hated second grade more than any other. When the school year began in September 1956, I was assigned to a remedial class for slow learners and problem children—the only predominantly Negro class in the school. Stone silent, I sat and stared. I knew why I was with the dummies: I couldn't read.

Propelled by my pouting, and the panic of a mother who had entered first grade already able to read, my parents arranged for me to be tutored by my first-grade teacher, Miss Spalo. With one-on-one instruction, her gentle encouragement, and my own stomach-twisting fear of being labeled stupid, I was promoted into the regular second grade by Christmas.

Grover and I stopped seeing one another altogether when his parents transferred him to St. Dorothy's Catholic School. Years later, I caught sight of him seated behind me on the South Park bus. I twisted in my seat, intent on jumping up and saying, "Hey, Grover." Then I remembered, slouched deep into my seat, and hoped he hadn't seen me.

Color Conscious

When I was a child, I would stand and gaze at the starry firmament and contemplate infinity. As I stood there, the boundary that is time dissolved; I expanded my spirit to fill the boundary that is space . . . Transcending boundaries was fun in those days. But, as I reached adulthood, it became more difficult. More and more, I was aware of the boundaries of race, class, age and sex.

—Yvonne Seon, "Transcending Boundaries"

Calumet Avenue was an unremarkable tree-canopied street lined with brick bungalows and well-kept front lawns wide enough to accommodate our touch football games. But we didn't live in a bungalow. Our two-story, pale-orange brick house rose above the others, and its large, shady front porch served as a spot for the neighborhood kids to gather. There was Tag O'Leary, a scrappy, little, dark-haired Irish boy. And Tommy Plutz, who was blond and good-natured. And gung ho Eugene Payton, white, a couple of years older than me, with a muscular build and thick, dark eyebrows. His father had been a sergeant in the U.S. Army, so Eugene was into all things military. A born leader, he ruled on the block and was president of the student council at school. Whenever I was sent to get Philip, I knew that he probably would be at Eugene's.

And there was my buddy, Nipper Nipson. We first met in the alley. "Where you live?" I asked.

"Down by the garage that's about to fall over," he said.

"Bet mine's worse." But one glance at how his leaned and I conceded.

A forerunner of today's nerds, Nipper had brown skin and long, dark, wavy hair that made him look a bit Mexican. He was a Negro, though he claimed to have Indian blood. Maybe it was true and maybe it wasn't. Everyone claimed they were part something, but for sure no one back then thought being colored was anything to brag about.

Actually, race was of no great concern as we tore around. A major embarrassment, however, was Mother's cowbell—as soon as we heard its clang, the gang would begin mooing. "Time for all cows to go home," Eugene would proclaim. They could laugh; their parents all used whistles. Philip and I were called home to an earlier bedtime than those of our friends, but our brooding, begging, and whining about the unfairness of it all made no difference. Our parents' stricter rules prevailed.

At bedtime, Mother would appear at our bedroom door to kiss us good night but only after we knelt and prayed:

Now I lay me down to sleep
I pray the Lord my soul to keep;
If I should die before I wake,
I pray the Lord my soul to take. Amen.

I saw God up above, sitting on a massive throne in a cloud-filled heaven, his brow furrowed, his long white beard flowing over white robes. Later in the dark, listening to the traffic on South Park and staring at the dark sky, I wondered: How far out in space is heaven? How does he keep it all afloat? And how can he listen to all our prayers at once? And . . . ? and . . . ?

And then one night I wondered: What color is God? Until that moment I had pictured him as a white man, but suddenly that didn't seem fair. Could he be brown like me? That didn't seem right either. Then I remembered grace at dinner:

God is gray.
God is good,
Let us thank him,
For our food.

Yeah, that was it. God was gray like the people on our grainy black-and-white television set. Another night I envisioned all the different kinds of people in the world—the Chinese and Indians, Pygmies and Watusi. I saw people with pointed noses and flat ones, with nappy black hair and blond locks, with red hair and no hair at all. What did God look like? I wondered. And what color was he? The question of God's appearance was a problem I couldn't solve until it occurred to me that God might be some mixture I couldn't imagine. Maybe God was what the world was moving toward; maybe God looked the way all people would look someday.

God and race were confusing. By the time I became conscious of race as a problem that extended beyond Mother's admonitions, almost all the white kids had moved away. One by one they fled, first Tag and later Tommy, as middle-class Negroes supplanted working-class whites. Eventually, other than a Jewish family across the street, Eugene's was the only white family left.

Arriving at Eugene's house one day, I spied a thin, old colored woman standing on the porch. *Housekeeper,* I thought as I dashed to his back door. "Yo, Gene," I yelled. He popped out, saying, "Not now, my grandma's visiting."

His grandmother? *Mark, you moron.* I ran home, brooding. How was I supposed to know that Eugene wasn't white? His family looked white, like Italians. I retreated to my room, opened the closet door, and looked in the mirror. How many times had I heard my Great-aunt Irene say, "Where'd we get this black child from?" She, like Mother and Granddad, was light-complexioned, but there was no denying that my skin was brown, and even a shade darker than Philip's and Carole's.

It wasn't fair. Paging through *Jet* magazine I would see advertisements for skin-bleaching cream and think to myself, *Maybe if*

I used some of this. . . . But it didn't matter whether these products would lighten my skin because I knew without asking that Mother wouldn't tolerate me using them. It just wasn't fair.

Of course, race shouldn't matter. Mother had often told me that all people are equal, but the world said otherwise. There weren't many colored folks on TV. There was Rochester on the *Jack Benny Show*; Buckwheat and Farina on *The Little Rascals*; and, of course, the raucous characters on *Amos 'n' Andy*, which I never missed. But TV was no antidote for my doubts; these were the "common Negroes" Mother fulminated against. Yet, if we were all equal, why should I have to bust my butt to prove I wasn't one of them? The scariest inference, too frightening to really consider but too obvious to ignore, was that Negroes were inferior. Was it possible? Overwhelmed by confusion and too daunted to ask for an explanation, I pushed the unbearable thought away whenever it surfaced.

Afro-Americans are excruciatingly color conscious. Slavery's legacy left self-esteem so fragile and nuanced it turned on whether you were a "free Negro" or a "slave," then turned again on whether you were "house Negro" or "field hand." Skin color was how you knew the difference, and it led to obsessive attention to subtleties of shade and hair texture. Unspoken, the dynamic still holds sway.

Although the calculus of color was never overtly taught, like most Afro-Americans, I just knew it. Eugene looked white and Nipper didn't, but Nipper had "good" hair and so did my sister Carole. That meant it was wavy, so she was spared Lauren's ordeal of having her hair combed straight until her scalp ached. And while mine wasn't "good," it wasn't nappy either. Mother made sure of that, with Ultra Sheen and vigorous brushing. Guys with "worse" hair than mine put on even more goo and wore stocking caps, or got rid of the kinks using a fiery, lye-based straightener and a hot iron. None of the neighborhood boys had hair like that. While some weren't as fair as Eugene, they weren't as dark as Nipper and me; they were what we called "yellow." In fact, Rodney Hammond was the only person we ran with who was darker than I was.

Four years older than me, Rodney was tall and lanky, with short hair and plump, protruding lips. I liked him, but nonetheless from the safety of my own yard I taunted him; in the perverse hierarchy of color, he was the only one beneath me. "Long legs, liver-lipped Rodney. Long legs, liver-lipped Rodney," I chanted—until the day he caught me. Afterward I slunk home and hid in my closet, in the fetal position, all the while muttering, "I hate your guts." But what I really hated was the skin I was trapped within.

Already world-weary, I withdrew further into books, the basement, the bathroom, under the bed, because I dreaded the gang of kids on our block. My standing in the pecking order was so low that even my brother, Philip, being as tough as I was timid, ranked ahead of me. I was sure to be picked last when we chose sides, and I didn't know about "doing it." "Chump, you don't know nothin'," they all hooted the day I asked what a boner was. When forced to go out and play, I'd hole up in Nipper's bedroom and lose myself in his stacks of comics. My heroes, Superman, Batman, and Flash, were everything I wasn't: powerful, fast, smart, and white.

My memories of elementary school are gloomy, and the feelings associated with it so unpleasant that I suppressed them until I visited St. Louis in my mid-thirties and called on Mrs. Hudson. For years Mrs. Hudson had tended to us while Mother, a caseworker for Illinois Children's Home and Aid Society, was busy advocating for needy children. She washed and ironed, cleaned and cooked. She was always there when we got home from school, there when we needed comforting, and there when being direct was called for. We called her our "Other Mother."

After hugging and kissing at our little reunion, Mrs. Hudson and I began to reminisce. She reminded me of how I always deferred to my younger brother. I hotly denied it. "Yes, you did," she shot back. "Whenever I asked you what you wanted, you'd turn to Philip and say, 'What do we want, Philip?'" I cringed as she mimicked my whimpering, but continued to shake my head in denial. "Okay," she said, pointing a finger at me, "how about Wednesdays?"

Choir practice took place on Wednesday afternoons, and we

were always late. Standing at the front door, I would whine, "Come on, Philip, come on." In response he would go slower, and I would whine louder, "Phil-lup, Phil-lup." As Mrs. Hudson reenacted the scene to remind me, I ached inside. She had my number—I was king of the wimps.

Our sister Carole once observed that Philip never had an older brother who could look out for him. From his point of view, my lack of assertiveness meant he had to fend for himself on the block and deal with the consequences of challenging our parents' rules at home. Although I was the elder brother, I was ill-suited for the role, and our parents made it worse by making me responsible for him. If I ignored Philip or left him behind when I set off for choir practice, I got in trouble. He didn't care about making my life easier. If I gave him orders, he paid no attention. If I tried to make him do anything, we fought. If I socked him he'd go crazy, flailing with his fists, kicking with his feet, and biting if he got a chance. And me? I ran.

The outcome was predictable: I'd get blamed and spanked when Dad got home. So eventually I just let Philip decide what to do. I figured, why fight? Instead I retreated into passive aggression and sly teasing. When Philip went wild, I'd simply lock myself in the bathroom and wait, leaving him pounding on the door, screaming, "I'm gonna kill ya!"

I spent a lot of time hiding from Philip, from the gang, and from life. Creeping into the house, I would sneak upstairs and hide in the comforting darkness of Dad's closet. There, next to the 8mm-film splicer and beneath his white tuxedo, I would crouch, muttering, over and over, "Everybody hates me, nobody likes me, everybody hates me, nobody likes me."

Our family ended up Unitarians because one Sunday morning Dad, observing Philip and me peering out the window at the families heading for church in their Sunday best, said to himself, "I don't like this void. We've got to be something." He had been raised Christian Scientist so that's where he took us. But when we got home, Mother said, "No more of that," and the two of them had it out. Dad reported the argument to his colleague, our uncle Pud, who invited our family to accompany him to the Unitarian church near the University of Chicago campus. Mother took Philip, Carole, and me; she liked it, and the next week Dad came with us. Fifty years later, he still attends that congregation and Mother is there as well, interred in the crypt beneath the church.

In 1954 Dad cradled infant Carole, while Philip and I, wearing matching plaid sport jackets, stood in front of the congregation to be christened—the first Negro children named and dedicated in the First Unitarian Society of Chicago since its founding in 1836. Once again we were on the vanguard of integration. By the mid-sixties the congregation was 15 percent Afro-American, and today about a third of its members are people of color.

At times my life felt like an excruciating experiment. Racial integration meant being one of a few Negroes in a sea of white; it meant awkward situations and embarrassment lurked near, and so fostered in me an almost aberrant cautiousness. At eight, I was a skinny, bespectacled soprano in the congregation's children's choir. Today it is known as the Chicago Children's Choir, a multicultural, multiracial chorus that has grown to more than three thousand children, but in 1956 there was only one Negro, a girl named Ermetra Black. The next year, Kris Yasutake and I joined, then Philip, Kris's brother Kim, and the Fuji sisters. Slowly the choir came to mirror the changing neighborhood, which was integrating despite the University of Chicago's resistance.

I knew a lot of the kids from Sunday school, and found in the choir a sense of camaraderie that I didn't experience on the block. Nonetheless, before Philip joined, when I looked around Woolman Hall the only other person I saw with brown skin was pigtailed Ermetra, and now and then growing self-conscious, I would look away, because I did not want to notice that we were the only ones. Let myself remember that we were different, and I would feel alone, apprehensive, and confused. Yet every time I looked up, there she was.

It was no accident that the choir later developed such rich diversity. In 1947 a light brown-skinned college student named Polly McCoo began teaching in the Sunday school. At the same time the congregation's Women's Alliance brought forward a resolution "to invite our friends of other races and colors who are interested in Unitarianism to join our church . . ."

The resolution set off a storm. The church bylaws included a clause that denied membership to Negroes. The minister, Leslie Pennington, threatened to resign unless the clause was changed and the new resolution adopted. This led to a board meeting that raged into the night, until finally the two board members who opposed integration caved in. At the end, someone suggested they sing "Amazing Grace," but however sweet the sound may have seemed that evening, once the congregation passed the resolution, the opposing board members left the church.

The next spring, when Polly joined the church, the president declared to her father, "We don't mind if members are like your daughter." With that disturbing welcome, the slow process of integration began: One Negro joined; the next year, another. My family started attending in 1953. At that time, only a dozen of the more than five hundred Unitarian congregations in the United States had five or more Negro members. Most had none, and other denominations were similar. No matter how much integration took place during the rest of the week, on Sunday mornings, the races went their separate ways. Unitarian minister Homer Jack, a founder of the Congress on Racial Equality, once called Sunday at eleven "the Segregation Hour."

No one had envisioned a children's choir, much less a multiracial one, when the resolution to invite "friends of other races" finally passed in 1948, but it created the conditions that made integration possible.

Beyond transforming the church, the choir opened worlds that normally would have been closed to me. In 1960 I was among a handful of boys from the choir who were chosen to sing with the Chicago Lyric Opera, as altar boys in a production of *Tosca*.

Of course, we had to know the music and cues, but on top of that we had to learn a lot of Catholic rigmarole: how to genuflect, cross ourselves, and bear the incense. On the night of the dress rehearsal we were wound up, bouncing off the walls as they tried to dress us in cassocks, surplices, and slippers. Then it was makeup for everyone—except me, the one Negro kid. But if makeup was part of the show, I wasn't going to be left out. I pouted. I whimpered. I whined. And they caved. Powder puff in hand, I gave myself the same treatment as the other kids; it also hid my blush when word came back afterward that I'd looked like a clown. Obviously, the Chicago opera scene wasn't ready for Al Jolson in reverse, and from then on, I went without.

At school I was slowly maturing. I won first prize at the school science fair in sixth grade and won the Negro history essay contest in seventh. With each accomplishment, my anemic self-confidence grew a smidgen. Then, as that school year drew to an end, I found a girl who was as interested in me as I was in her, and that set me vacillating between ecstasy and terror. Dushka Hawkins was her name, and she lived one block north on Calumet. She had big brown eyes; her hair was gathered in a bun and her skin was a soft, luscious cinnamon. We talked as we walked home from school, which gave me hope that soon she'd pucker up and give me some sugar. She'd have to; after all, I was going away to Switzerland. My father had been granted a one-year appointment to the Physics Institute of the University of Bern. I just knew she'd do more than shake hands and say good-bye—all I wanted was to kiss her pretty lips.

On the last day of school, as I rushed out of class looking for Dushka, some black-assed high school student picked my report card out of my back pocket. I whirled about. "Give it back, man," I pleaded. Back then, you didn't call anybody "black" anything unless you were ready to duke it out.

"Go fuck yourself, motherfucker or I'll give ya this!" he said, shaking his fist in my face.

I backed off, hesitated, then dashed away. I wasn't about to get my ass kicked over a piece of paper. My folks could get a copy from the office. Dushka was the only thing on my mind, and I didn't want to miss my last chance to walk her home.

I found her near the corner. She smiled sweetly as we strolled up Prairie Avenue. A half block from school there was a commotion behind us—a gang of boys crossing 78th Street. I returned to our conversation, her eyes, her luscious lips.

"That's the nigger that's goin' to Switzerland. Kick that sonofabitch's ass," someone shouted. My stomach clenched. A hand slammed down on my shoulder. Jerked around, I cocked my arm, ready to throw a punch that never landed. It rained fists. Dushka screamed. My glasses went flying. Red flashes filled my eyes. Clutching hands ripped my shirt open as I was hurled to the ground. I instinctively covered my head with my arms and curled into a ball, while they kicked, stomped, and cursed me. Then nothing, except the sound of sneakers running away.

Wrapped in pain, I remained curled up until the silence enticed me to peek. Nothing happened. I struggled to my knees and groped around until I found my glasses. Blood from my nose and cut lips filled my mouth with its thick, salty taste. I staggered to my feet and scanned the block. The boys had vanished, and so had Dushka. Holding my side like a wounded soldier, I limped home, tears blurring my vision.

We were soon to leave for Switzerland, so I holed up at home—no way I was going outside again. Just one week. Just a few more days. My hiding ended when I balked at running an errand to the corner store. Dad blew up, "Don't be silly, boy. Nobody's going to bother you." Heart pounding, I sped down Calumet and past the basketball court where the gang that had beaten me hung out. "Calumet" is a Native American word for "peace pipe," but whatever sense of security my block had provided was gone.

The next day, gathering my courage, I slipped out our back door and sprinted up the alley to Nipper's to say good-bye. Meanwhile, Dushka hadn't called. The day before we left, I stole up Calumet and stood opposite her house, staring at the shady porch while I stood in the glaring sun. The heat made the minutes drag.

I wanted to knock on her door, but unnamed fears fixed me there, watching, waiting, praying, and finally retreating. I could only hope that things would be different when I returned in a year.

Bon Voyage

*I am black and was born and raised and lived in America,
and the fact that race prejudice was one of my reasons for
leaving it is inescapable.*

—Chester Himes, *The Quality of Hurt*

In 1962 President Kennedy's so-called "New Frontier" was proving
to be more rhetoric than reality as civil-rights protests mounted
across the South and elsewhere. In Chicago, black parents dem-
onstrated against de facto segregation, double shifts, and mobile
classrooms in the public schools, and University of Chicago students protested racial discrimination in off-campus housing.

Yet these events made little impression on me, for my thoughts
were on Dushka and my family's impending voyage.

Dad's professional reputation had been built on research that
shed light on the origin of the solar system through the dating of
meteorites. The invitation to work at the Physics Institute of the
University of Bern was well deserved. The miracle was that my
father, who grew up in a starkly segregated society as the son of a
working-class family, had become a respected member of an overwhelmingly white scientific community.

"I was just an inkspot," Dad said. "That was the case with
everything I did because there were no other blacks in nuclear
chemistry or meteoric science." The same had been true for the

handful of Afro-American scientists who had gone to Europe before him.

The morning we left for Switzerland, I found my way down the front stairs of our house in the dark, crossed the yard, and flopped into the backseat of our pale-green 1951 Mercury. Heavy under its load, the hand-me-down from Great-uncle Harry rolled south down Stony Island and roared onto the Skyway, where it arched above the Windy City. Looking back, I saw the South Side spread out behind me, a grid filled with blocks of bungalows and treetops, apartment buildings and church spires. Far away in the first light, I could just make out the silhouette of the downtown skyline. We were on our way.

I had wanted to go to Europe ever since 1958, when Dad returned from the Second Geneva Conference on the Peaceful Uses of Atomic Energy with white chocolate and picture slides that I never tired of viewing. But my yearning for far-off lands was first kindled by Great-uncle Lloyd.

Great-uncle Lloyd had traveled the world exploring places we couldn't imagine and his many souvenirs had accumulated in the mystery-filled basement of 114 S Street. If we kids persisted in asking questions, he'd turn his blue eyes toward the ceiling, roll his dentures around in his mouth, stroke the stubble on his pale chin, and in a slow gravelly voice tell us a story.

Once he had sailed down the coast of West Africa with a group of doctors, but when they arrived in South Africa he was forced to remain onboard. The government wouldn't allow him to accompany the other doctors on their tour because he was "colored." And so, in response to my indignant queries, I learned about apartheid.

Then there was pipe-smoking, yarn-spinning Great-uncle Harry, who had seen Europe from the trenches. Only later did I realize that most of the Afro-American men I met who had been to Europe had been there to fight the Nazis. Ironically, the war had provided new opportunities for Afro-Americans, even if in a segregated army. They returned with changed expectations and fortified confidence, ready to take up the battle at home. Men forged anew at a terrible price. Some 909,000 served in the U.S. Army, largely in the quartermaster, engineering, and transportation corps.

Harry's all-Negro battalion arrived on Omaha Beach six days after D-Day, when, as he told me, "they were still bulldozing dead men and body parts into burial pits." At thirty-six, he had been deemed too old for combat, but still came under fire when the Germans attempted to repel the invasion. "Two days after we landed, they said to us, 'You got ten minutes to strike them tents.' Man, then, they turn us right around and send us back to the coast," Great-uncle Harry said. "And we can't go on them roads because they're full of mines. So we're skirting round between the road and the open fields when them antiaircraft guns cut loose. Boy, them big guns were talking. Heard that friendly fire comin' in and that was it." The blast buried him beneath a hedgerow. He awoke two days later in an English hospital, deaf in his left ear. After convalescing, he was stationed as a guard in a transfer camp outside Paris. He was promoted to sergeant, but only briefly. "Man, I got busted for missin' reveille one morning when I didn't get back in time and they demoted me to corporal. Of course, I never obeyed my mama neither."

Uncle Lloyd enlisted. He was trained in Utah before being sent to Camp Lee, Virginia, and then Elgin Field, Florida. There segregation was enforced; colored soldiers were barred from the movie theater and store at the base—yet the German POWs were served. Lloyd's unit, the 1898 Aviation Engineer Battalion, landed in southern Italy shortly after the Allied invasion and began building airfields for Allied bombers. As the battle line shifted north, his unit stayed put and watched the troops move to the front.

In Italy Uncle Lloyd saw the Colored 366th Infantry Regiment (the first all-Negro regular army unit commanded only by Negro officers), the Nisei 442nd Regimental Combat Team (made up of second-generation Japanese Americans and praised as the most decorated in the army), and the Brazilian troops, which stood out because they were completely integrated.

When the United Service Organizations (USO), which provided R and R for the troops, refused to serve Negroes at their centers, the colored soldiers went to the British equivalent instead. Indeed, outside the USO, Lloyd didn't encounter discrimination in Italy. "Over here," he wrote home in March 1944, "it is good for a change. There is no obvious racial prejudice from the Italians. They could not afford it now, and there is none from the white troops around. That is a relief from the bigotry in the States, particularly where we come from."

All of this seeped into my consciousness. A vast world lay beyond Chicago and D.C. and somehow I knew without understanding that Europe was a better place to live if you were a Negro. This in itself was odd because my siblings and I had never known overt discrimination or poverty. My notions about prejudice had been formed indirectly, and my fears fastened on to what might happen but never had.

Much of what I knew about the Negro world came from our feisty, white-haired Great-aunt Irene. She told it like it was, and it took no prodding to coax a tale from her. She would enthrone herself before us, as fair-skinned and blue-eyed as Great-uncle Lloyd, but more regal than any of her siblings.

"Now let me tell you children how it used to be when your daddy was your age," she would say. "Back then Negroes had to sit in the balcony of the movie house. Of course, that was before the Republic and the Booker T were built and we had our own places to go."

Great-aunt Irene was definitely the source of the most interesting facts about how it had been, and the most dramatic were always about herself. "Did I ever tell you about Admiral Niblack's wife?" she would ask. She had, but it didn't matter because I was eager to hear it again. "Must have been 1917. I went to work one afternoon and there my lady is packing and crying. I said, 'What's happened?' She says, 'America's entered the war and Admiral Niblack has to go to Norfolk. I'll be leaving the apartment,' she says, 'and I don't know what's going to become of you.'" Great-aunt Irene leaned toward us and her eyes flashed. "Well, that didn't make any difference to me because I planned on going into government and had already taken the examination, but when she found out that I had taken it, she got very angry with me because she didn't think that a colored woman had any business working in the government. She says, 'I hope you fail.' And I told her I can't fail. It's just a second-grade examination. Well, I passed. She broke up her apartment and I went to the Bureau of Engraving. Oh, well," Great-aunt Irene sighed, "you know, people have always been prejudiced, my dear, and they'll be prejudiced until they die."

That is how I learned about prejudice. Not firsthand, but from stories leaping out of other people's lives, dashing in black and white across our television screen, jumping at me from headlines, and simmering as rage in Mother's voice. I couldn't escape knowing about segregated water fountains, lunch counters, buses, and schools. After watching a hateful white mob yelling at colored kids integrating Little Rock Central High School in 1957, I had gone to bed with a stomachache. I knew about the Ku Klux Klan and lynchings and especially about Emmett Till—a fourteen-year-old Chicago boy who had gone to Mississippi to visit his uncle during the summer of 1955. He had allegedly whistled at a white woman. For this act of adolescent swagger, the woman's husband and his half brother kidnapped, tortured, and executed Till, then sank his mutilated body in a river. Distressed by the brutal slaying, tens of thousands of Chicagoans converged on the South Side chapel where the funeral was held. His death filled the newspapers and dinner conversations, and the older boys on the block elaborated on the grisly details. I was six at the time, and just a little older when the two murderers were tried and acquitted, but I still knew something terrible had happened. What I felt was terror, terror of the South. My first trip there didn't take place until 1968, six months after Dr. King was assassinated. Philip was attending Morehouse College and I flew to Atlanta to visit him. As I stood in the queue at the taxi stand, a cab pulled up, a white man at the wheel and a Confederate flag emblazoned on the door. Dread gripped me. The knot in my stomach returned. *No way!* I looked down the lane. Seeing a black cabby, I quickly stepped aside and waved along the people behind me.

Even though my childhood had buffered me from directly experiencing the harsh reality of racism, I still lived in fear. But now, on the eve of our trip to Europe, the possibility of experiencing prejudice seemed further away than ever.

We disembarked from the SS *France* in Le Havre. Traveling made Mother nervous, I saw it in her searching eyes and heard it in the rising tone of her voice crying, "George, George, George." It was a relief when her second cousin, Mabel Smythe, met us at the train station in Paris. Another descendant of Catherine Clevland, Mabel was fair-skinned and sophisticated. She was returning to Damascus to join her husband, Hugh Smythe, the U.S. Ambassador to Syria. Ten years later, she would become an ambassador in her own right and represent the U.S. in the United Republic of Cameroon, but to us she was just Aunt Mabel.

Placing us in two taxis, Aunt Mabel spit out instructions in French and our drivers took off, cutting and screeching through the traffic. Our eyes fixed on the toy-like automobiles that sped and honked around us. The French drove the way Philip and I did in the bumper cars at Riverview Amusement Park. Then at the hotel I made a mistake. I used a bidet as a toilet and Mother, our live-in Emily Post, delivered a lecture about bidets and more. Europe would give her new reasons to correct me and more rules to dispense. Rules for situations I didn't even know existed.

Paris. Richard Wright called her a "city of refuge" and James Baldwin described her as a "European haven." She had drawn generations of Afro-Americans. Artist H.O. Tanner arrived in 1892. In 1919 scholar W.E.B. Du Bois organized the First Pan-African Congress there. A young Langston Hughes hung around for six months in 1924, found it "an endearing city" and kept returning. Activist and singer Paul Robeson performed in Paris during the winter of 1930, and Wright settled there in 1946. Baldwin followed two years later. Novelist Chester Himes, who had called for a Negro revolution a decade earlier, arrived in 1953 on the *Ile de France* as did Vincent O. Carter. Carter, an aspiring writer, gave Paris a crack but finding it inhospitable fled and circuitously ended up in "unfashionable" Bern, Switzerland, where he would spend the rest of his life laboring in obscurity.

Despite this history, I didn't warm to the city. Most of what adults like about it was lost on me. While our parents went out on the town, we were in bed and never saw any of the Parisian night-life. The ritual of sitting in outdoor cafés bored me. Yet everywhere we looked, people sat at small, round tables, nursing their drinks, their *Gauloises* passing between yellowed fingers and searching lips, their conversations dispersing into the air like smoke, their gaze following the passersby, and it seemed to me, our family in particular. The tribulations of Paris outweighed the pleasures and after three days I was eager to leave.

Traveling with my parents was not easy for an adolescent. We looked like refugees carrying everything we owned—suitcases of every shape, size, and color; a shopping bag full of cheese and crackers, fruit and candy, coloring books, crayons and toys, playing cards and magazines; plus an extra jacket or two. Mother had an air of disarray about her and fearing Carole and Lauren would go astray, she towed them along while Dad was either looking for or supervising a porter.

Philip and I kept our distance. We strode along, our new berets cocked. We played it cool, hoping no one would think us a part of the embarrassing circus fifty feet behind.

Arriving at the French-Swiss border outside Basel, Dad got off the train to find a money exchange. I watched his tall, bald figure hurry across the platform and disappear. He still hadn't returned when the train lurched forward. Mother bolted from her seat. She was about to head into Switzerland with four children, a thousand pieces of luggage, no money, and no husband. She pulled down the compartment window; flailing her arms, she leaned out and began to scream in her feeble German, "*Halt! Halt! Mein Mann! Mein Mann! Halt!*"

Heads turned. Everyone stared as she pointed and yelled, "Stop my husband!" The Swiss must have thought he was deserting her.

"Stop it, Mama," we implored. "Be quiet!" we begged as we tried to tug her back into the compartment. But she kept right on yelling, "*Halt! Halt!*" I looked at her and said, "Oh, God." Then glancing sideways, my eyes met Philip's, and we darted out of the compartment and down the corridor, putting as much distance as possible between her and us. A moment later the train, having moved a few feet while hooking on a new engine for the mountains, stopped.

Babes in Switzerland

EVERYBODY, Men, Women, Children, Dogs, Cats and Other Animals, Wild and Domestic, Looked at Me—ALL the Time!

—Vincent O. Carter, *The Bern Book*

When the train pulled into Bern, several faculty members of the Physics Institute and their wives waited on the platform. Whisking us through the old, dark, cavernous station, they deposited us at a taxi stand, where we were crammed into a black Mercedes-Benz taxi and dispatched to Finkenhubelweg 8.

At the end of the first block, I peered at a police officer directing traffic, his white-gloved hands in perpetual motion. He waved us on. We turned right, left, right again, then quickly left and up a shaded, narrow, cobbled street. We children were still jockeying for a good view when the taxi stopped halfway up the hill. Already? I couldn't believe it. I looked around and saw nothing but a huge green hedge. Scrambling out, we ran through the hedge's cavelike entrance and stopped. Our heads tilted upward. Before us stood a grand, pale-yellow stucco apartment building.

It was a long climb to the third floor. Sunlight streamed through the windows as we rushed from room to room, seven in all. Philip discovered the balcony, but when I stepped out on it, I froze; I reached the railing only by crawling on all fours. Slowly,

I stood up. Before me lay Bern and beyond it the mountains. In Chicago the only soaring peaks had been the spires and antennae sitting atop some of the highest skyscrapers in the world. In Bern on clear days when the *Föhn* was blowing, the visual effect made the Alps seem so close I felt I could reach out and touch them. We hadn't been in Switzerland long when we first heard the Föhn mentioned. "It's the Föhn," our downstairs neighbor would say, with a shake of his balding head. Whatever it was, it was something serious, something to do with the weather, and something of a mystery. Everything would seem fine, and then people would begin complaining. It was just a breeze, a gusty warm wind pouring over the Alps from the south. But to the Swiss, it was more than a wind; it had something to do with atmospheric pressure and gave some people headaches, made others' joints ache, caused still others to feel bad in unspecified ways and to do something utterly unSwiss: call in sick. Chicago is called the Windy City because of the winds that sweep in from the prairies to the west. Funneled between the canyon walls of the towering buildings, these create a blast that stop you in your tracks and steal anything unsecured; but this Swiss wind was different. When it was "Föhning" doctors canceled operations, and I would later learn of even more serious consequences.

Archaeological findings indicate that Bern may have been a Roman outpost, but its permanent settlement dates to 1191, and the old part of the city seemed more ancient to me than anything I had ever seen. The gray buildings, dark arcades, and narrow cobbled streets made it mysterious.

What a contrast to Chicago, which sprawled along Lake Michigan's southwestern shore. From our home on the South Side, its Loop was a solid forty-five-minute ride on the bus and the El. Bern, focused on a little bend in the river Aare, was compact. The center of the city was only a four-minute ride downhill on our bicycles over brain-rattling cobblestones.

Poverty didn't seem to exist in Bern—no rundown tenements or vacant lots, no rusty jalopies, and no poor people. There was no dirt either, except in gardens, and even there it was contained in immaculately kept plots. Any litter in the streets was regularly swept up by lean men in dull blue work uniforms. Broom in hand, a man in blue would appear from nowhere, sweep together whatever manure, leaves, and trash he found, scoop up the pile, and dump it into a barrel that sat on a cart attached to a black bicycle. Then off he went, leaving everything behind clean and tidy.

The afternoon we arrived, Bern was festooned with long colored banners and Swiss flags hanging from buildings and waving from the windows. The next day, August 1, was the Swiss National Day—a celebration of the 1291 defense alliance between the Uri, Schwyz, and Unterwalden communities, considered the beginning of the Swiss Confederation. Parades marked the early evening and fireworks filled the night. My sense of wonder grew as we stood on our balcony and watched the darkening sky explode.

All through August, Bern served as an amusement park for Philip and me. On the way to the bear pits by the Nydegg Bridge, we would zip through the middle of town, across its squares, and past flower-decked fountains crowned with statues. Sometimes we stopped on Kornhaus Square to marvel at one fountain in particular. *The Ogre* has a huge oval mouth from which protrudes the flailing legs of a boy he is devouring; another boy is tucked under his arm and others are pinned beneath his feet. At first I thought it an odd statue, perhaps taken from one of the Grimm brothers' fairy tales. But then I intuitively discovered its usefulness. Whenever we walked past that fountain with our mother and sisters, I'd grab Lauren and hold her above my head as an offering to this beast. She'd squeal "Mommy, Mommy," like a piggy going to slaughter until, inevitably, Mother ordered me to put her down. Twenty-five years later when I did the same to my four-year-old son, he started giggling and couldn't stop.

In Swiss German the fountain is called *Chindlifrässer*, and that doesn't translate as "ogre"—it means "child-eater." A closer look at this figure shows it to be neither a giant nor a monster but simply a man with a gigantic mouth. I didn't know at the time that this statue allegedly portrays a Jew and the fountain purported to commemorate a ritual murder attributed to the Jews in 1287. What I'd been having fun with wasn't at all amusing; it was the Swiss anti-Semitic underbelly.

Philip and I often visited the museums in nearby Helvetia Square, and for a while we were enamored of the wave machine at the swimming pool, but then we discovered we could float down the River Aare on inner tubes. Plunging into the river felt like jumping into an ice bucket, but the excitement of riding the surging, gray-green waters was more thrilling than any carnival ride. The river was so fast that life-saving poles, which looked like extra long shepherd's crooks, hung along its banks. Exploring Bern with Philip was exhilarating; in Chicago we'd never had such freedom to roam. As the months passed, for the first time I began to feel as if my life was my own.

If you were brave enough, Bern offered great opportunities for mischief. I wasn't. My friend, Jan Luss, was. He had moved from Yonkers to Bern with his mother, Rhoda, an artist; his stepfather, Henry Isaac, a translator for a Swiss bank; and his younger half brother, Jeff. Jan's eyebrows rose to a dark, devilish peak when he looked over the black frame of eyeglasses that sat halfway down his ample nose. "Come on," he would implore whenever I balked at one of his schemes, which was every time.

Franz Carl Weber, a marvelous toy store in the old town, never failed to turn Philip and me into bug-eyed, finger-pointing kids, repeating "Oh! I want that and that and that . . ." We never had any money, but loved going there nonetheless, until Jan ruined it. "Wait for me outside," he directed. Two minutes later he rushed by and winked. When we caught up, he flipped open his jacket, revealing a plastic bag. He had cased the store earlier, brought a shopping bag to stuff his booty in, and made his move when he saw there were no clerks in the basement. I peeked inside the bag and my stomach turned. There it was—the air gun he had coveted. "Holy crap, man," I said. I was certain they would think I, a colored kid, had stolen it and that if I ever walked in there again I'd get nabbed for his crime; that ended our excursions to Franz Carl Weber.

Before we arrived in Switzerland, the sum total of what I knew about the country amounted to mountains, St. Bernards, William Tell—and, of course, chocolate. To our delight, there was a Tobler chocolate factory a few blocks from our apartment. When the wind blew southward, the sweet, vanilla smell almost satisfied my craving. I loved chocolate. I would stop on the way home from school at the kiosk on Helvetia Square to buy a bar: milk chocolate, bittersweet, white, with raisins and rum, with hazelnuts, or liqueur-filled. The best place to binge was the supermarket Migros. Philip, Jan, and I would pool our francs and skip down the street singing, "Migros for Negroes and Jews, tra la . . ." Once there we would buy a huge cheap kilo bar, or maybe three *Mohrenköpfe*.

Mohrenkopf was a cookie topped with marshmallow and dipped in chocolate—a fancy Oreo—and it was delicious. Unfortunately, its name meant "Moor's head." I wouldn't ask for one because its wrapper displayed Sambo, a shiny black face with white teeth. It felt wrong that the Swiss found it appealing, and I was convinced that the girl in the kiosk would look at the wrapper and then at me and think, "You've got one already," snickering behind my back as if I were a cannibal. I tried to enjoy eating a *Mohrenkopf*, but only when someone else bought it. Even then, my self-consciousness spoiled it. The *Mohrenkopf* wasn't an aberration, for the Swiss had very strange notions about Negroes, and sometimes so did I.

Going to the movies proved to be a challenge. At twelve and thirteen, Philip and I were too young to get into the more interesting films. Tired of being hassled, I came up with a plan to see *Irma La Douce*, a comedy about a prostitute. I carefully darkened the fine hairs above my upper lip with Mother's eyeliner. At the box office, I pointed at the movie title, held up two fingers, and said, "*Zwei*." The cashier looked us over and hesitated, but not knowing how to judge our ages she let us in. If she hadn't, it would have been time for my emergency plan—a plan I dreaded carrying out. In loud indignation I was prepared to yell, "Ooga, booga, boo!" and whatever other nonsense words came forth as long as they sounded angry and African. It was a plan I never stooped to using.

One afternoon, Philip, Mother, and I walked down to the city center to go shopping. Ahead of us, the traffic officer was poised on a rostrum above the cars, controlling all the comings and goings with the deft authority of his hands. Suddenly a man on the other side of the street stopped, grabbed his companion's arm, pointed at us, and yelled, "Nigger, nigger." I gasped and froze.

Philip clenched his fists, moved to the curb, and said, "Mama, they're calling us niggers."

Before Philip could utter another word or make another move, she grabbed our wrists and dragged us away. "Stop it," she snapped. "They're saying *Neger*. That's how you say Negro in German. It's no reason to get angry. Control yourselves."

"But Mama—" I protested.

"Hush up," she hissed, obeying a Negro mother's protective instinct—a hair-trigger instinct that squashed any move to confront a white man. "People are simply surprised to see Negroes. They've never seen people like us before, so get used to it."

Getting used to it was hard. It happened constantly—on the street, in a tram, or in a store, and it made us mad. Children, in particular, pointed and whispered loudly, "*Lueg, Negerli!*" (Look, little Negroes.) We stared them down. We crossed our eyes. We stuck out our tongues. Adults were nearly as outrageous as children: They would stop whatever they were doing to stare. A few even asked to touch three-year-old Lauren's braided hair and reached for her little pigtails without waiting for an answer.

The Swiss were curious beyond the point of rudeness, and in response Philip and I developed a strategy. A culprit's eyes would shift as he passed by, eager to stare but intent on doing so surreptitiously. Glancing at each other, Philip and I began the countdown— *eins, zwei, drei*—then we'd whip around and glare. Sometimes our death-look would land on an innocent back and leave us feeling foolish, but more often we pranced gleefully away after seeing the mortified expression on the face of some gawking jerk.

That's the way it was: Philip and I staring at them staring at us. I had no idea what they thought they saw, but I saw a stiff, somber people whose formality didn't hide their lack of tact. Greetings were mandatory except in crowds. Whether encountering a neighbor or a stranger on the street, one was expected to say *grüessech*, the Bernese equivalent of "hi." So we walked around saying *grüessech* but speaking the local dialect didn't make anyone stare less; we were still *Negerli*.

Something else bothered me—Swiss women couldn't vote there, and it was impossible to imagine why. In 1920, my great-grandmother had been the first Negro woman to vote in Montross, Virginia; in Chicago, Mother had served as a poll watcher; and across the South Negroes protested poll taxes and other practices that kept them from voting. But in Switzerland, a country proud of its democratic tradition, women still were denied this fundamental right.

My suspicions about the Swiss were further reinforced by a story told to us about Prince Wilson, a Ghanaian studying at the University. He had been shopping at Loeb, a large department store in Bern, when he overheard a man tell his son that if the boy didn't wash he'd end up as black as that man over there. Drawing himself up to his full height of five feet, Prince Wilson marched over and, in his best German, said that he had heard what the man told his son and that, for his information, he, Prince Wilson, showered every day and was cleaner than any Swiss he had ever met. His skin was black and beautiful and had nothing to do with *Schmutz*. Having straightened the man out, Prince Wilson proceeded to walk away, until he was suddenly lifted off the ground. Two brawny Swiss women wordlessly marched him to the train station and dropped him there, and as they walked away, Prince Wilson realized that they must have overheard him correct the errant father and were letting him know he was not welcome in Bern.

I didn't like the Swiss: their rudeness and rules, their BO— they didn't seem to know about deodorant—and tough-textured toilet paper. But when I complained, Mother cut me off. "I imagine," she said, "that we look as strange to them as their habits do to us," and suggested I learn to be tolerant. But since hardly a day passed without an incident, it remained a struggle.

One afternoon while I stood outside the train station, a man walked up and asked, "Where are you from?"

"Chicago," I said.

"Oh! Chicago in Africa?"

"No, in America."

"In South America?"

"No, in the U.S.A."

"*Ach so*, I understand. Chi-ca-go! Gangsters! Gambling! Al Capone! Rat-tat-tat!" He sputtered while his imaginary machine gun mowed me down.

Another time Philip and I were crossing the little bridge by the Dälhölzli Zoo when an entire family—father, mother, and three children—stopped, pointed, and began shouting, "Look there at the Negroes," as if we were new acquisitions.

In actuality, we didn't know many Swiss. There were Dad's colleagues, of course. They generously loaned us bicycles and skis, but we didn't actually see his co-workers. The neighbors weren't particularly friendly, except for the family living on the first floor of our building—a widow, Frau Tobler, and her middle-aged son, Walter.

Wizened and stooped, Frau Tobler reminded me of the witch in "Hänsel and Gretel," but she doted on us and when she invited Philip and me to tea Mother drilled us on manners—when to say thank you, when to say please, how to hold a teacup. Forever hectored about elbows and etiquette, we already knew.

Frau Tobler led us into her sunny parlor. The table was covered with a lace tablecloth and set with a china tea set and little silver spoons. We sipped tea and snacked on cookies and little chocolates. She shuffled about, getting whatever we wanted, just as our own Great-aunt Irene would have done. Pampered, we felt good even as we struggled to communicate in German. We talked about school; she fretted about Walter, hoping her only child would soon finish his doctorate, get married, and have children.

I associated every good experience with the Swiss with a particular individual such as Frau Tobler; I universalized every negative

experience to the Swiss in general. As my anger mounted, my prejudice grew and sometimes even Mother stopped being tolerant.

One day the window display at Loeb was full of American
products and this caught Mother's attention because of our inces-
sant whining about things we wanted and couldn't get. However,
her curiosity turned to outrage when she saw, there in the middle
of the display, a large, ugly, and sensual picture of a Negro couple doing a dance. Dad wrote to the ambassador in protest: "The
contorted bodies and distorted faces reflect nothing that is really
reflective of the Negro in America." When the embassy refused to
act, Mother recruited the wife of a professor at the Physics Institute as her translator, then marched back down to the store and
gave it to them. The next day, the picture was gone.

On October 4, 1962, the *International Herald Tribune* announced:

SCHIRRA ORBITS SIX TIMES, PICKED UP IN PACIFIC
3600 PARATROOPERS PULL OUT OF OXFORD, MISSISSIPPI
U.S. CURB ON CUBA STIFFENED

I regularly bought the *Herald Tribune* to scan the headlines,
read the sports section, and enjoy the comics, but when the Cuban
missile crisis mounted, I became interested in the news itself. A
Gallup poll showed that 51 percent of the American public thought
that if the United States invaded Cuba war with Russia was likely.
Grim thoughts occupied me. For as long as I could remember, we
had prepared for this war back home—sirens whining across the
sky, school drills requiring us to line up in the corridor and then
sit against the lockers with our heads between our knees. Now,
with apprehension, I obsessively watched the headlines and eaves-
dropped on my parents' conversations.

Oddly, despite Kennedy's denouncements of communism and
Khrushchev's railings against U.S. imperialism, I felt safe. If war
began, Switzerland—with its fabled hollow mountains and huge
stockpiles of supplies—was a better place to be than Chicago. But
what about my family and friends? If the world I knew did end,

we'd be stuck in Switzerland, maybe forever. The possibility that this quirky, infuriating Swiss world might become our permanent home didn't sit well.

"George and Carole are home every day from 12:00 to 2:00," Mother wrote in a letter explaining another Swiss peculiarity. "Needless to ask what my program is with a two-hour lunch and an icebox that looks like a toy for Carole. I am fortunate to have an automatic washer at my disposal. I am trying to keep ahead of the ironing but with six of us it mounts up fast." After working outside the home all her married life, Mother struggled to fill the role of the fifties-style housewife. No longer a social worker, she was Frau Professor Reed, wife of a prominent scientist—a high-status role in class-conscious Swiss society, but nonetheless one without an identity independent of her husband.

Yet it didn't matter that Mother knew no one; it didn't even matter that she couldn't speak German. With Mother, no one stayed a stranger for long. She befriended the butcher, the green-grocer, and the baker. This was a good thing, from a teenager's perspective—life at home revolved around food. Until Switzer-land, Mrs. Hudson, our "Other Mother," had done most of the cooking. Since she was from Mississippi, ours had been a typical American diet, with more than a touch of soul—spongy Wonder Bread; cooked-to-death, catsup-drowned meatloaf; stewed pork chops; and on Sunday stringy pot roast, but also tangy collard greens, buttery grits, and golden corn bread. On New Year's Day, we would scarf down ham hocks with black-eyed peas and very rarely, thank God, chitterlings—slithery, smelly white pig intestines.

Now we were in Mother's hands. She served us yogurt, which was new to us. In 1962 it was not yet a staple in American homes, but we liked it. There were *Chäschüechli*, which were like miniature quiches, and more cheeses than we knew existed: Emmentaler—which everyone thinks of when they say Swiss cheese—Gruyère, Appenzeller, Raclette, Saanen, Hasliberger. *Wurst* resembled bloated hot dogs and *Spätzli* looked like misshapen noodles. For dinner we rarely saw a whole cut of meat, because meat was expensive and

Mother frugal. She made sauces—and we tried to fish for the meat without getting caught.

Whatever the situation, Mother had her personality going for her. A consummate extrovert, within one week of arriving in Bern she met Marion Richter, an American Jew who was an artist and the wife of a Swiss traffic engineer. Mrs. Richter introduced Mother to the Roletts. Ron Rolett, another American Jew, was a medical student and his wife, Karin, a lively Swede. Within a month we had become part of a small expatriate community that also came to include my friend Jan's family, the Isaacs. That this network of friends was largely Jewish was never commented upon; indeed in 1962 it was still taken for granted that Negroes and Jews were allies.

"Been spending a lot of time looking for schools for the kids. . . ." Every letter to our grandparents discussed the options: "Carole is the only child [in her class] who speaks English . . . We are afraid she may lose a year but we won't worry about it now . . ." "We are still trying to find something for the boys. We've just about been convinced that if the boys go to a German school it will be a complete waste. We are now investigating the English Speaking School whose quality is poor . . ." "Carole likes her school but we're a little concerned as to whether or not she'll get enough out of it. She doesn't care to read so we have a hard time trying to supplement . . ." In the end, Lauren went to a Swiss nursery school, Carole to the Rudolf Steiner School, and Philip and I enrolled in the English Speaking School of Bern.

At the English Speaking School, most students were the children of diplomats. There were only ten in our room: Mona, an Egyptian with shiny, dark hair and creamy skin; chunky Ralph Petty, an American; a girl from India; an English South African lad; four American girls; and Philip and me. In mid-fall, devilish Jan joined us.

A friendship blossomed between Sheila, one of the American girls, and me. She had broad shoulders and a dark tan, and played softball; we talked about sports, about the States, about school. Then one day the way she looked up into my face as we stood in the stairwell invited a quick, soft kiss. I felt it on my lips all the way up the stairs, and my thoughts never returned to schoolwork.

Sheila lived in Muri bei Bern, the well-to-do suburb where most U.S. Embassy personnel resided. Her father was the military attaché. One afternoon late that fall, I accompanied her home. The day was gray and brisk but it didn't matter. Her step had a boyish bounce and her long, dark hair moved across her shoulders in response. We talked. The conversation flowed easily as we wandered. I was lost in the warmth of her hand and the glow of her hazel eyes. When it grew dark, we hid deep in the shadows of her back yard and kissed—it was deliberate, tender, absorbing, and easier to do than what I did next.

"Sheila, would you like to go to a movie next Wednesday?"

"Have to ask," she said, and grinned. Her hair bounced as she ran inside.

Sitting on the stone wall that enclosed her yard, brittle leaves swirling around my feet, I couldn't help but smile. I waited and watched the door. The time dragged. Finally she appeared on the porch. Then I saw her father's silhouette through the screen door. The spring was gone from her step as she crossed the yard. Her eyes were fixed on the ground. A chill ran through me.

"Daddy says I can't go to the movie with you." She paused and I tried to catch her eye. "And I can't see you anymore."

My stomach sank. "Why?" I whispered.

"He won't let me go out with you because you're a . . ."

"What?"

"Because you're a Ne . . ." Her voice trailed off.

I looked at her, but her eyes wouldn't rise to meet mine. We just stood there in silence until she turned and left. *Please, please* formed upon my lips, but I just stood frozen until her silhouette passed into the house. Then, slipping over the stone wall, I slunk away up the street toward the train stop. My face felt flushed but I was cold inside. I rubbed my hands, almost pulling at the skin. I stared at them. They were brown. I was a Negro—couldn't change that. Like a drum in my head the protest beat: *It's not fair! It's not fair!*

Winter came. The snow fell and kept falling until it piled up higher than we imagined possible. The cold came too, severe enough to make Lake Zurich freeze over—a once-in-a-hundred-year event. Talk of skiing started one November morning when we awoke to find the top of the Gurten covered in white.

One Sunday Dad drove the whole family to a ski slope near Spiez. Eager to show off what we had already learned, Philip and I herringboned up the slope, then skied down, yelling, "Look at me." No one paid any attention.

Mother was prone on the slope, her arms and legs spread wide, her butt in the air. "Help me, George, help me," she hollered.

"Mommy, Mommy," Lauren cried.

"Just a second," Dad said and then, rather than help, kept shooting photographs of her misadventure.

Philip rushed over to untangle Mother. I, however, had only one urge: to put as much distance as possible between them and myself. Seeing Carole head off in one direction, I went the other. Right, left, right, left, back up the mountain.

In our enthusiasm, Philip and I swiftly graduated from snow-plow turns to ski jumping. We met our classmate Ralph in Muri, on the bank of the Aare, and in no time built a ski jump. I watched Ralph bomb down the slope, jump, sail into the air, land, and skid to a stop with a nifty little twist of his hips. Philip was already sidestepping his way up the hill; he lined himself up, pushed off, crouched, and as he reached the lip of the jump, launched his tough, skinny body. He soared, landed, and a moment later was lying in a heap at the bottom of the slope. He didn't know how to stop, but falling proved effective. It was my turn. While Ralph and Philip sidestepped up the slope, I stood there looking down. Me, do that? I wasn't budging.

"Chicken, chicken," one yelled.

"Jump or move your ass out of the way," said the other.

I pushed off. I leapt. I landed and fell in a tangle. But my moment of floating in midair was fantastic. I brushed myself off and started up the slope again.

Mom and Dad took ski lessons at a school on the Gurten. However, before January was over, Mother had run into a signpost and, as Dad wrote to his parents, "managed to gouge out 4 stitches worth of flesh from her leg." His letter continued: "It seems to be a fine sport if you can get the hang of it. But I'm not sure Lee should keep at it." Two weeks later catastrophe struck again. Dad tore a ligament in his knee and our parents' experiment with skiing ended.

But Philip and I were crazed. Propelled by second-child syndrome, Philip fearlessly schuss-bombed straight down every mountain. I followed. Inching my way to the bottom of the slope, I would spy Philip pumping his arm, signaling me to speed up and join him in line. Arriving home after a day of skiing, I should have been exhausted. Instead I would yell, "Christy, christy," jumping around with my legs together, a technique I was far from mastering on a ski slope. Mother never missed getting a little dig in by telling their guests, "Oh, Mark's a great skier—on the kitchen floor."

Philip and I went from resort to resort and hoped winter would never end. Our longest trip was a visit to the Ecole d'Humanité, a boarding school attended by the son of one of Dad's colleagues. We spent the first week in January there, skiing, sledding, and hanging out. The meals were a boisterous free-for-all, and I found the absence of Mother's constant hen-pecking to be liberating. As the week passed, an idea possessed me. While it took another six months to orchestrate, I eventually would find a way to attend the Ecole.

But the Ecole was just a dream when I left the school I was attending to go to Villa St. Jean. In a letter to his parents, Dad wrote: "Carole was getting too far behind in reading and arithmetic so last week we switched her to the English Speaking School . . . Mark is going to a school in Fribourg about an hour by train. It's a parochial school but it's in English and offers a more advanced program than he was getting here."

Traveling to Fribourg took hours, and I was anxious about attending a Catholic school, but leaving the English Speaking School was a relief. I wanted to forget Sheila. Against my will, I had kept sneaking glances at her, hoping she would respond with just a nod. But nothing came back, not even eye contact. There was no returning to the moment before we lost our racial virginity. Yearning, aching, and anger dominated my school days, and I never knew what it was like for Sheila because we never spoke again.

Oblivious to the reforms of the Second Vatican Council, my idea of the Villa St. Jean was based on the catechism I'd heard from the nun-terrorized kids I'd known in Chicago. Preparing for the Villa meant steeling myself to resist every effort to convert me. As a Unitarian, I knew that Jesus was not God, but human—a guy like other guys, but better. My God was a God of love. My God, and I wasn't 100 percent sure there was one, didn't send people to hell because they held beliefs different from those of the Catholic Church. The only belief I felt certain about was that what really matters is how we act toward one another.

The teachers at the Villa belonged to the Order of the Brothers of St. Mary, and the only female teacher in the school was Miss Flynn. She was not a nun, but she was Catholic, young, enthusiastic, and nice looking enough; and she taught an ethics class that was mandatory for non-Catholics. They called it Ethics; we called it religion in disguise.

One afternoon her topic was marriage, and as she explained that the Catholic Church didn't recognize marriages performed outside the Church, there was a commotion in the back of the room. Carlos, a boarding student from South America who had somehow escaped being raised Catholic, waved his hand. She called on him.

"Teacher, teacher," howled Carlos. "I'm a bastard. Oh, my God, I'm a bas-tard." Laughter filled the room.

"Stop it!" Miss Flynn screamed. "Stop it right now!" But her growing hysteria just provoked more mirth. Tears were streaming down her face by the time the monsignor appeared in the doorway, only to find us as quiet as angels.

Class at Villa St. Jean began with prayer, and since my Unitarian upbringing left me respectful of other faiths, I always stood when the eighth grade recited the Our Father and Hail Mary, prayers that would never cross my lips. One day Brother Gerard wasn't pleased with how the prayers were said in French. He told the class to write both prayers twenty-five times by the end of the day. My classmates scribbled madly all day long. At four o'clock, Brother asked for the assignment; the others handed theirs in and split. I stared hard ahead, waiting to be released. Another student behind me, also a Unitarian, hadn't written the prayers either.

"Where is your assignment?" Brother asked.

"I beg your pardon?"

"The Our Father and Hail Mary written in French twenty-five times."

"Excuse me. Did that include me?"

"It did."

"Well, I don't believe the same things your sect does and if you don't like it you can call my parents." With that I stood up and walked out, with the other Unitarian trailing behind.

I rushed home and told my parents. I knew they would set him straight. Then I waited but the call never came. The next morning, Brother said nothing. All day long I waited for the monsignor to call me into his office, but nothing ever happened.

I had never been to a Passover meal before, and as the train headed toward Bern from Fribourg I didn't know what to expect. My family had been invited to celebrate the holiday with the Isaacs— gentle, jovial Henry; short, sharp Rhoda; my friend, devilish Jan; and his little brother, Jeff. That afternoon, Jan and Philip went straight from school to Jan's house. As soon as they appeared, Rhoda fished some money out of her purse and sent them out to buy matzo. "Hey," Philip said, "how come I have to go with Jan to buy some Jewish stuff? It's tough enough being a Negro." Rhoda's mouth fell open, but before she could say anything, Philip laughed and Jan hooted and, money in hand, off they ran.

Dusk had fallen by the time we gathered around the dining room table. Candlelight lit the food and our faces; all else disappeared into darkness. Henry began by blessing the candles. Then he blessed the wine: "*baw-ruch a-taw ado-noi elohay-nu me-lech haw-olawm bo-ray p'ree ha-ga-fen.*" The words, as guttural as German but more melodic, sounded strange. He repeated it in English: "Blessed art thou, O Eternal, our God, King of the Universe, Creator of the fruit of the vine." We drank some wine; this was going to be fun.

Henry explained that by custom the youngest literate child asked four ritual questions. He turned to seven-year-old Jeff, and Jeff read from the Haggadah, the book of Passover readings: "Why is this night different from all other nights? On all other nights we may eat either leavened or unleavened bread, but on this night only leavened bread; on all other nights we may eat any species of herbs, but on this night only bitter herbs; on all other nights we do not dip even once, but on this night twice; on all other nights we eat and drink either sitting or reclining, but on this night we all recline." Not realizing I should wait, I took another sip of wine.

Henry read the response: "Because we were slaves unto Pharaoh in Egypt, and the eternal, our God, brought us forth." Being rather easygoing in their religious practices, they made quick work of the plagues and the slaying of the firstborn, and then we took ten drops from our wineglasses, symbolizing the suffering of the Egyptians. Next we improvised and sang the Negro spiritual "Go Down Moses," before rushing through the flight into the desert and the drowning of Pharaoh's army in the Red Sea. Celebrating the Jews' escape from slavery was something with which I could identify.

I had some more wine. My cheeks felt as if they were glowing as brightly as the candles. I was nearly fourteen but had never been allowed to drink alcohol before. Mother gave me her you-had-better-behave look, then hissed, "Now, Mark," but there wasn't much else she could do without making a scene. I smiled and took another sip.

That evening it felt natural to celebrate freedom, and as the years passed and other Jewish friends invited us to celebrate, I came to anticipate Passover. Yet, over time, an unrest grew within me. Behind this unease, which sweet wine couldn't soothe, was a question I couldn't answer. Languishing in slavery, black folks had told the story of the Exodus, named their children Moses, sung about the river Jordan, preached about the promised land and known that we, too, were God's children. I couldn't understand why my Jewish friends gathered in their homes to recall that they had been enslaved and to thank God for delivering them, yet Grammy denied that we were ever slaves. For Jews the story of their past was a source of strength, while we treated our enslavement like an embarrassment. In my family, the Newmans called themselves free slaves and the Reeds had always been free, as far as we knew. The stories passed down to us always emphasized that we were free. Perhaps my family came to believe the masters' justification that slaves were ignorant, shiftless brutes and therefore used the word *free* as a shield to guard our self-respect. But doing so required us to deny we were slaves and to consider bondage inherently shameful.

It was my Great-aunt Irene who had told me the truth about her mother, Mary Elizabeth, being a slave. As she continued to reminisce, especially as I grew older and more discerning, the world made sense in a way it hadn't before. I could see that Grammy's denial and my mother's admonitions not to act like a common Negro were both fueled by a need to bolster our self-esteem.

Where were the stories, songs, and rituals that preserved our history, instilled pride, and taught us to cherish freedom? Listening to Great-aunt Irene was as close as I have come to having an Afro-American Passover. Through her, as a living Haggadah, I learned to cherish my roots and caught a glimpse of how I became who I am.

She was far away the evening I celebrated my first Passover at the Isaacs' house, and I had not yet formed my conviction that Afro-Americans must also draw upon their experience in slavery as a source of strength. That evening, celebrating the Jewish experience was an adventure. I loved the matzo ball soup and kept sipping that sweet wine.

After nine months in Switzerland, the new had become familiar and the offensive ordinary. Inquisitive stares became everyday events, as did questions about where I came from and what had brought my family to Bern. Since I never took into account what white people saw when they looked at me, I answered the question that was asked, rather than the one that was camouflaged for the sake of politeness: What are you, a Negro, doing here?

Their mistaken beliefs about black ability and social status blinded them to the truth but remained unspoken—while my own naïveté hid that same truth from me. My family landed in Switzerland because the Captain had built a one-room schoolhouse, the General had insisted that all her children graduate from high school, and my father dared to dream of becoming a scientist. Our success came from taking advantage of unusual opportunities, matching great expectations with high achievement, persistent effort across generations, and a faith in education that made school a necessity rather than an option.

This was the answer to the question I was never directly asked. I misunderstood the coded conversation. I thought people were expressing honest curiosity, and certainly some were. But I hadn't learned to distinguish curiosity from incredulity. How naïve I was—open, quick to smile, eager to please, and trained to be polite.

"Do you come out of Africa?" the Swiss would ask. That's what having dark skin, broad features, and curly hair meant: the Dark Continent. "No, Chicago," I replied—and the gambit began once again. I could have said, "Yes, Africa, yes," and perhaps I should have. I knew enough about Mother's heritage to know that we came from Sierra Leone. But in 1963 I wasn't proud to claim Africa as my birthright.

I simply said, "Chicago."

"*Ach so*," the Swiss would reply, while Americans would say, "With the army!" Everybody knew there were lots of colored GIs.

"No, my dad's at the university."

"Oh. Your father is a student."

"No." This second contradiction left them confounded.

"So what does your father do at the university?"

"He's a scientist."

"Oh. What kind?"

"A chemist."

Stymied, they would pursue another tack: "Do you like Switzerland?"

They probably didn't care. They were really trying to find out how the improbable had occurred.

From a white American point of view, my family's presence was an enigma. Negro families didn't live in Europe and colored men didn't work as scientists. Negroes had a place in society and we were living above it. A real conversation rather than a polite one would have exposed this prejudice, and a truly candid exchange would have bared a deeper truth: In America you can be a complete loser and still be redeemed by an accident of birth—the unearned virtue of being white. This was also true in Switzerland—every Swiss, no matter how remote the valley they lived in, knew without reflection that their culture and race was superior to everything black. This is what racism does for white people—their preeminence is buttressed by their belief in black ignobility.

Attending Villa St. Jean liberated me from my parents' tendency to treat Philip and me like twins. It also forced me to stand on my own feet and develop my own friendships. Among the gang I traveled with were the Frenchs, three chain-smoking, red-haired American brothers. The Frenchs led the pack that rode the train to and from Fribourg, and all three cruised through life with a bravado that amazed me. They smoked, so I tried to as well, but I couldn't stand the taste or the guilt. The Frenchs drank. I didn't dare. They were all humping their English nanny, or so they claimed. I listened and snickered and, wanting to be included, kept my moral wincing (and my lust) to myself. I smiled so hard my cheeks ached, but I was accepted, for it seemed that their still-forming worldview included room for a Negro friend.

Their father, like Ralph Petty's, was a diplomat at the U.S. Embassy in Bern. They lived in Muri, in a large suburban house and their cupboards were filled with American products, delivered every Saturday from the PX in Heidelberg. The French brothers talked big and despised the Swiss, and the train conductor had to tell them to take their feet off the seats every time he went through our coach.

One day, en route to the train station, we were horsing around in the back of a streetcar when a Swiss man speaking British-accented English accosted us. In a flash, Mike French had his middle finger in the stuffy old fart's face. "Go fuck yourself," Mike said, and then swaggered away, boasting that no one could do anything to him because he had diplomatic immunity.

My first impulse was to cheer Mike on; my second was to act as if I didn't know him. The Swiss often made me angry enough to want to say what the Frenches dared to say, but I never acted on it. If I did, I would be a disgrace to my race. But these cocky white boys sure saw the world differently. We're Americans, and if you don't like it, up yours, buddy.

My mother's admonitions not to act like "white trash" or a "common Negro" had partly been about public behavior. She meant that my behavior always reflected on more than me and my family; it reflected on the whole Negro race. Whatever I did, however magnificent or mortifying, people didn't see *me*. They saw a Negro. And when Mother said, "I won't have you acting like a common Negro in my house," she meant that vulgar, loud, and disrespectful behavior wasn't permissible at home or anywhere in the whole wide world. If you were angry, you set your teeth and smiled, and I did just that. In our home, the Frenches' antics would've been unpardonable, but there was no danger of my acting that way, for Mother's voice was embedded deep in my psyche.

Hanging out in this American ghetto was more comfortable than struggling to speak German or deal with the uptight Swiss culture. There was, however, a downside. While the gawking Swiss were aggravating, our interactions with the American diplomatic community left us more deeply wounded. The ache I felt after Sheila's coerced rejection lingered—and I wasn't the only one to experience prejudice for the first time from the child of U.S. Embassy personnel.

My sister Carole was in fourth grade at the English Speaking School. One of her classmates was the ambassador's daughter (the same ambassador who received my parents' letter of protest six months earlier). A frail little girl, Robin was chauffeured to school in a limousine. As her birthday approached, the class was abuzz. The embassy briefing room contained a movie screen and the highlight of the party would be American cartoons, and everyone was invited except Carole. At age nine, my sister, with her gap-toothed grin, was used to being persecuted by Philip and me, but this was different. She could assume only that she had been excluded because of her race, which left her feeling more an outsider than she had ever felt at the Rudolf Steiner School.

With spring came softball, and Ralph Petty invited me to play against a team from the U.S. Consulate in Geneva. I stood on the sideline, hoping only that I not make a fool of myself while at bat. I was still waiting to bat for the first time when a white fellow— they were all white—yelled from the outfield, "What's that nigger doing here?"

It felt like I had caught a line drive in the stomach.

Ralph turned red. "Who does that ignoramus think he is? He can't say that," he said, grabbing my arm and dragging me across the diamond toward this beefy-looking guy in left field.

"Forget it, man, just forget it," I pleaded. Terrified, I really dug in, pulling in the opposite direction—it must have been something to behold.

Of course, Ralph was right, but it took me decades to see that. The scene kept replaying in my head until one day my shadow stepped forward and said, "We'll show that motherfucker. Get a bat." If I had taken a stand on that outfield, it might have changed my whole life; it might have been the moment I stopped fleeing, ceased seeing myself as a victim, and started to defend my own dignity. I didn't need to bash that cracker's brains out, although I enjoyed imagining it. I needed to conquer my fear and stand up for myself.

But on that spring morning in Switzerland, being dragged across the infield by an enraged white Virginian boy, I shrank from the confrontation. Breaking free of Ralph's grip, I retreated to the sidelines. When my turn at bat came, I popped up and was called out. I drifted back to the sideline, then to the street. Once home, I managed to avoid Mother's inquisition, slipped quietly into my room, closed the door, and buried myself beneath a blanket.

Summer arrived, and then fall, and we should have been preparing to return to the United States, but the future was uncertain. My parents considered staying for another year, if a particular apparatus Dad needed at work was available. Another opportunity arose as well. "George was cabled an offer from Washington to be a senior scientific officer with the State Department in Geneva," Mother wrote to Dad's parents. "The salary is tempting—a job never held by a Negro . . ." Toward the end of the letter, she added, "Mark wants to stay."

Perhaps surprisingly, I had been buffered from the reality of racism in our liberal, middle-class Chicago environment, and pristine Switzerland had at first seemed a fairyland. Yet it was there I finally experienced racial prejudice. However, the events at Sheila's house and the baseball game, while traumatic, weren't as important to me as what I had found in Switzerland—freedom.

I had a plan, and when the opportunity came I acted. Carole and I were sent to a summer camp at the Ecole d'Humanité, the boarding school I'd been smitten by six months earlier. The day after we arrived, I approached Edith Geheeb, who had founded the school with her husband. "I want to attend the Ecole year-round," I told her, and this old woman with a kind face and dancing eyes took up my cause. My parents fretted; fourteen was too young. They came for a visit and met Edith and Natalie Lüthi, the director of the American program. I would be too far away—it was just one year. The school was too expensive—they offered financial assistance. Finally my parents consented.

The machine Dad needed to continue his work wasn't available and realizing that the position in the State Department would take him away from his real love, research, he turned down the offer.

Toward the end of August, my family began packing to leave. All kinds of borrowed paraphernalia, including Ralph's sled, needed to be returned. On the bus that took me to Ralph's, I looked around and realized everyone was staring at me—a colored boy wearing shorts and holding a sled was a phenomenon, not a person. I fixed my eyes on the floor and endured the whispers and titters all the way to the end of the line. Happy to escape, I started down the path toward Ralph's. A man came toward me, a father holding the hands of his two sons. Beyond pleasantries, I didn't understand much Swiss German, but I could make out what he was saying: "Look, there is a Negro. He comes from Africa. He is looking for snow. He doesn't know any better." As they proceeded past me, I nodded and greeted them in my best Swiss German: *Grüessech mitenand.* That was like saying, "Hi, y'all" in vernacular American, and I was still laughing when I knocked on Ralph's door.

When the time came for my family to depart, they left me with the Isaacs. Mother, in a fit of anxiety, issued instructions at an incomprehensible speed. I agreed without listening, then steeled myself for a last round of hugs. Philip acted cool, holding his tears until after they drove off. But as the car disappeared on that late August day, I had no regrets. I felt more free than sad, for I was finally and happily on my own.

Between the time my family left and when I went to the Ecole, the March on Washington took place. As I savored my newfound freedom, more than 250,000 people congregated before the Lincoln Memorial to demand freedom too long deferred. In Martin

Luther King Jr.'s words, "I have a dream today," all of us found a voice.

I had a dream, too—to be free from my fear of Chicago, from a mother who suffocated me, and from a brother who felt like an unwanted appendage but whom I used as a crutch. While King spoke of transforming the state of Alabama into a place "where little black boys and black girls will be able to join hands with little white boys and white girls and walk together as sisters and brothers," I imagined the Ecole to be such a community—a place where girls and boys from all over the world held hands as they danced and sang and thought of one another as brothers and sisters. As King's voice climbed toward his conclusion: "[Let us] speed up that day when all God's children, black men and white men, Jews and Gentiles, Protestants and Catholics will be able to join hands and sing in the words of the old Negro spiritual, 'Free at last! Free at last! Thank God Almighty we are free at last!'" I was about to flee into the mountains so that at last I too might be free, never guessing how elusive that freedom would prove to be.

Ecole d'Humanité

This belief in the oneness of humankind . . . has existed within me side by side with my deep attachment to the cause of my own race.

—Paul Robeson, *Here I Stand*

As the train from Bern pulled into Interlaken, I began to fidget. I had felt more confident when traveling with Philip, but now I was on my own and more anxious than I would admit. When Philip and I made the first trip to the Ecole d'Humanité, we disembarked at Interlaken. A jittery traveler like my mother, I egged Philip on until he inquired where we could catch the train to Brünig. "You want Interlaken East," came the reply, and realizing that the train was about to depart without us, we frantically threw luggage, skis, and ourselves back on board. Recalling that mistake, I scanned the platform, hunting for the name of the station. Spotting "Interlaken West" on the wall, I relaxed back into my seat.

The train wound along the shore of the Brienzersee. From Meiringen, a cog-wheeled locomotive climbed the 1007-meter-high Brünigpass. In Brünig I transferred to a bus and began the nine-kilometer traverse of the Hasliberg. As the bus snaked its way through a dark wood, beams of sunlight broke through the green canopy to cast golden spotlights upon the mossy, boulder-strewn floor. Enchanted, I thought, *Surely if dwarves exist I'll see one now.*

73

My eyes probed the shadows until we came out of the woods and suddenly I was looking down, down, down. Beyond the narrow road there was nothing between us and the valley floor. As the bus clung to the asphalt, I looked at the vista. Far away on the opposite side of the valley, a stream of water surged over the Reichenbach Fall, a foaming white ribbon that fell until it disappeared behind the peaked tops of the pine trees. Above the falls the Rosenlaui Glacier lay like a blue-tinged white carpet and behind it a massive wall of mountains. Atop these stood the Wetterhorn. It means "storm peak," and living on the Hasliberg, my eyes perpetually returned to that majestic mountain sitting high above the valley, a view I still carry within.

In 1910 Edith and Paul Geheeb founded the Odenwaldschule. The first coeducational boarding school in Europe, it was located in a forest in southwest Germany and became well-known as an experiment in educational reform. Edith was Jewish, and facing the National Socialists' escalating control over their school and Hitler's increasing denunciation of Jews, the Geheebs fled Germany in 1934 to begin a new school in Switzerland.

The mood across Europe was foreboding, and the conservative Swiss populace, always suspicious of the outside world, regarded the school with distrust. The war began. Families called their children home. The student body dwindled to nine. The school edged toward bankruptcy, its survival hinging on the stipends paid by the Swiss government for taking in refugee children and the meager contributions sent by alumni and friends. The school moved four times over the next twelve years. By this time Paul was seventy-six years old, with a chest-length white beard and a walking stick always nearby, while Edith was a kind-eyed woman whose round face had a thousand wrinkles. They were driven on by their compassion for the refugees and the resolve that their life work should not perish. Finally, in 1946, the school settled—to the local inhabitants' dismay—in Goldern, a tiny village on the mountainside between the Hasli valley and barren peaks. It inhabited three rustic wooden buildings, and they named it Ecole d'Humanité, the

School of Humanity. Paul Geheeb, always referred to as Paulus, died in 1961, but by then the school's future was secure.

Now I was returning. My bus would pass through the villages of Hohfluh, Wasserwendi, and Goldern on the way to Reuti. There the road turned into an unpaved lane, and then a gravel path that narrowed into a trail before dropping off into the next valley. That was Switzerland—another valley, another impenetrable wall of mountains, and here and there a pass between them, but always many more valleys and mountains than passes. In Goldern the bus headed downhill, its gears whining to slow its descent, and then stopped at the post office just beyond the school.

Luggage in hand, my head held high, I threw back my shoulders and for a moment sent timidity fleeing as I strode back up the road. I walked up to the building called Haupthaus, which was bedecked with green window boxes full of red geraniums and a sign reading, "Ecole d'Humanité." Because it meant a whole new life to me, the Ecole felt enormous. In fact, it was unprepossessing, the seven buildings so primitive that today only two of them remain. To my right stood a dark brown, ramshackle building with a workshop on the first floor, a classroom on the next, and an apartment in the attic. It was named Stöckli, meaning "little beehive." Further along sat creaky, old Turmhaus, named after its bell tower and containing the main hall where school-wide gatherings took place—community meetings, singing, dancing, and theater. The center of the action at the Ecole, Turmhaus housed the majority of the student body. To its right lay a playing field, and beyond it Waldhaus—the newest residence. From there the gravel road narrowed and continued until it came to a dead end in a barnyard.

I knew the school's layout, and I knew what to do next. Instead of following the gravel road, I turned left to a walkway, passed a little fountain, bounded up the Haupthaus steps, and stood in line to see Frau Varga, the office manager, whose brusque façade thawed for a moment before my beaming smile.

The directors of the school were Armin and Natalie Lüthi—he was Swiss and she American. His voice was stern but soft, her bear-

ing direct and mannish. I was taken into their family; the entire
school divided itself into family units, each family composed of
several adults and up to a dozen students. A "family" sat together
in the dining hall and lived together in one of the main buildings
or in one of the houses scattered throughout the village. I moved
into Waldhaus and my first roommate was Jörg Luyken. A slender,
blond, blue-eyed German, he had a quick mind and quicker tongue.
His mother had attended the original school the Geheebs founded
in Germany. After Christmas, Philipp Hostettler joined us. He was
Swiss and had a complicated but not atypical background for an
Ecole student—he had been abandoned by his mother when she
ran off with an actor, following a young, mismatched marriage
to his father. His father, who owned Wine Shop Hostettler AG in
the old town of Bern, sent Philipp to live with his grandparents.
But when eleven-year-old Philipp proved too wild, his grandfather shipped him off to the Ecole. Philipp, whom Jörg taunted and
called Phipu, was deliberate but adventuresome, hard-working but
not humorless, thick-featured with eyebrows that merged in the
middle of his forehead. We bickered like brothers, but this didn't
keep us from scheming together about how to sneak out at night,
or planning the feasts we'd buy with our meager allowances.

We lived adjacent to weatherworn Turmhaus, which was the
next best thing to living there. The old building swayed and creaked
when the gusty Föhn wind blew against it. When the winds fell
silent, you could hear the underlying rumble of 130 students—
the constant murmur of voices through thin walls, the giggles
and squeals, the shouts directed from the first- to the third-floor
balcony, the trampling feet thundering down sagging stairs, the
swoosh of rear ends sliding down banisters.

A crashing gong announced when to get up, to clean up, to
eat, to go to class. Awakened at 6:20 a.m, Phipu, Jörg, and I began
the day by arguing over whose turn it was to brave the cold and
close the window to the frigid alpine air. The appearance of Herr
Lüthi, as tall and lean as his humor was dry, ended all debate and
sent us scampering, pulling on shoes and shorts before rushing

outside for morning calisthenics. When the school first began in Germany, the students pranced around nude—segregated by sex, of course—and called it an air bath. After the local farmers complained, the students stopped running around naked, but the exercise continued.

Calisthenics was followed by cold showers. For me this meant hopping in to quickly wet myself, hopping out to soap up, then back in to rinse off. When I didn't shower, I splashed and hollered enough to make Herr Lüthi think I had. Cleaning up meant dumping our clothes on the floor of our narrow closets and shoveling everything else under our beds before stampeding to breakfast. Breakfast never varied: cocoa, porridge, bread, one pat of butter each and jam—molasses on Sundays only. Then we peeled potatoes, the skins flying everywhere as we filled bowls with potatoes, whole, quartered, or sliced. Afterward, each of us scurried off to do housekeeping chores: washing dishes, sweeping, emptying waste baskets, folding laundry, chopping wood (and the occasional finger tip), hauling coal, stoking fires, or shoveling snow. Because of the school's communal nature we were called Kameraden rather than students.

When the gong rang again at 8:30, we meandered off to class. There were three one-hour classes, six days a week, but no grades or report cards. Hooray! Instead, Kameraden wrote self-evaluations. The Geheebs envisioned an atmosphere of learning without fear, something I had never known. This approach was a consequence of a pedagogy which understood learning to be an inborn process, the motivation coming from within and leading to a natural unfolding of each individual's unique personality. To nurture this process of individuation education began with a young person's own interests.

Afternoons were reserved for skiing and other sports, music, clay modeling, dramatics, woodwork, and drawing. While the school offered plenty of free time, it forbid the casual use of radios or record players, and kept its only television locked away. Many complained, a few resisted; I, however, relished every moment. Whether singing or skiing, clearing timber or jogging up the mountainside by myself in the early morning, I felt safe, sound, and finally free to be myself—free to choose my own classes, free from my mother's all-seeing eyes and controlling hand, free of my daring brother and my clandestine dependency upon him, and free from my fear of Chicago. I embraced that freedom, tempered as it was by the demands of living in a community where the lifestyle was spartan, the meals plain, the responsibilities many, and the joys simple.

In Switzerland the Geheebs applied the educational innovations they had developed in Germany; however, fleeing the Nazi regime had altered their philosophy in one significant way. "We will be neither a French, nor a German, nor an English, nor a Swiss school . . . but a school of humanity," Paulus had said during the first days of the school's Swiss incarnation. The student body I joined, although largely Western European and white, was international—Swiss and German, Dutch and American, French and British, Swedish and Danish, Arab and Israeli, Canadian, Yugoslavian, and Central American. It never occurred to me at the time that my presence as the only American Negro brought the school even closer to the Geheebs' goal. Living in this idyllic community, race seemed to be of no concern, for in such a cultural jumble a friend was a friend, and a turkey a turkey, regardless of nationality.

After a few weeks, I settled into my new life, which included devotedly reading the *International Herald Tribune*. On September 17 the banner headline announced: BOMB IN BIRMINGHAM CHURCH KILLS 4 NEGRO GIRLS. I flattened the paper across the green Formica table and read on: "A dynamite bomb hurled from a passing car blasted a crowded Negro church today, killing four girls in their Sunday school class and injuring dozens of other Negroes. Thousands of enraged Negroes poured from their homes into the area around the shattered 16th Street Baptist Church. Police fought for two hours, firing rifles into the air to control them . . ."

I ripped the paper open to the next page.

"Across the street from the church, M.W. Pippen stood outside his badly damaged dry cleaning store. 'My grandbaby was one of them killed,' he said, 'Eleven years old. I helped pull the rubble off her . . . I feel like blowing up the whole town . . .'"

I buried my head in my arms.

Like nearly all space at the Ecole, the dining hall served multiple purposes. It doubled as a classroom and the library, and for me it came to fill a private function—where I maintained my emotional involvement in the struggle for freedom in America. I needed to feel connected to the civil rights movement, and my only means of doing so was the *Herald*. In moments snatched between classes, I slipped into the dining hall to read the newspaper, paying attention for the first time. Reading about the Freedom Rides and sit-ins, beatings and murders, my confusion deepened. Distance didn't provide an escape; it only intensified my fixation on the race problem. News of the movement reached across the Atlantic and grabbed hold of me. Or perhaps I, not wanting to lose my identity, grabbed onto it. It didn't matter how good I had it at the Ecole; I couldn't free myself from the knowledge of the injustice that reigned at home. Guilt ate at me, perhaps contributing to my first English assignment, when I wrote a character sketch of a Negro who was passing as white.

Great-aunt Irene once explained "passing" to me when reminiscing about her older brother, Stacy. In 1907, when Stacy was twenty-seven, their father died and their mother, the General, informed him that he was now the man of the house. Instead he ran off to sea, and then to the West Coast, before settling down in Connecticut with a Canadian wife and having a "pack of children." Great-aunt Irene explained all this while building up to the point of her story—her last trip to visit Stacy's family and why we'd never met any of them. "After I came home, Stacy's boy, Billy, calls up and says, 'Aunt Irene, please don't be coming around here no more because we're going over.'"

I didn't know what she meant. "Because they're passing," she said. But I still didn't get it. "Child, it means they're pretending to be white folks."

Some studies estimate that 75 percent of all Afro-Americans have European ancestors and, of these, some have enough white ancestry to allow them to quietly blend into the white world and disappear from the black. Other studies estimate that 20 percent of all white Americans have black forebears; similarly an English researcher asserts that one in five white Britons, including the Queen, has a black ancestor. Most scholars agree, however, that a reliable number is not ascertainable. By its very nature, hiding makes data hard to come by and the essence of passing is hiding.

"Going over," like skin-color hierarchy, is another racial reality that is never explained to Afro-American children, but which everyone knows and gossips about. As a child, I didn't know much, except that Eugene Payton's family, the fair-skinned people who lived at the other end of the block in Chicago, could have passed but didn't. Sometimes I wondered why.

As I grew older I became aware of the family skeletons on my mother's side as well. The most mysterious of these was the tale of John Moreau Maxwell Jr.

"Man, Moreau Maxwell was a good-looking guy who could have passed," Mother's first cousin Andrew had said. He went on to explain that after graduating from the University of Wisconsin early in the 1930s, Moreau returned home to Orangeburg, South Carolina, to work in the family business, a well-known general store used by blacks and whites alike. After a while Moreau began disappearing on weekends. No one knew where he went, nor would he say. "Around 2 a.m. one morning Moreau showed up at our house [in Patterson, New Jersey] accompanied by a young woman who looked white, but who could tell. Well, Pops whisked them in and started cooking up somethin' to eat. 'Fine, fine,' Pops says, 'you got married. I know all them families down there but I don't recognize your name. Burns? Cathy Burns? The only Burns I know is Senator Burns and . . . that can't be!'

"And Moreau said, 'Oh, yes it can.'

"And Pops said 'Oh, my God!'

"'This is his niece and we're about to leave the country. We've got to go away. Some place where we won't be known. They've threatened me. Senator Burns called Papa and said, "Have him bring Cathy back and leave the South and everything will be okay because we are going to forgive her. But if we ever find him down here, I'm going to have him killed. I've known you Maxwells for many years and you are good people and Moreau is a fine young man. But he's still a nigger. Bring my niece back.""

So Moreau and his wife disappeared, and his younger cousins were told—to make sure they didn't make the same mistake—that he was at the bottom of Edisto River. Some figured they moved to South America, but those who knew never talked, and died without telling.

History and common sense tell us that race mixing began as soon as Europeans and Africans joined Native Americans on this continent. However, that was just the precondition for passing. Since the advantages of being white and the disadvantages of being black are real—life threatening in ways subtle and not—there is a great temptation to quietly assimilate into the dominant culture. To escape the stigma of being black, some completely submerge themselves into white culture, while others do it partially, essentially leading two lives. And when one person goes over, cutting him- or herself off from kin and culture, the next generation is rarely told. As a result, the majority of Americans who have black ancestry probably don't realize it. But going over exacts a price. Donning whiteness requires exchanging truth and honesty for pretense, and forsaking family, closeness, and black culture for fear, isolation, and shame.

Going over and *passing* not only mean disappearing into the dominant culture, they are also euphemisms for death that aptly describe a form of suicide in which people kill their own blackness, tearing up their roots in an act of self-annihilation—and the side effect is a soul sickness.

Since this blending and hiding has been underway for four hundred years, and given the fluidity between classes in American society, there may be more white folks walking around who have black ancestors than there are identifiable Afro-Americans. This is American yin and yang, in which white includes blackness, and black, whiteness. Since so much integration has already taken place genetically, one wonders whether race any longer has meaning.

While some of my relatives had passed for white, there was no way I could. Nonetheless, in some ways I felt as if I were passing, since I lived a privileged life and had little interaction with other colored people or our culture. What I did have, and kept turning to in my turmoil, was the *Herald*.

PUPILS STRIKE IN CHICAGO RACIAL Row read an October 23 headline. The article continued, "Thousands of students played hooky in Chicago today to support demands for the removal of the public school superintendent and protest what their leaders called 'growing school segregation.'"

I wondered if Dad was involved, and whether Carole had skipped school. He was. She had. The article, however, misrepresented what had happened. Over 100,000 had participated in the one-day boycott and Carole hadn't played hooky. She had attended an alternative program called Freedom Day School, and the lessons were about oppression, politics, and racial pride.

Such headlines only fed my unrest, but no matter how disturbed I felt, the demands of our bustling community life drew me back to the Ecole. A walk in the evening on the Reutistrasse, the road that traversed the Hasliberg, set another mood—brooks gurgled, cowbells rang, and sometimes the low, lingering tones of an alphorn would drift down from the high pastures. Against a deep, dark blue sky on its way toward blackness were white ghost-like mountains; ahead stood the whale-backed Planplatte, across the valley the serrated peaks of the Engelhörner, and looming above it all, the massive Wetterhorn.

The Geheebs had sought isolation, and they found it on this mountainside nestled between the peaks and alpine pastures above, and the woods and cliffs below. Their educational method relied on the school's distance from the lights, the free and easy morality, and the many diversions of city life. Yet, as we all knew, the world beyond could never be completely kept out.

One evening, folk-dance music blared from the main hall. Hendrick, a young American teacher, was leading the weekly folk-dance evening. The music bounced up to the room where Richard, another Lüthi family member; big, blond Bob Matson; and I were hanging out. The door swung open and in rushed Kenny Kronenberg.

"President Kennedy's been shot," he said.

"Nice try," said Richard.

"What?" said Kenny.

"Not funny," added Bob.

"Listen, you guys, I'm not kidding," yelled Kenny.

"Right," I offered, for once trying not to be the most gullible one in the Ecole. It was the wrong moment. Kenny opened his arms, almost pleading. Shit. This was no joke.

We flew down the stairs, passed the woodshed, rounded the corner, and dashed into the main hall, yelling for Hendrick to unlock the closet where the big Blaupunkt radio was kept. Everything stopped. We knelt over the radio, spinning the dial. A crackling, barely audible voice said that President Kennedy had been shot while visiting Dallas, Texas. Cries of "What happened?" and "How bad?" and "What about Jackie?" surrounded us. We didn't know the answers and realized we probably wouldn't until the next morning.

Hendrick headed over to Waldhaus to tell Armin and Natalie; we took off in the opposite direction, toward the Reutistrasse. I felt numb, while Bob, all six-two and 250 pounds of him, cried. Tears streamed down his face. Then suddenly he picked up a large wooden bench, screamed "Damn!" and heaved it across the yard. In the darkness I heard it crash as we disappeared into the night.

Glumness hung over the Ecole for several days, but it was never long before the regimen of school life reasserted itself—classes, cleaning, and family evenings.

One Tuesday evening's family gathering started out as a particularly tedious affair. To my ears, the conversation sounded like the circling of droning deerflies, its meaning darting in and out of the reach of my weak German. The gathering included my roommates Phipu and Jörg; the heads of our family, Armin and Natalie Lüthi; their three children; teacher Herr Cool; and our housemates. Everyone buzzed away until the group reached a decision about what to do. I remained clueless. Exasperated, Herr Lüthi stood up and said something else I didn't understand. His pesky younger son, however, squealed and bounded up the stairs. Everyone laughed.

"What's so funny?" I asked as they surrounded me. "Come on, you guys," I said, laughing, as they lifted me out of my chair. "Help! Help!" I cried in feigned distress as they carried me up the stairs— after all, what could they do?

"Race riot, race riot," bellowed Richard, who had remained seated. As we reached the top of the stairs, I heard Natalie hiss, "Stop it, Richard."

The next moment we burst into the bathroom. I still didn't understand, but there was that brat, the Lüthi's son, jumping up and down by the bathtub—which was filling with cold water. As I descended, pleading "No, no," I figured out that *Badewanne* meant "bathtub."

Just before Advent, a group of us headed up the mountain to collect boughs. We trudged along until we reached a recently logged clearing. We gathered evergreen branches from the ground, while one of the braver souls climbed up a tree and brought down some mistletoe. The next day we assembled Advent wreaths, and by the first Sunday evening of Advent we were ready.

Full of anticipation, we milled about outside the dining hall. The doors opened to a dazzling sight. Candlelight flickered everywhere—on the tabletops, on the windowsills, on the counters— while large paper snowflakes hung from the ceiling. A wreath lay on each table, surrounded by a feast. Ecole meals were simple and hearty, meat once a week and all the potatoes you could eat. But at Advent the tables were laden with assortments of cheese and sausage and pickles, white instead of coarse brown bread, hot punch instead of the regular tea, and baskets full of peanuts and tangerines. We gorged. Boisterous voices filled the room until the bell rang, a signal to be silent. A hush descended, then quiet conversation resumed, building to a crescendo until the bell rang yet again. In the midst of this revelry, I grabbed a tangerine, stopped, and stared. Looking up at me from its thin tissue wrapper was a jet-black Sambo with red lips as large as liver-lipped Rodney's, my childhood target. I flinched. I looked around. No one else had noticed my reaction or the racist caricature; they just kept wolfing down supper. But for me, in that moment, the celebration lost some of its magic.

We gathered silently in the main hall. All was dark except the halo around a small table ablaze with candles. We remained quiet because of the mood, but also because of Herr Lüthi's stern face and watchful eyes. The chairs were arranged in a half circle for *Andacht*—a nonsectarian devotional hour held every Sunday evening. But these four Sundays leading up to Christmas were different from all others. After a long silence Herr Lüthi began: *Die Räuber-Mutter, die in der Räuberhöhle im Göingerwald wohnte* (The Robber Mother, who lived in the Robber Cave up in Göinger Forest). In the dark I was transported by Selma Lagerlöf's story, "The Legend of the Christmas Rose." He read this story every year, followed by three additional stories. My brother, Philip, heard them when he attended the Ecole the year after I left, and I heard them again when I returned as an adult.

There were other rituals, among them the Christmas play. I was given the obvious role. I suppose everyone else knew before I did that I—the only Negro student—would play Kaspar, the Moor, one of the Three Wise Men. My lines were simple enough, and translated into English, they meant: "And I am the king from Moorland. My name is King Kaspar. But even though I have a black face, fear not, dear children. I am known to be a good king." Calming children's fear of my black skin was the least of my problems. Every time I delivered my lines, the cast burst out laughing because I kept pronouncing the German word for fear (*Furcht*) so that it sounded like the word for fruit (*Frucht*). I kept saying, "fruit not, dear children," and when the roar subsided we would start over again.

Winter that year was disappointing; it turned cold but the snow never really arrived. To go skiing, we hiked fifteen minutes to the cable car, which took us to the top of Käserstadt; from there we walked to the far side of the alpine huts, where we packed the snow to create a practice slope and proceeded to tramp up and ski down all afternoon beneath Aurobindo Peak.

We had named this peak, the rise just beyond our ski slope, after Aurobindo Bose, a squat, seventy-year-old Bengali who followed Edith Geheeb like a shadow. One day, having sidestepped halfway up the practice slope, Auro took off his skis and schlepped them around back of the hill. There he proceeded to get lost, and no one noticed until a shrill call—"Oh! Help me, help me, please,"— came from above, and there in the distance he stood frantically gesturing from what was known forever after as Aurobindo Peak.

Aurobindo was the school joke. He was a plump man with medium–brown skin, who looked to me like a cross between a cherub and dwarf. His thinning hair came down to his shoulders and tufts of it stuck out of his nose. The high-pitched cry, "Oh Edith, oh Edith," signaled Auro was about, and sure enough, he'd appear shuffling along in bedroom slippers, waving his hand above his head as he tried to catch Edith's attention. When it was cold, he wrapped a shawl over his head so that it covered his ears, and tied it under his chin like a man with a toothache. When it was warm, he wore it backward, so that it flapped behind him. Culturally Bengali men often wear scarves but not knowing that I just saw it as additional proof of his weirdness. None of us knew exactly how he came to the Ecole or why Edith tolerated his presence, but every mimic in the school could imitate Auro. Others snickered as he passed, but I moaned and lamented that the only brown-skinned man in the school was a fool.

Days forsaken for night, liquor-lubricated lack of inhibition, and misguided romance would come in time, but at fourteen I was a dutiful young man who spent his vacations in Bern with the Isaac family. That year during the Easter break we headed for the Ticino, the Italian-speaking region of Switzerland where palm trees and unbelievably mild weather are wedded to Swiss tidiness and punctuality. The Isaacs rented a villa near Lugano that was spacious enough to accommodate us and the Roletts, another family who was part of the expatriate community that had included my parents the previous year.

The Roletts had a new baby boy, Jonas, and wherever we went we lugged him about in a portable bassinet. One afternoon we drove across the border to Como, Italy. Blond, Swedish Karin Rolett and I took in the town piazza, holding the bassinet between us. She had one strap and I the other as we rocked Jonas to sleep. After a while we realized that everyone who came near us—and many went out of their way to cross the cobblestone square and stroll past—craned their necks to peek inside the bassinet to see "our" baby. Amused at having become an attraction, Karin and I began making up the questions we knew they were dying to ask: "What color is your baby?" "Café au lait? Milk chocolate?" "Does the baby have stripes, checks, or polka dots?" "Is the hair like a scouring pad?" "And where do you come from, Africa?" We laughed, took a peek beneath the blanket at pale little Jonas, and laughed harder. Then it dawned on me that the people must believe we were a couple. Suddenly I stood just a little taller. Ron Rolett later wrote to my folks about it, saying he thought I was flattered. But I don't know if he guessed it was more at being taken as Karin's lover than Jonas's father.

After Easter, when the Föhn came, what little snow remained disappeared overnight. The creeks swelled, the waters in the Brienzersee churned, the pastures turned green. Yet this dry wind from the south was no soothing breeze; in 1962 a Föhn storm had uprooted half the forest that stood upon a nearby mountain pasture. Fierce as a hawk plunging upon its prey, it would charge down the valley, sounding a constant, low-pitched whistle that mounted to a roar, keeping me awake late into the night. The Ecole, of course, forbade smoking. But during the Föhn teachers kept reminding us about the laws against smoking out-of-doors. One statute, dating from 1736, forbade bakers from baking during the Föhn. As the wind continued to howl, we were served stale bread, and eventually no bread at all. And when we performed our annual Christmas concert in the Protestant church in Meiringen, we were told that the building was one of the few that survived the Föhn-stoked fires that destroyed the town in 1879 and 1891. The Föhn was called the worst arsonist in the country.

Some idiots went right on smoking, but I found pleasure in going for walks along the road that led toward the next village, leaning into the wind and feeling it flow over the contours of my face. On the way back the wind pushed so hard that if I spread my arms wide, to catch as much as possible, I could sail along with my feet flying to keep up. The wind supported me, curled and swirled about me, carried, caressed, and surrounded me; but sometimes it also blew within me, turning my life topsy-turvy.

June came. Time to go home. Time to plead my case with my parents, face to face—I didn't want to leave the Ecole.

When Dad's teak-brown, bald head and broad smile came weaving through the crowded waiting room at Chicago's O'Hare Field, I let out a sigh of relief, but then catching a glimpse of Philip behind him, I instantly reassembled my cool. I had no intention of acting hyped up about being home in front of my brother. "Hey, boy," Dad yelled and, ignoring my posturing, lifted me off the floor with a bear hug that left me breathless.

We collected my luggage and headed home. Traveling down the Kennedy Expressway, we passed steeples and onion-topped churches, warehouses, and, for a South Side kid, some not-so-familiar street names—Ashland, Division, Armitage. Downtown Chicago came into view and I saw that the skyline had changed during my two-year absence.

"Mark," Dad said, breaking through my chatter in a way that told me something was wrong. They hadn't wanted to tell me in a letter. Mother had had a serious operation. How was she? Recovering fine. What kind of operation? A mastectomy. I didn't know what that was. Doctors had found a lump in one of her breasts and removed it. Where was she? Anxious questions poured forth until they trailed off into silence, and then there were the questions I didn't dare ask: Would she die? Did it mean going back to the Ecole was out of the question? Anything seemed possible. Instead of going home, we drove directly to Chicago Lying-in Hospital.

When Mother appeared at the end of the corridor, wearing a light blue robe, it felt as if everything moved in slow motion. She shuffled along, and I wanted to go to her but had been instructed to wait. As she came closer, I could see her brave smile. When she got to me, I said, "Mama," and she threw her arms around me. "Oh, Mark," she whispered, sliding into my shoulder and beginning to cry. I held her. Caught between childhood and manhood, I didn't know whether to cling or comfort. Eventually she straightened, stepped back, looked up, and said, "My, how you've grown."

The conversation continued. I wasn't to worry. She'd be okay, but still needed another week of radiation therapy. I listened but didn't really understand. And I worried, but not for long. Soon I was caught up in the busy swirl and sweltering summer heat of 1964. Summer school began several days later. I had promised to go—I would have promised anything as long as they let me return to the Ecole. So, despite the financial strain and Philip's complaining, I'd be going back in the fall.

The summer swept by. After a few awkward attempts, I let old friendships go. What could I say about ocean liners and traveling, Switzerland and skiing, without sounding haughty? And how could I explain the Ecole? I couldn't talk about television—in two years of living in Switzerland, I hadn't watched a single show. Folks in Chicago couldn't believe that my school banned televisions and radios. I couldn't talk about clothing—dirty jeans were de rigueur at the Ecole. I couldn't talk about dancing, because we mostly did folk dancing at the school, which I didn't dare admit. And I couldn't talk about music because the kids at the Ecole were into the Beatles, not the Four Tops. So it was that my hope of kissing Dushka Hawkins's luscious lips turned into a fear of being ridiculed, and died.

The America I returned to didn't feel like the America I had left. While sit-ins, marches, and voter registration drives continued to challenge discrimination in the South, chaos and conflagration consumed Northern cities. The "long hot summer" of 1964 began: Harlem erupted, then Bedford-Stuyvesant, next Rochester, New York, followed by Jersey City. America burned. I spent hours transfixed before our television. Later that summer, I watched with horror when the bodies of three civil-rights workers, James Chaney, Michael Schwerner, and Andrew Goodman, were found near Philadelphia, Mississippi.

I watched the streets with different eyes, too. The fear remained. Ready to bolt, I scanned the schoolyard looking for the boys who had beaten me. It had happened so fast that I hadn't seen any of them, but the event had grown within me until, like an edgy white person, I was scared of every young black gouster.

Wary-eyed, I examined the crowd that hung out along the curb at 79th and South Park. There, between the Rexall drugstore and Price's Barbershop, I saw something I didn't expect: young Negro men in dark suits, white shirts, and black bow ties. Clean-shaven, with short cropped hair, they held themselves erect with a fierce dignity. The first time one greeted me with *Salaam alaykum*, I became even more confused. Then he offered to sell me a newspaper, *Muhammad Speaks*. I rushed home and asked Mother who they were. "Black Muslims" she said, and went on to explain that their temple was the old Jewish synagogue on Stony Island Avenue and they were followers of the Honorable Elijah Muhammad. They worshipped Allah, considered Christianity a tool the white man created to keep black people enslaved, and viewed integration as an anathema. Their solution: Separate the races. That meant giving black Americans their own country somewhere in the southern United States. A strict code of morality guided their lives—no tobacco, liquor, or pork. I was incredulous, but Mother assured me that, as crazy as their ideas sounded, they were industrious, thrifty, self-respecting, family-oriented people who did good work. In particular, she admired their efforts with prison inmates. I wasn't buying her take, especially after learning they held the utterly preposterous belief that whites, being the product of genetic engineering, were inherently evil. All their color had been bleached out—the revenge of an evil scientist who had been driven from Africa.

In September, having returned to the security and sanity of Switzerland, I returned to my ritual of reading about the civil rights movement in the *International Herald Tribune*. From the haven of the Ecole, I couldn't understand the bombings and killings, riots and arrests. Either I was in the only sane place in the world, or we at the Ecole were the deluded ones. While I enjoyed a Swiss boarding-school education, the *Herald* kept reminding me that others were suffering and dying to end discrimination. Back in Chicago, I had yearned to return to this hillside utopia, but now, having returned, guilt tormented me. But as quickly as my turmoil escalated, it would abate. Indeed, we were so busy that I would forget about it all, but never for long because the next newspaper article would set the tempest in motion again.

One day an emotional Föhn arose within me—I'm not certain why—and I acted precipitously. I made a poster which read: END COLD SHOWERS. Then I began marching back and forth in front of Waldhaus. We all hated those icy showers and everyone should have joined me, but that's not what happened. The first Kamerad laughed. The second took the other side and before long I stood alone against a bunch of pretend rednecks.

That day, an American professor and his wife, there to visit their three children, looked up and saw me charging toward them, followed by a swarm of Kameraden.

"Get him! Get the nigger!" someone yelled.

"Wh . . . what's going on?" he exclaimed.

"Oh, we're having a race riot," somebody piped up as the mob swept past.

I raced through town and down the Reutistrasse. My lungs burned, my legs would go no faster. Then they caught me and jostled me, and since the make-believe race riot was over, everyone drifted away. The word *nigger*, even used in jest, jolted me. Feeling sick and troubled by a mood as threatening as the clouds above, I slunk into the woods to be surrounded and hidden by its darkness. People usually saw my gregariousness, they heard the ring of my laughter, they remembered my enthusiasm. But I kept hidden how alone and conflicted I felt.

My protest, and there was a real protest going on behind the acting out, was meant to call attention to my reality. Look at me, goddamn it! I am a Negro. The trouble with the Ecole was that in the effort to be color-blind people ignored a fundamental piece of my identity. How could these white people act as if race didn't matter when the *Herald* screamed racial injustice and unrest? They seemed oblivious, yet in subtle ways their attitudes said that race really did matter.

"Oh, I forget about your color," was a typical comment. I would glance at my brown skin. *I beg your pardon? What are you talking about? Is it possible?*

"How's that?" I blurted out more than once.

"I just think of you, Mark, as another person."

"But how can you think of me as a person and not as a Negro?"

"Because it doesn't come to mind, because it doesn't have anything to do with anything that we do together."

And while I agreed that most of the time it didn't, I felt sure there was more to it than I could explain.

Despite people's disclaimers, they held plenty of stereotypes. I saw glimpses all the time—the assumption that I had grown up in a ghetto, that of course I could sing and had rhythm. But my dance moves, which these off-the-wall white folk thought cool, had sent my siblings to the floor in fits of laughter. Most outlandish, however, was their admiration of my basketball savvy, which was non-existent. But I wanted approval so desperately I actually did my best to act out the stereotypes, faking it all the way.

I held within me a question that I didn't know how to formulate nor had the courage to ask: What hides behind white people's claim not to notice race?

During the fifties and sixties, as social mores liberalized and racial intolerance became stigmatized, white liberals chose color blindness. Not seeing race at all proved—to themselves at least—that they were not prejudiced, and served as a way to say, "I'm not a bigot." For white liberals, facing glaring racial inequities and knowing the game was rigged in their favor, the feeling of guilt was unavoidable—as was the suspicion that blacks couldn't help but hate them for it. Saying "I'm color-blind" was like an incantation invoked to ward off these feelings. It was more a defense than a virtue, a willful naïveté which, like so much else, served white self-interest. If you ignore my color you can't understand the oppressive social reality that impinges on Afro-American lives at every moment. Yet if you notice only my color you misread who I am. Color blindness protects whites from knowing that which they have to labor not to know. And at the Ecole their need not to know kept them from simply asking me, "How is it for you?"

A Negro teacher named June Long arrived at the beginning of my second year. Chocolate-colored and round-bodied, she wore her hair in a bun and hailed from Berkeley, California. She had been a radical at home. At the Ecole, this take-charge woman was free to teach what and how she wished, but had little influence and no system to fight. It never worked for her. I noted how sharply she dressed at first; but when she realized that no one else did or cared, she began to wear jeans like the rest of us. The day she was to learn how to ski, she huffed, puffed, and complained all the way to the practice slope, put on her skis, fell down from a standstill, broke her leg, and spent the winter hobbling about school in a cast—a situation made worse because she lived in Gelbeshaus, on the other side of the village.

Her school family consisted of older American students. I hung around Gelbeshaus because of them, but also because I remained intensely aware of June and sometimes caught her staring quizzically at me. Perhaps I perplexed her, being a brown-skinned youth who reveled in this odd foreign world. She must have wanted to ask me questions, or deliver a lecture about how I was supposed to act. The silence between us was pregnant. I wondered what hope had drawn her to the Hasliberg. After the first exhilarating breath of mountain air, perhaps she had imagined herself as another James Baldwin who, a decade earlier, had written "Stranger in the Village" while residing in a Swiss village as remote as Goldern. Could she have imagined encountering natives so naïve that they rubbed her skin to see if the color came off? (At least no one asked, as they had earlier about a student named Sue, "Would you say she is black all over, you know what I mean, *all* over?") June must have lamented her decision at times. I wanted to confide in her— thinking that she would see what whites folks couldn't and under- stand what they didn't—and it almost happened. One evening as I lingered about Gelbeshaus, I sensed that she wanted to say some- thing, but my fear of being judged triumphed and I deflected her approach. The evening slipped away and the opportunity did not come again—not with her or with Gamey Bowman.

Gamey, who arrived from New York City that fall, had a quick smile, crooked teeth, and processed hair, and was a shade lighter than I. "How's it been?" I could have asked Gamey, as I had asked others. I had buddies, confidants, and girl friends. I had learned that the best way to make friends was to be a good listener. I had even befriended the school handyman, Herr Horcher. But I, who boldly claimed to love everyone, didn't reach out to June or Gamey. Instead, I colluded with them to keep our fragility hidden. From within a loneliness none but they could understand, I watched them as I had watched Ermetra in my church children's choir in Chicago. And they, I'm certain, watched me.

That November, when the school produced Shakespeare's *The Merchant of Venice*, I was the obvious choice to play the Prince of Morocco, one of Portia's three suitors. My attire was regal— purple satin pants, golden chains about my neck, scimitar hanging from a yellow sash, turban upon my head. Unfortunately, I lacked a royal bearing. I practiced hard holding myself erect and proud. But without the inner conviction of my inherent nobility, it felt like faking rather than acting. Indeed, living in a white world, I often felt as though I were posturing. The question lingered— sometimes in my mind and sometimes in the attitude of others —about whether I belonged. I postured because being black compounds the self-doubt that burdens every adolescent. Nonetheless, I swept onto stage, bowed deeply and spoke:

> Mislike me not for my complexion
> The shadow'd livery of the burnished sun
> To whom I am a neighbor and near bred.

I, too, was dark and concerned that people would not accept me, and so the words rang true even if my bearing was not entirely princely. As I exited a scene in the second act, having failed in my effort to win her hand, Portia said to her attendant:

> A gentle riddance. Draw the curtains, go.
> Let all of his complexion choose me so.

Those words bit deep every time Portia spoke them, and that feeling took me back to the painful memory of Sheila, the girl whose father wouldn't allow her to go out with me, and to the anger.

Two scenes after Portia sends the prince of Morocco packing, Shylock berates Salarino, a comrade of the merchant: "I am a Jew. Hath not a Jew eyes? Hath not a Jew hands, organs, dimensions, senses, affections, passions? Fed with the same food, hurt with the same weapon, subject to the same diseases, heal'd by the same means, warmed and cool'd by the same winter and summer, as a Christian is? If you prick us, do we not bleed? If you tickle us, do we not laugh? If you poison us, shall we not die? And if you wrong us, shall we not revenge?"

As he spoke I echoed, "Hath not a Negro eyes? Hath not a Negro hands . . ." and knew why Shylock wanted his pound of flesh.

Dwarves, those mythical, magical beings, did, indeed, reside upon the Hasliberg and would teach me unexpected lessons. Aurobindo Bose, Edith Geheeb's pet and school laughingstock, and Herr Horcher, the school handyman, were nicknamed the *Zwei Zwerge* (two dwarves). Short, stocky Herr Horcher wore a little, gray, square Hitler mustache that put me off, but as the leader of the student work crew, I depended on his guidance. Decidedly different from Auro, he was just as strange. He wore a stocking cap underneath his wool ski cap, its tassel dangling behind him, a hearing aid in his ear, and a curved pipe in his mouth. His hands had dirt in every crease, and his left index finger was missing above the first knuckle. He used a cat's hide to grease his tools and wore a carpenter's apron over his charcoal-gray wool pants, which were held in place by suspenders that pulled the waist nearly up to his armpits. And like every Swiss laborer I had ever seen, he wore a dull blue cotton work smock. He had hobnailed boots, a cane, and walked with a steady but peg-legged gait—his shoulders dipped down, and as they rose up again, his little leg swung forward. As he walked through the middle of the school on his way home, his wife, Frau Horcher, followed eight paces behind, muttering. I couldn't tell if she was talking to herself or to him, but while her lips moved and her white-haired head shook the whole time, I never saw him respond.

I knew where to look for Herr Horcher. His workshop was up the road. Failing to find him there, I used my nose, for the odor of his pipe was unmistakable. He knew where to find me, usually in the woodshed chopping wood. We needed each other, but I needed him more than he needed me. When the work crew started clearing the forest above the Ecole for the construction of new buildings, Herr Horcher taught me how to fell a tree and split a log. I had never replaced a windowpane, but he led me through the process and my fellow students guaranteed endless opportunities to replace more. We needed a new retaining wall for the ski shed, and he taught me how to build a mold and pour concrete. We needed a garden wall, and he showed me how to place the stones.

My father, having spent every summer on the farm in Zacata, had developed manual know-how, but passed none of it on to me. The summer he built an addition to the back of the house on Calumet Avenue he had shipped the whole family off to D.C. I wasn't handy and felt inept, but Herr Horcher taught me with great patience in a slow, deliberate Swiss way. Sometimes, if I got it right, he would nod, his eyes lighting up as he flipped open the lid of his pipe.

Once, at the end of the work day, he took me home to the two rooms he and his wife occupied in the wing of a farmhouse just beyond Waldhaus. We entered and climbed a half flight of stairs, and as we did I caught a whiff of the toilet, an indoor outhouse. *Jeez!*

At the top of the landing, I ducked beneath the threshold to the kitchen. Heat rose from the wood-burning cookstove, and the smell of smoke hung in the air. The log walls were dark with soot, the room full of shadows. He motioned for me to sit down at a rough-hewn wooden table, then called for Frau Horcher to heat us some coffee. When it was piping hot, Herr Horcher pulled out a bottle of pear schnapps and poured some in each mug. *All right!*

We talked. Talking was easy; understanding one another wasn't. He spoke his dialect of Swiss German, while I spoke my own brand of German. He wasn't a local, and I got the impression that he had been a chicken farmer before coming to the Ecole. Now he kept rabbits, and on special occasions, Frau Horcher cooked up rabbit stew.

I looked around and mused that, a hundred years earlier, others had lived in this farmhouse in the same way. Probably not much had changed. Was this what it meant to be poor in Switzerland? They didn't seem to lack a lot, nor was there any sign that he thought of himself as poor. Yet, when I recounted my adventure to my roommate, Jörg, he sneered and called Herr Horcher a peasant. Feeling honored to have been invited into my mentor's home, I got royally pissed off.

Herr Horcher was handier than we knew. One Sunday evening when the entire school gathered in the main hall for *Andacht*, the devotional hour spent listening to inspirational stories, thoughtful readings, and music, Herr Horcher was invited to play the spoons, a heretofore hidden talent. Seeing him dressed in his Sunday best, I couldn't keep from smiling. He parted his gray-tinged hair and wore a white shirt with a string tie and an embroidered jacket over a vest from which a long watch chain dangled. As soon as the record of Swiss music came on he set to work with the spoons, showing moves I had never seen before—clackity, clack, clack, clack, the spoons struck one another. With a sharp, metallic rhythm, they vibrated between his palm and his thigh. He rubbed them across his knuckles, bounced them off his knees, then against his hunched shoulder. I tapped my foot, a few snickered, but at the end of the evening we all applauded lustily. Whether the roar signaled appreciation or relief that it was over remained unclear.

On another evening, we heard a performance from an opera singer from Zurich who was the mother of one of the Kameraden. She sang songs from around the world. I was sitting toward the rear of the hall, my mind elsewhere, when I heard her say, "Und now I vill sing a Negro spiritual." That caught my attention. I listened. The song lacked a spiritual's flowing, melodic, mournful tones. This Brünhilde was slaying the song with her German-accented English and cadence.

"Vade in da vater, vade in da vater, child-rren. Vade in da vater. God's going to trrrr-ouble da vater."

I repressed a chuckle because a teacher sat to my right. But when Herr Poeschel, who I thought of as the stuffy Latin teacher, rolled his eyes and gave me a quick little grin, I lost it. Laughter burst forth and I couldn't stop. I held my sides but when I looked up again I saw Herr Lüthi looking over his shoulder, giving me his famous death stare. I understood. Struggling to gain control, I clamped my jaws shut, but my chair kept shaking and tears streamed down until she finished. Thankfully, she sang only one Negro spiritual.

My second winter at the Ecole was a real one. The snow piled up higher and higher, forcing us to excavate a series of trenches between the Ecole buildings. The nights were bitterly cold.

One frosty Tuesday evening after dinner, I bounded into the school kitchen and bellowed at Jörg and Phipu, "Hustle up, so we can get the hell out of here."

Other school families would be scampering off to sit in front of cozy fireplaces but the Lüthi Family was going sledding. We had put the best sleds aside, the moon was full, the snow fresh and cold, the road icy, and there would be no traffic. We planned to hike straight up the zigzag path by the brook, but follow a much longer route down. Everything was set; the only problem was that Phipu and Jörg were assigned to wash the dishes.

"Listen, man, I'll do the big pots," I hollered, and they renewed their efforts loading the plates into the dishwasher. Behind me someone else cleaned the serving bowls. I dove into the huge cooking pots. Merry with anticipation, I didn't care that it wasn't my night to wash. I wrestled with each pot—scraping, scrubbing, slamming it around in the metal sink, then rinsing it as fast as I could. Due to my furious pace and soapy hands, one of the big pots slipped and crashed to the floor.

Utta, the Kameradin in charge, was an older, taller, beefy girl with short blond hair and a clipped North German accent.

"Vhut are you doing?" she yelled.

I looked at the floor. It was obvious. I shrugged and said, "Sorry."

"Get out," she said.

"No!" I said, staring back at her.

"Leave now!" she screamed.

"Can't make me. I'm a volunteer."

Smack! My head jerked as she slapped my face.

Whack! I hit her back. *Oh shit!*

Hand on cheek, she turned and ran to the front end of the kitchen crying, "Herr Wiesman, Herr Wiesman!"

Herr Wiesman was the cook. Originally a pastry chef, he had somehow ended up at the Ecole with his Algerian wife and their three children. With forearms as big as hams and dressed in a white apron with the main course smeared all over the front, he came charging across the kitchen yelling at me to get out. *Good idea!* I thought, but before I could budge he was upon me. I pushed him away. Actually all I did was stick out my arms, but remnants of dinner had mixed with the soapy water upon the floor and become a slippery mess. He lost his footing and his feet flew from beneath him. I had never seen anything like it except in a Charlie Chaplin movie. He didn't just fall; rather, for a moment his whole body seemed suspended in midair before he landed flat on his back.

Time to leave. One step and I was at the back door, but it was locked. I leapt over him to get to the other door, only to find that it was latched, too. As I fumbled with the latch, Herr Wiesman crawled to his knees. By the time I had unlatched the door, he was barreling around the stove. The door popped open. But before I could bolt, he swung his foot and kicked me dead in the ass. I slid down the hallway on my stomach, then crawled, and finally ran toward the front door. As I jerked it open, I heard him yelling, "*Du schwarzer . . .*" (You black . . .) The words were lost as I bounded down the stairs. I raced along the side of Haupthaus, then skidded to a halt and fell into a stroll when I saw Natalie Lüthi coming toward me. For an instant I thought of throwing myself on my knees and confessing. Then indignation struck, and I wanted to complain that he had called me black. I took a deep breath, said, "Ciao, Natalie," and kept on walking. I was up shit's creek, and hurrying down it made no sense.

That evening the sledding was great—Jörg and Phipu told me so when they got back.

I grabbed the February 22, 1965, edition of the *Herald Tribune*, flattened the paper on the dining hall table, and read the headline:

Malcolm X Dies Shot 4 Times at New York Rally

I rushed into the article. "Malcolm X, 39, the apostle of violence as a solution to the American Negro's problems, was murdered today. He was shot as he addressed his own organization on the edge of Harlem . . ."

I knew that Malcolm X had broken away from the Black Muslims, but otherwise I was barely aware of him, and what I had read of his fiery rhetoric disturbed me. Not until I read his autobiography as a college freshman did I come to appreciate him, and not until long after that would I accept the depth of my own rage. So on that wintry day as I read about his assassination I felt he had gotten what he preached.

On March 11, another headline caught my attention:

THREE CLERGYMEN ARE CLUBBED IN SELMA, ALA.

"Three white ministers who came here to join a civil rights march were beaten with clubs last night by five white attackers. One was near death in a hospital . . . All three are members of the Unitarian Universalist Association . . ."

Unitarian Universalism was my religion, and those three ministers were my people. One of them, James Reeb, died soon after the attack. The Unitarian Universalist Association Board of Trustees, which was meeting in Boston, adjourned and traveled to Selma along with hundreds of Reeb's colleagues to memorialize Reeb and march with Dr. King. Two weeks later, another Unitarian Universalist protestor, Viola Liuzzo, a white Detroit housewife and mother of five, was shot and killed. These events galvanized white liberal support for the civil rights movement, propelled people into action, and assured the passage of the 1965 Voting Rights Act shortly thereafter.

As I read about events back home, confusion reigned within me. Witnessed from afar, it made no sense—not the way the Ecole did. I knew in my heart that people could live cooperatively with one another. After all, we did.

By tradition, everyone at the Ecole ventured forth on a three-day hike in the fall and a six-day hike in June. Summer was coming, and this would be my last hike before returning to Chicago for good. I was leading a group with Jack Bierschenk. Blond Jack had a nose nearly as pointed as Pinocchio's, the laugh of a hyena, the organizational compulsion of a German, and the aura of a Boy Scout. I'd adopted him as my older brother.

On the second day we climbed over the Hahnenmoospass and descended to Lenk. After shopping, we headed out along the Simme River then up the west slope. Halfway up the incline I saw a dark, little figure moving up the trail as slow as cold molasses. We overtook him easily, passing with a nod and the obilgatory *grüessech*. We stopped to examine our map and he passed us. A couple of minutes later we set out again, passing him. Later, as we lay sprawled along the side of the steep path moaning and panting—it was a very steep path—I saw him coming up the trail. Step, step, step. He was wiry, wore a tattered green felt hat, brown vest, and dark brown pants held up by suspenders; from his mouth hung a curved pipe. Step, step, step. His pipe, steady gait, and suspenders brought Herr Horcher to mind and I smiled. He nodded but his huge hobnailed boots never stopped. When we set out again I looked ahead, hoping to spot him; I never did. But after a while I fell into a pace that was new for me. Step, step, step. More deliberate, slower, sustainable.

The last leg of the six-day hike included the long climb from Meiringen to Goldern. Anxious to get home, we surged up the trail, sweaty, dusty, and smelling like cows since we had been sleeping in haylofts. I marched beside Jack, and when we passed a cluster of three farmhouses, we knew we were halfway there. Around the next turn, the path narrowed, passing through a large stone wall. A little boy stood in the opening, pop-eyed, mouth agape. In all likelihood he had never seen a real live Negro before. As we came closer, he turned, cried "*Mutti, Mutti!*" (mother) and ran for his mother.

I no longer remember exactly what he said—*Ein Schwarzer kommt* (A black is coming) or *Ein Neger* (A Negro)—but it was clear he was scared and fleeing from me.

"Man, look at him go!" crowed Jack.

The lines I had spoken as the Moorish king in the Christmas play jumped to mind, and I yelled, "*Fürchte dich nicht*" (Fear not), and then "*Hab' keine Angst*" (Don't be afraid). But on he sped. Perhaps it was some story he had heard. There were many. I might have been Black Peter—St. Nicholas's companion who visited bad little boys and girls—or even the devil, for they all knew Satan was black. Perhaps it was some primal fear of the unknown that drove him. I would never know, but there was no doubt he was terrified.

Unable to bear watching his frantic scramble up the trail, I lowered my eyes, and although I had done nothing except be there and be black, I felt guilty.

When he reached his mother, she stretched out an arm and I felt relieved. Then his head jerked as she slapped his face. He whimpered. She dragged him to the side of the road and turned her face away as I went past. Heedless of her shame, I glared without speaking. My mother would have scolded me if I had done as that child had, but I identified so strongly with him that I saw nothing but hardheartedness in his mother. As I redoubled my pace, the focus of my indignation shifted. Why should I feel bad about myself, about who I am, and the color that is my birthright? In that moment of righteous anger, I saw that something was wrong with the world, not with me. From that came a realization: The world must change! I think it was then that I first felt called to try to help make it happen.

The majestic Wetterhorn was hidden from sight as we marched through the woods. As I brooded about the state of the world, I couldn't imagine that before the end of July I would be marching on the streets of Chicago.

Homecoming

The only thing we have to fear is fear itself.

—Franklin Delano Roosevelt,
first inaugural address

When summer came, I returned to Chicago and, of course, to summer school, but my real education came in preparing to march on the Chicago Board of Education. As the day approached, Philip and I spent our time making posters and distributing flyers.

The Chatham Avalon Park Community Council (CAPCC) had been working with the Coordinating Council of Community Organizations (CCCO) to remedy the problems caused by school segregation, including prefab classrooms, derisively called Willis Wagons after the superintendent of schools, Benjamin Willis. The Chicago Board of Education had placed these in school playgrounds and called them an answer to overcrowding. In the meantime, as white flight accelerated, many white schools were left with empty classrooms.

As co-chair of CAPCC's schools committee, Dad was deeply involved. CAPCC, realizing that the only way to maintain residential stability was to provide excellent schools, proposed establishing a new region on the southeast side of Chicago. The region's five high schools would specialize in either academics, vocational work, or commerce, and one school would offer special psychological and remedial services for students who were drop-out risks. A decade later, similar programs called magnet schools became popular in other school districts. However, Ben Willis, committed as he was to keeping the school system segregated, refused to meet with CAPCC.

An ad hoc group of parents hired Paul Zuber, a Negro attorney who had helped to sue the New Rochelle, New York, school board. He did the same in Chicago and won. The court settlement established the Advisory Panel on Integration of the Public Schools. In March 1964, the panel reported that 84 percent of Negro students and 86 percent of the whites attended essentially segregated schools, but in the year since the report's release, little progress had been made in implementing its recommendations. School boycotts and marches became a regular part of CCCO's effort to get rid of Ben Willis and bring the Board of Education to the negotiating table.

The day of the march arrived, and we gathered by the lakefront near the band shell in Grant Park. As the marchers surged ahead, I hovered close to Dad. We poured down Columbus Drive, then left onto Jackson Avenue and headed toward the Board of Education. "Ben Willis must go! Ben Willis must go!" we chanted and kept chanting until it grew into a roar. Heat radiated from everywhere: the sun, the asphalt, the people, and the speakers—whom I couldn't see through the crowd even when standing on tiptoe. I felt trapped with Dad on one side and Philip on the other, and as the rally went on and on, boredom replaced enthusiasm. My eyes wandered until they rested on Philip. I was astonished; his face was fixed in concentration as he strained to listen. I said to myself, *You can do this*; then I dug down and tried again.

I hadn't wanted to leave the Ecole, but the choice wasn't mine. There was a fairness factor—a year later Philip would get his turn—and a fear factor: Stay away longer and readjusting to Chicago would be that much harder. I didn't care. Wanting no part of Chicago, I withdrew. I sulked. I resisted, refusing to adapt, eschewing old friends, offering my family a sullen adolescent silence.

Clinging to the Ecole, I phoned big Bob Matson, the only other Ecole Kamerad in the Chicago area, and he invited me to visit him in Libertyville. The day came. At Union Station, I caught the Chicago and Northwestern to the affluent, white northwest suburb where his family lived. All the while, I worried it would be a place where a black South Side kid wasn't welcome. I stepped off the train into a crusher of a hug from Bob, but his enthusiasm couldn't smother my anxiety. As we drove past a small lake, I scanned the beach looking in vain for someone—anyone—who wasn't white.

My experience in Libertyville was typical of balkanized Chicago. There were places I went—Chatham, Hyde Park, the Loop—and many more that I didn't. To the west, white working class Gage Park was a no-go-zone (Dr. King would be jeered and stoned there a year later), while to the north Woodlawn was black but nonetheless another area I would have avoided if possible. Woodlawn was a poor neighborhood being gutted by urban renewal—which actually meant Negro removal—that was backed by the University. I had to traverse it on my way to and from the University of Chicago Laboratory High School.

If I were going to encounter gang members, it would be in Woodlawn and my fear, which had abated, intensified. Philip ridiculed me, but from my perspective, surviving in Blackstone Ranger territory meant the day-to-day challenge of getting my timid, terrified butt home in one piece. Heading south to catch the bus home, I crossed the green expanse of the Midway, separating the University of Chicago from Woodlawn. To me, it also divided the known from the unknown. The hospital in which I was born, the Unitarian Universalist church my family attended, my dad's lab in an ivy-covered neo-Gothic building, and the dour-looking white students who populated the north side of the Midway all disappeared as I walked south past abandoned buildings, empty lots covered with rubble and weeds, cracked sidewalks, and few people. One side was familiar and integrated, the other foreign, black, and frightening. My heart would pound as I scanned the block ahead, picking a route with a clear view so I could see anyone approaching. The bus stop on 61st Street was across from a drug-store where, if necessary, I planned to retreat. I would strut, fak-ing coolness, but my teeth were set, and as the autumn days grew shorter I dreaded what might loom out of the dark. That ordeal ended when we moved to Hyde Park, but the fear remained.

Fighting our way into Hyde Park had been difficult. As Dad put it, "We had a hell of a time finding housing." Restrictive covenants had proved ineffective even before being ruled illegal in 1948, but after nearly two decades of civil rights battles, the U of C, as Hyde Park's major landlord, continued to resist. At the same time, the Hyde Park-Kenwood Community Conference, led by Leslie Pen-nington, the minister of our church and one of those pushing to integrate First Unitarian Church, worked to create a genuinely interracial community. When the well-known black historian John Hope Franklin was hired by the University in 1964, hous-ing couldn't be found for him in the neighborhood. Dad recalled that "Walter Johnson, the head of the history department, began to throw his weight around in an unbelievable way" to get Franklin housing. "And I didn't have a ghost of a chance despite the fact I was working at the University. The university housing office made no effort to help us. In fact, anything I turned up, the University would preempt. I remember this place on 52nd and Greenwood that went for five thousand dollars less than we were told we would have to pay for it. We ended up buying one block east in an urban renewal project the University didn't control and where antidis-crimination laws applied."

The First Unitarian Church, halfway between our new town-house and my high school, became a natural place for me to hang out. Its sixty-member youth group, part of the national Liberal Religious Youth (LRY), was a happening place, and it became my raison d'être. I stayed past ten on Sunday evenings, helping Leroy, the janitor, clean and lock up. I hung around church all the time, especially when I should have been at school, and within a year the church had hired me as assistant janitor and the youth group had elected me its president.

That fall we organized the first dance of the school year. The one responsibility no one ever wanted was standing at the door to bar crashers. As president, I got stuck with it. I stood there, backed by our adult advisors, turning people away. No one appreciated it, and I had already taken a lot of abuse when three homeboys approached. By the way they pimped up, I knew they didn't belong. "Sorry, man. Members only," I said. Well, they cursed me up and down and were just leaving when I reached my limit.

"Ya mama," I muttered.

The one closest to me whipped around and shouted, "What you say, nigger?"

"Nothin," I lied.

"Man, you dissing me? We gonna get ya motherfucking ass. You just wait, you jiveass sonofabitch. We gonna jack you up." Hearing the commotion, an advisor stepped forward and the guys swaggered off. Then someone who attended Hyde Park High School sidled up to me and whispered, "Those were Rangers." I felt like throwing up.

I began running scared again. Giving my paranoia full rein, I varied my routes between home, school, and church. I never left by the same door two days in a row. I slid out back doors and side doors; I cut through backyards and dashed down alleys; I stuck myself in the middle of crowds of students, and still my heart raced. Then slowly, as winter came on, I wearied of my own neurotic behavior, and my angst tapered off.

As my senior year progressed, two dreams grabbed me, and both came to naught.

By then I was also the church's Sunday office manager and was so immersed in church work that I practically lived there. The idea of becoming a minister was inescapable. The church had been there for me. I had gone there lost and faltering, and found a home and a purpose. It was a place where I was nurtured, and so I grew; having grown, I could give; and the more I gave, the more I grew.

Setting out to test my intuition, I stopped by Wylie's. He had been one of my teachers at the Ecole, and now was completing a master of arts in teaching at the University of Chicago. "That's very interesting, Mark. You go right ahead, if that is what you really want to do," he said. Then, mumbling something about an appointment, he disappeared down the hallway. Feeling unheard and unsatisfied, I crossed the living room and knocked on his roommate's door. Michael, a longhaired, bearded grad student in high-energy physics, answered and I explained my idea. He listened, but only briefly.

"Sit down," he said taking on a professorial tone. "You know, Marx once said 'religion is the opiate of the masses' and he's right."

Stunned into silence, I sat as he paced the floor, wagging his finger at me. I tried to speak, but he spoke over me. I disagreed, but he argued me down. I had never heard him speak with such vehemence. "I just don't want you to get caught up in this religious hocus-pocus," he said. Then, placing his hand upon my shoulder, he softened and counseled, "Besides, why waste your life on a dying institution?"

"Thanks a million," I stammered, and fled down the stairs. I mentioned the ministry one more time during a visit to Madison, Wisconsin, to see the Pinocchio-nosed Kamerad, Jack Bierschenk. Robust-living, ultra-organized Jack would understand. But when I told him of my interest in the ministry, he began to laugh and kept on laughing, and was still laughing when he fell breathlessly to the floor. "Forget it," I said, and never brought up ministry again.

It went without saying that I would go to college and I had dutifully mailed applications to Swarthmore, Earlham, Kalamazoo, and Beloit. By then, in addition to all my church activities, I had also picked up a job as a waiter at the U of C faculty Quadrangle Club, but I was failing typing and barely maintaining a C average overall. In May, the college rejection letters began arriving. I compared myself to the others at U-High, a school full of brainy types, and began to consider not going directly to college. Besides, my girlfriend, Sharon Wang, was putting off college to go to Taiwan and learn Chinese.

Standing at the door to my dad's study, I peered in. Mother sat on the piano stool. Behind her stood an upright piano with

cherrywood veneer and above it a gallery of family photographs—
babies, grandparents, and my warmhearted, hard-talking Great-
aunt Irene. Across the room, light shone through the window,
silhouetting the figure of my Great-uncle Lloyd, the retired vice
dean of Howard University Medical School. Father sat on a swivel
chair in front of his paper-strewn desk. The walls were covered
with over-loaded bookshelves.

"I, ah . . . I'm, ah . . . not ready for college. I wanna to take a
year off."

They stared at me as if I had lost my mind. "Boy, what are you
talking about?" Dad erupted. "Delay college? Absolutely not."

"No. Listen, it's like this. I need some time to be on my own.
A chance to find myself. I don't know what I want to do, so why
waste all that money? Instead I thought I'd get a job, save some,
then travel. Switzerland, maybe Israel? I could—"

"What's this stuff about finding yourself? Where'd you get that
crazy idea?"

"Well, you know some of the other kids are going to wait a
year before they start college and Sharon's going to Taiwan and I
just—"

"Boy, what . . . are . . . you . . . thinking?"

What had I been thinking? I must have been brave or stupid or
deluded to suggest delaying college to this august group, in whose
footsteps I was expected to follow. "I just thought that maybe—"

"Listen, Mark," Mother said, speaking softly and slowly, as if
I were ten years old, "you have to understand you don't have the
same luxury those white kids have. You're a Negro. Their options
aren't your options, or even Sharon's. Finding yourself? Well, those
white parents can let their sons and daughters do that if they want,
but we . . . Maybe we brought you up the wrong way. I mean staying in Switzerland and being around all those white children. Now
you think you're just like them, but you're not."

"I don't care. I just don't wanna go." And with those words, my
face turned hard as I looked past them and out the window, knowing they would never understand.

Great-uncle Lloyd broke in. "Stop talking nonsense, boy. I'll tell you what you need to do. Don't worry about finding yourself. What you'd better worry about is getting into college and getting an education so you'll be able to find a good job."

"Yes, sir," I whispered, "You're right, sir. I'm sorry." Too scared of the consequences to defy them, and feeling utterly ashamed and defeated, I couldn't tolerate standing there another moment. "May I be excused, please?" I mumbled and without waiting for a response, backed out of the room. In an instant, I sped around the corner and out the back door. It was the last time I asked for permission.

I didn't want to go to college but I looked forward to leaving home, getting out of Chi-town, and getting free from Sharon—particularly after she and my mother, as a not-funny joke, turned my eighteenth birthday into an engagement party.

Beloit, the only college that accepted me, was about a hundred miles northwest of Chicago, in a region of Wisconsin called Little Switzerland. The city of Beloit sat at the confluence of Turtle Creek and Rock River, where the Winnebago tribe once camped. Beyond this industrial town of thirty thousand lay rolling hills, cows, and dairy farms. I thought that there I would escape the pressures and dangers of living in Chicago.

During the first hour of my first day at Beloit, I met Art Perkins, who would change my life. He was white, spoke with a down-home Midwestern twang, and strolled up to me asking where to find Haven Hall. His short, plump, graying parents came right behind him. Since his room was next to mine, I was able to guide them to the red brick Georgian dormitory that would be our home for the next year. Somehow Art and I fell into a relationship that endured. Fortunately, friendships aren't like romances—hormones don't flow, bells don't go off. You ease into it. Hang out together, have a good time. Art's almost goofy lack of pretense made him easy to be with and four decades later we remain friends.

We were an odd couple. Art, the son of a Presbyterian minister, had spent his life moving from one rural parish to another—always an outsider, always viewed with some suspicion, and at the same time held to a higher standard. A chubby boy sandwiched between four sisters, he quietly bore his cross. Eventually, however, his smarts won him a full scholarship to Phillips Academy in Andover, one of the country's most prestigious prep schools. Landing there at the beginning of his junior year, he was a hick among the sons of America's elite, and more an outsider than ever. Meanwhile, I was good-natured, grew up with advantages but didn't belong to the elite either; I was black but not street-wise, and nobody's scholar. I nurtured a scruffy beard, wore bell-bottom pants, a London bobby's cape, and wooden clogs. I loved being high and flirted with being a hippie, but was too cautious to seriously plunge into the counterculture. Art and I both felt like misfits—awkward, self-conscious, and guarded.

In those first days, I noticed that Art actively avoided mentioning Andover, and whenever the truth came out, he responded to the raised eyebrows with an embarrassed shrug. I, on the other hand, enjoyed telling these white kids—in a casual sort of way—that I had attended the U of C lab high school, and before that a Swiss boarding school. That turned their heads around. Yet, I concealed this same information from black students. Hearing I had lived in Europe, blacks, like everyone else, assumed I was an Army brat. Of course, I rebuffed that. But then only one option remained: I was a boojee—an uppity bourgeois Negro—or at least, that is what I imagined they said behind my back. So I avoided mentioning it, becoming evasive when pressed. For if whites thought, "He's not one of *them*," I feared blacks would think, "He's not one of *us*."

The class of 1971 at Beloit included twenty-two black students, and most hung with the black upperclassmen, who had laid claim to a round table near the main entrance to the student union. Neither U-High nor LRY had been like that; these students reminded me of the sturdy, stolid farmers of the Hasliberg gathered around the table reserved for regulars at the local inn, smoking their pipes and playing cards. Similarly, almost any time the Beloit Student Union was open, a group of black students sat jawing and playing

Bid Whist. They had created a small, safe, and lively haven in a white world. I dropped by from time to time, and it didn't bother me particularly that the space was off-limits to whites. However, I was troubled by another unspoken decree: Real blacks sit here. And, in truth, few black students sat anywhere else. I, however, refused to conform, and so every time I entered the Union I faced a dilemma: Where to sit?

Wanting to be accepted, I never passed the table without joining in the banter, but their refuge was just too confining. With feigned indifference, I sat where I pleased, taking in the comings and goings out of the corner of my eye, while in a corner of my heart, my yearning warred with resentment.

Then, on April 4, 1968, the day Martin Luther King Jr. was assassinated, all middle ground vanished and an unbreachable wall of hostility went up between blacks and whites.

The King Is Dead,
Long Live the King

*We have left the dusty soils of Egypt and crossed a Red Sea
whose waters had for years been hardened by a long piercing
winter of massive resistance. But before we reach the majestic shores of the Promised Land, there is a frustrating and
bewildering wilderness ahead.*

—Martin Luther King Jr.,
Nobel Lecture, 1964

I recall King's assassination as clearly as President Kennedy's,
but everything else was different. After the initial shock of Kennedy's death, my life had carried on as before. After King's death it
didn't—not mine nor any member of my family's. We staggered, as
inconsolable grief gripped the black community, shook our lives,
and changed everything. But the changes—which were wrenching
and dislocating—were already in motion before the moment of
King's death. Whether he lived or not, difficult choices loomed.
The upheaval of 1968 was, of course, cultural but also very personal. We struggled with developmental and relational issues, and
would have struggled with them even if that tempest hadn't swept
us all up. Each of us had to respond and each did, sometimes in
opposite ways.

When my family returned from Switzerland, Mother became the director of the Social Work Department at the University of Chicago Bob Roberts Children's Hospital and an instructor at the University's School of Social Service Administration. As the activism of the sixties built, her own activism intensified, and six months before Dr. King's assassination she had flown to New York City—over Dad's protest—to attend an emergency conference called the Unitarian Universalist Response to the Black Rebellion. The conference did not go as planned. Thirty-seven of the 150 attendees were Afro-Americans, and soon after the conference began, thirty of them withdrew from the planned agenda and moved to another room to hold their own meeting. Mother was among them.

As they met through the evening and into the night, seeking a purpose more compelling than getting by, this black caucus tapped into the raw emotion hidden behind middle-class reasonableness. They started searching for an identity more authentic than the futile attempt to be carbon copies of white people. They saw white liberalism's emphasis on integration as a one-way street that elevated white and debased black. Civil rights had changed the law but proven ineffective at remedying black poverty, and liberal religion had failed to address the experience of blackness. The group called for a new agenda, and by the time they emerged from their meeting, the Black Unitarian Universalist Caucus [BUUC] Steering Committee had been formed.

The conference sent shockwaves through the Unitarian Universalist Association. Ben Scott, a long-time family friend who also attended, said, "I am not the only UU who was irreversibly shaped by it. Thousands were born again. They came to a thrilling sense of the awesome potential of human society and lifelong friendships crumbled, marriages dissolved, careers were ended and congregations factionalized." That included my parents' marriage, for powering mother's natural gregariousness was a new, almost defiant, assertiveness and increasingly manic activism. This new cause gave direction to the anger that had long simmered within her, and she came home saying, "For the first time in my life I feel black."

Following the conference, Dad picked her up at the airport. She was traveling with George Sykes, a white member of First Unitarian Church who, realizing he couldn't do what had to be done, told her, "You're going to have to carry the ball."

And she did, despite knowing that the formation of a black caucus would scare whites. At a meeting of forty black Unitarian Universalists, Mother, who was chair of the Church Council at First Unitarian, spelled out BUUC's demands and told of the commitment the participants had made to return to their communities and organize local chapters. They formed a Chicago area chapter, and with zeal began preparing for the National Conference of Black Unitarian Universalists. It gathered in Chicago in February 1968, and two months later Dr. King was dead.

Three years earlier Dad had participated in another meeting of blacks and whites to discuss race, a local gathering at First Unitarian. What he heard annoyed him so much that he stood up and said, "Listen! You white folks can all walk out of here and you can do whatever you want. We walk out of here and we are still black. You can do whatever you want but we can't." Later he said, "I'll never forget how cavalier their attitude was. Like it was no big deal and somehow the Civil Rights Act had changed everything. And it hadn't. I was amazed because a lot of them weren't aware of all the subtle ways bigotry plays a role in determining black people's whole lives. That every aspect of our lives is controlled by people who are unsympathetic and not about to treat people of a different color in an equitable way."

After that event Dad made a decision. Realizing that he couldn't spend the same amount of time as he had before on social activism and remain competitive as a scientist, he chose to back off from the former and recommit himself to the latter. In the spring of 1968 Dad had just returned to Chicago after having spent the winter as a visiting professor at the University of California in Irvine and was extraordinarily engrossed in the early stage of preparation for the Apollo 11 moon mission. He was also about to be promoted to senior scientist at Argonne National Laboratory. Amidst all this, he didn't notice that Mother's activism was on the verge of spreading from the streets into their marriage.

By April 1968, the ground had shifted beneath the civil rights movement, among the younger generation most of all. Earlier Stokely Carmichael, former leader of the Student Nonviolent Coordinating Committee (SNCC), had called for the right of self-defense. Then in 1967, he left SNCC to join the Black Panther Party, which Huey P. Newton and Bobby Seale had founded. In that same year, the Congress of Racial Equality (CORE), an avowedly integrationist organization, made an about-face, became militant, and embraced a black nationalist agenda.

This was the climate Philip returned to in 1967. Having spent his junior year at the Ecole d'Humanité, he was now a senior at Hyde Park High School and about to graduate. Hyde Park High couldn't have been more different from the Ecole. It was predominantly black. Fifty percent of its students were Blackstone Rangers, and by their junior year more than half of them had dropped out. Philip discovered that most of his black friends had gotten involved with the Black Power movement; one was even selling Black Panther newspapers. "If you didn't hang out with them you weren't considered one of their crowd," Philip said. "Instead you were considered a problem and that could be dangerous for your personal well-being, so I had to learn to speak the language of the streets if I was going to survive."

Carole's story was similar to Philip's. As a freshman at Kenwood Academy, which like Hyde Park was predominantly black, she also experienced lots of peer pressure. "I chose to go with the in crowd," she said "since I was having enough trouble with some of the black students because the color of my skin was too light and the texture of my hair too straight. I had some friends who were real radicals in the movement and most of them were real fair skinned. One was very fair skinned and both her parents taught at the University, and she became the most radical of all. Mama said she was overcompensating; that she had to be more militant in order to prove she was black enough."

For Carole it was a hard choice: "I really struggled during those years because the world in which I had grown up was a mixed world of diverse cultural groups. Our house was open to people from around the world. I would sit at the dinner table with Mom and Dad having long, interesting conversations with all kinds of people—East and West Indians, Africans, Asians, Europeans, Cubans, Haitians, and Panamanians. Now my peers were telling me that I had to make a choice; that it was either all Black Power or nothing; it was either black or white, but all I had ever known were shades of gray. The choice I searched for was a choice that offered diversity. As I matured, I recognized that I could have that and in the end my shades of gray won out, but that came later."

Even Lauren, who had just turned nine five days before King's assassination, couldn't help but be swept up in the whirlwind of her mother's activism and her siblings' dilemmas. The tempest following the awful news that King had been murdered left no choice; each of us just had to cope.

I looked up as the door slammed open. "The stupid fuckers! Stupid fuckers, they shot him." Peter, one of my two college roommates, a blond, southern, good-time boy from Virginia Beach, snarled as he burst into our room with my friend Art Perkins trailing behind.

"Who?" Keith, my other roommate, and I asked at once.

"King, man! Martin Luther King Jr. Somebody killed him," Pete said as he sank onto his bed.

"Oh man! No, no, no," I said, shaking my head as if to deny the truth. Then, in a haze, I spent the rest of the day in front of a television, watching pictures of the Memphis motel where the shooting took place, seeing riots break out across the country, and hearing the world's reaction to his death.

Philip's description of the day was almost surreal: "The principal of our high school came over the loud speaker and said that Martin Luther King Jr. had been shot. There was an eerie silence, then hushed whispers, and all at once people started filing out of the classrooms and heading for the doors. The students dismissed themselves from school and there was nothing the administration could do about it.

"Some of my white friends came up to me and said that there was going to be a rally in the lunchroom and I should check it out with them. I told them that as of right now, 'I don't know you and if I were you I'd go home and fast.'

"I went to the lunchroom alone. There were students crowding around a table and a young black man was standing on it, shouting and ranting. By the time I left the lunchroom and headed home, people were dashing down 63rd Street. There were cries for the revolution to begin. People were throwing bricks and rocks through storefront windows while others followed behind them looting. . . . The police, who had a reputation for their extreme brutality, came out in full force, backed and supported by Mayor Daley's order: Shoot to kill. The National Guard was eventually called in.

"I can remember coming home at dinner time. It was a very quiet night. We sat and listened to the news. So much had happened, so much turmoil, shock, and sadness."

My father didn't even know about it until he was driving home and heard it on the car radio. "People were rioting," he said. "They were burning down the Westside and all sorts of stuff like that and [your mother] was talking some nonsense about going out on the street to try to stop it and I said, 'Absolutely not.'"

Dr. King's life and death were all that we discussed in class the day after the assassination. Averting their eyes, the white students remained silent, except for commenting on how awful it was. Walter and Charles, two other black students, dominated the hour. They warned that an armed struggle was inevitable. I disagreed, but no one else really dared. I argued that violence couldn't succeed. Class ended and the white kids fled, perhaps hoping to escape a sense of guilt they felt but didn't understand. Our voices were still raised as Walter, Charles, and I walked across campus.

"What about King's way?" I asked. "What about nonviolent resistance?"

"Hey, what about it?" Walter said, shaking his head. "Reed! Don't talk to me about King. Sure, he was peaceful, and they offed his ass. Protest doesn't mean diddly to honkies. We gotta have a revolution."

"Tell the man about it," Charles chimed in. "Tell him what the white man's game really is."

When we reached the gravel parking lot between Haven Hall and the field house, we were still arguing. "Let me get this straight," I said. "Blacks are going to organize cadres, procure arms, and begin guerrilla warfare, like Che Guevara. And then what?"

"We commit acts of sabotage that'll bring the system to a standstill."

"Walt, it's futile. How are we going to beat the most powerful army in the world? With all its weapons, how are we gonna be more violent than they can be? Not to mention they'll have the support of the majority of the people. Come on, how are we supposed to win?"

"Man, we don't have to beat them. We just start the revolution, hit the strategic locations. Then the Red Chinese will come to our aid."

"What you been smokin'? The Red Chinese? Get real!"

"Reed, this is how it is. The white man gonna just keep us down, just gonna keep killing us when we try to stand up, just keep abusing us until black folks rise up and overthrow this goddamn oppressive system."

"Think about what you're saying. Even if the Red Chinese did come to our aid, and we should win, what then? Would it be black over white? So we're going to be running things, and we're going to do it better? Out of the ruins we're going to make a better society? And the Red Chinese are simply going to say, 'Glad we could help' and go home? Man, come on. Think about what war would mean," I pleaded. "There's got to be another way."

He pointed his finger at me and said, "What you need to think about, Negro, is what side you gonna be on."

"Man, I don't believe this shit. Let's drop it. You haven't convinced me and I obviously haven't convinced you." I turned away and bounded up the stairs before they could see the tears welling up.

Nothing in that time was simple, not even friendship. For Carole, as for me, the impact of King's death on her relationships was immediate: "The day after Martin Luther King Jr. was killed, I was to sing with the Chicago Children's Choir at a memorial service for him downtown at City Hall. There were two other members of the choir at my school. They were my friends and they were white. I'd grown up with both of them, but because of the Black Power movement I had begun to pull away because it was becoming dangerous to have white friends.

"I came to school a little late that day. A lot of black students were hanging out in front of school. The tension, you could feel it, it was like walking the gauntlet. I was hearing all these threats: 'No white people better show up today,' 'We're gonna kick some ass.' Even though I had begun to separate from my white friends, I was still close to them, even though it was now behind closed doors. I didn't want any of them to get hurt so I ran through the school telling my white friends to get out and go home. I explained that some people were threatening to beat up the white people at school. I told them that I thought there was going to be trouble and that fighting was going to break out. Most whites did go home and a few blacks and whites did get beaten up. And that night I decided to stay away from my white friends."

That same day the wife of one of Dad's colleagues at Argonne called him up and said, "Wouldn't you like to come out here and stay where it is safe?" "And I get home that night," Dad said, "and Lee has gone somewhere. It turns out she went to Oakland, just north of Kenwood, to some sort of rally related to King's death. I remember being real annoyed because she was so late getting in, and I didn't know what was going on, or what had happened, or if she was okay or not."

The very next day, a memorial service was held at Rockefeller Chapel on the University of Chicago campus. The sanctuary was packed; Dad was in the audience and Carole in the choir when Mother, who delivered one of three eulogies, stepped into the pulpit:

Did he dream the impossible dream?
Did he fight an unbeatable foe?
Can we right an unrightable wrong?

I keep thinking of two biblical passages, "Ye shall reap what ye sow," and "He that lives by the sword shall die by the sword." The words of the late existentialist author Albert Camus [sic] are also prophetic today: "We must learn to live together or we shall all perish together."

The first time I saw Dr. Martin Luther King Jr. in person was in 1956, right here in Rockefeller Chapel. The occasion was the celebration of Thomas Jefferson's two hundredth anniversary by the Chicago Area Liberal Churches.

Dr. King was only twenty-seven years old but it was clear even then that he was old and wise beyond his years. That meeting stands out clearly in my mind. When he ascended the podium, a hush settled over the audience of two thousand people, and everyone present rose in unison to pay silent tribute to the experience in Montgomery— and we were awed by the presence of a man who inspired simple black folk to walk over 370 days for the right for a seat on a bus.

Dr. King said many southerners falsely interpret the Bible or use false logic to support their stand. "They set up an Aristotelian syllogism like this: All men are made in the image of God. God is not a Negro. Therefore, the Negro is not a man. This is a philosophy of hate," he said. "We will not respond with violence or hatred. Our weapons will be the instruments of love and passive resistance. We will refuse to cooperate with injustice."

And in referring to the work that lay ahead he said, "If you can't fly, you must run; if you cannot run, you must walk; if you cannot walk, you must crawl, but the most important thing to remember is that you must keep moving."

I wonder how many of us who were present on that occasion have kept moving. So many of us decent folks feel that if we do not throw bricks, and if we live in an integrated neighborhood, or send our kids to an integrated private school, or attend an integrated church, then our slate is clean.

It was Whitney Young who said recently that our sin is not that of commission but of omission. We have abdicated our responsibility and we have permitted our country to be racist, and then we wonder why this terrible catastrophe has befallen us.

In grasping for some ideas to make this tribute meaningful for all of us, I asked my son [Philip], "What do you think of when you think of Martin Luther King?" He said, "I think of marching on a hot summer day, of singing 'We Shall Overcome,' of protests, of nuns, of black people and white, of Jews and Protestants, of walking tall and feeling good inside." It is hard to understand what it means to black people to lose a man who has for a fleeting moment given them a chance to feel good inside.

We are shocked at the looting, burning and self-destruction that has occurred during the past twenty-four hours—that only a fraction of black people have engaged in this is not relevant. It frightens all of us and we are repelled by it.

We are all greatly repelled today—but were we repelled when four little girls were killed in a Birmingham church in 1963?

Are we repelled enough by the landlords who charge Lake Shore prices for rat-infested apartments where children become permanently brain damaged because of lead poisoning?

Are we repelled enough by the storekeepers who mark up the prices in the market the day the AFDC mother receives her welfare check? Are we repelled enough by the fact that she pays more for inferior food than the mother in Winnetka or any other suburban area?

Are we repelled enough by the recent deaths of three black students from Claflin College, who were murdered because they had the audacity to want to bowl in a bowling alley across the street from their campus? A requiem for them was held in this chapel and there were fewer than a hundred people attending—mostly students. It was a lengthy program given by the Black Students Alliance of the University of Chicago. Some of the tributes were beautiful, some creative, and a few of the things they said were frightening.

I was compelled to attend the service, I must confess, not just to commemorate their death—but also to honor the memory of my mother who attended that same small college in Orangeburg, South Carolina, but who was never given the opportunity to teach after she moved north to Pennsylvania.

Are we repelled enough by the many comments we've heard on *The Jerry Williams Show*, such as "He deserved it," "He asked for it," "He did not obey the law," or "It's the best thing that ever happened to this country." My pastor [Jack Kent, minister of the First Unitarian Society of Chicago] received a call last night from a former parishioner who was sickened by the fact that in his officers' club in Tennessee toasts were being raised to celebrate the death of Martin Luther King Jr.

There is a cancer in our nation—and no one wants to look at cancer. Believe me, it is hard to look at—but doctors must look at it in order to treat it—and we must treat our own sickness.

We decry this senseless looting, but is it more moral to deny a black child a chance for a better education because of the color of his skin? Is it more moral to deny a man the right to buy a home so he may offer his family a better life?

And are we repelled by our legislators, both local and national, who play games with one-tenth of the population? And what about our churches?

I fail to see the difference in this morality—one strikes me as far more open and honest and moral if you will. Less damage is done to the psyche and the soul by the more primitive, impulsive response.

But we know this is not the answer. The primitive response would not be evoked if our country had permitted our black brethren the right to be men.

If we had said, "You are human and precious and you are worthwhile because you are human"—but the message has been clearly conveyed in so many different ways that the black man is not a man. The politicians want his vote but he need not honor his promises to a mere black man. One quarter of the army fighting in Vietnam is black—fighting for freedom—but they are not permitted to exercise their freedom to live or to die as men of dignity in their own country.

Martin Luther King Jr. believed in white America. He was the man who said we must go the nonviolent route, but he was also a militant.

Dr. King knew that if America did not respond to the needs of blacks, they would be forced to go underground in order to achieve some sense of equality—even if this meant risking the destruction of this nation. Better this than being destroyed as a people.

If Martin Luther King Jr. had a choice, he would prefer his death if our response to his death is to have many more people reevaluate and reexamine their own role in obtaining freedom for all.

Dr. King was a man who really knew who he was. He was proud of being a black man.

You know we allow Greek Americans to be proud of their Greekness. The Irish Americans to have their Irish pride. We do not let the Mafia destroy the image of the Italian Americans because we know they have their Fermis and Toscaninis. The Jews certainly have no problem with their identity. But when blacks begin thinking of black identity and black consciousness, it suddenly smacks of Black Nationalism. One cannot be a good American until he knows who he is.

The problem is defined—let us face it. Let us be honest with ourselves and with one another. Let us confess that we did indeed participate in Martin Luther King's death.

The last opportunity that I had to see Dr. Martin Luther King Jr. was this past winter at a dinner for the Joint Negro Appeal. He was speaking to a predominantly black audience and he said many stirring things. I was again impressed with the militancy of this peace-loving man. He said, "They tell a man who has no boots to pull himself up by his boot straps. Even a man leaving jail is given a suit of clothes and carfare to his destination, but the slaves were only given empty promises of freedom. They tell us to stand up, when someone is standing on our shoulders." He also said, "Let us not be like Rip Van Winkle. The picture of King George III was on the inn door when he went to sleep, and when he awakened it had been replaced by George Washington." He said, "There is a revolution going on," and then admonished us, "Don't sleep through it as Rip Van Winkle did."

Our nation has been asleep, and only when the black man finds his manhood can we awaken. Your black brother must take his rightful place in the sun. It is his rightful place. He has earned it through blood, sweat, and tears. He has earned it in building this nation, and if we don't know this, it's because the history of black people has never been honestly written.

If we can permit twenty-two million black people to have their manhood, they will have gained a country, and America will have gained a soul—for only when racism has died can America begin to live.

In the days following King's death, as Carole reexamined what it meant to be black, Lauren got swept up in her older sister's reorientation. She said, "Carole and her radical friend followed me and my friend Derrick home from school. They were talking about the assassination of Martin Luther King Jr. and about the rioting and bomb threats at their high school following his death. They also talked about wanting to join the Black Panther Party and how real change was now going to start taking place.

"When we got in front of our house, Carole asked me and Derrick to take a seat on the front steps. She began to ask us all kinds of questions about where we came from and who we were. When I said I came from Chicago, she said that wasn't what she meant. Then she asked Derrick what was the color of his skin. He took a real close look at his hand and said, 'It looks kind of yellow to me.' Well, that was definitely the wrong thing for Derrick to say. Derrick and I got a very long lecture on black pride. They made us repeat 'I'm black and I'm proud' over and over. They told us we needed to go to school and teach our friends about the movement and about the color of their skin. They warned us to never forget where we came from and if anybody asked us what color we were we should let them know we were black, not Negro or colored. I remember feeling proud afterward."

Word of the Black Student Union meeting passed in whispers among the black students at Beloit. Though I suspected the gathering would be nothing more than a political diatribe and a call to rash action, my yearning to be included drew me. I wavered, then decided to go at the last moment. Duty rather than desire compelled me, that and my fear of being labeled Uncle Tom.

We drifted into Bushnell Lounge, and once every chair and every spot along the wall of the large, long lounge was taken, a guard was posted and the door closed. *Ridiculous*, I thought.

Only then did Mike Young, captain of the football team, fraternity president, and big man on campus, stand up. I hadn't thought about him until I heard a fist slam into a palm. I turned and there he was in the shadows at the opposite end of the room. As he rhythmically pounded away, I grew tense.

"You know the revolution is coming (smack) . . . We gotta rise up against these honkies (smack) . . . Time to get the Man off our back (smack) . . ."

Sure, know-it-all, the revolution is about to begin. I rolled my eyes and considered slipping back out into the hot, humid July night.

"Time to arm ourselves (smack) . . . Prepare for war (smack) . . . Use any means necessary (smack) . . ."

Arms flew up in Black Power salutes and shouts of "Right on, right on!" echoed all around. *What bullshit,* I thought. *Time to drop it and get on with planning a protest or rally or whatever.*

As he paced in my direction my eyes fixed on his biceps and forearms—dark brown, scarred, powerful from playing football. They bulged, and I flinched every time his fist punctuated a phrase.

"First we gotta take care of business (smack) . . . Root out them vanilla lovers (smack) . . . Cuz we got some Uncle Toms right here (smack) . . . Got some Oreos (smack) . . . Black on the outside but white on the inside (smack) . . ."

A shiver threaded its way up my spine, and I slouched back against the stone fireplace, trying to disappear. As Mike's advance brought him closer, I looked away.

"We got some niggers with processed minds (smack) . . . And Reed here is one of 'em."

His hand shot out, grabbed my shirt collar, twisted tight, and jerked me off the hearth and out of my wooden clogs. Dangling in midair, I reflexively reached for his wrist, his arm, anything to hold on to and ease the constriction. I couldn't breathe.

Pulling my face an inch from his, he growled, "Why don't you get out of here, nigger?"

He was massive and strong and right there, his hot breath in my face, but he sounded far away. All I could hear was the wild pounding of my heart, and all I could see was the dark, bumpy stubble on his face. As I dangled there, trapped, my mouth agape, time stood still and the whole world, except my racing heart and his stubble, disappeared.

Then from behind one lone voice said, "Man, let the brother loose."

Mike released me and I stumbled back, sucking in great gulps of air.

"You . . . you know where I stand," I stuttered, eyes locked on the floor and knees shaking inside my patch-covered bellbottoms. *Now shut up and sit down.*

"I d- d- don't hold with th- this violence stuff," I stammered on. "Love is the an- answer an- and the white man ain't the enemy." *Negro, do you have a death wish?*

Philip, my brother, was too savvy to ever get caught in this sort of situation, but if he had, he would have said, "Go to hell" and stormed out. But I, having been tried and convicted of being an Oreo, just slumped into a heap, too numb to move, my eyes fixed on the carpet.

The meeting carried on, but I was in shock and the words were part of someone else's conversation, something that no longer had anything to do with me—something about preparing for the revolution, about the brothers learning to defend themselves, and the sisters needing to learn first aid; and something about the Revolutionary Action Movement.

Everyone left when the meeting broke up, and no one spoke a word to me. When I finally looked up, the room was empty, but my body felt incapable of moving. Tears leaked out and slid down my face, then suddenly I shuddered and sobbed. One deep sob followed another while the old mantra pounded in my head— *everybody hates me*—for a very long time.

Drained of tears, I staggered up from the hearth where I'd collapsed. I peeked out the door. No one there. I felt like hiding but the urge to bitch was stronger. Tim, the only other black student in my dorm, had been at the meeting. His room was down the corridor from mine and, desperate, I just walked in. The blinds were drawn, and he sat hunched over his desk. He stayed there on the other side of the room, and all I could see was his receding hairline; the features of his face hidden by the shadow above the lamp. Before I could say more than "Man, that good-for-nothin' s.o.b. Mike. You see wha–," he said, "Hey man, that was bad, man. No shit, that was baaaaad. That was really, really bad, man." He didn't ask how I was doing or invite me to sit down. I paced instead and tried again, and he repeated, "That was bad, man, heh, that was bad."

I broke in and rambled, but he kept talking over me. I couldn't even make eye contact with him, and then I realized that Tim wasn't listening at all. He just kept shaking his head and saying that one line, over and over. We were pitiful.

Trembling, I returned to my room. *Fuck all you black-ass sheep. You motherfuckers let him fuck me over and don't say diddly-squat.* My relationship with black students was over. The next day Greg, who had been at the meeting, said to me, "Hey bro, you know I'm with you, man. I really wanted to say something last night, but you know how it is. I'm sorry, man." All I felt was scorn. I wanted to spit in his face and say, "Fuck you, nigger!" Instead I nodded in a way that said, "Hey, sure."

But that evening I felt I'd go crazy. I had to find someone who would listen. But who? If I went to a white person, I'd be exactly as Mike Young claimed: Only an Uncle Tom would spill it all to whitey. In the darkness of my room I remained curled tight, my stomach knotted, until desperation drove me out.

Art's room was three doors down at the end of the corridor, just past Tim's. He was the only person I felt I could turn to. I peeked out into the hallway. It was empty. Feeling every bit the traitor, I walked quickly to his door, knocked, entered, and carefully closed the door. Art was on his bed, his hands behind his head, dim midsummer evening light shining through his window. He looked up and said hello.

I didn't bother to reply. I just began ranting and pacing. "Man, you got to listen to this shit. That asshole Mike Young is already the big man on campus. Why fuck me over? Like I don't know what he's up to." My hands shook. "Some status thing. Some blacker-than-thou thing. Make everybody think he's some badass radical." On and on I verbally vomited up the rage. "Kick my butt in front of every goddamn nigger in school and nobody says jack. Chickenshit motherfuckers."

Art later told me that he hadn't understood much, but all I cared about was that he sat and listened until I was spent and done.

As the summer progressed, I disintegrated. Art witnessed the turmoil and confusion—my room smelled of old socks and stale beer and I spent my nights smoking weed and eating pizza. I stopped attending the Negro History course we had enrolled in together. In fact, I stopped doing anything at all. Finally, he took it upon himself to get me out of bed and walk me to class. At the end of the summer term, my grade was a C/D, but that was better than the D/F I received in Introductory Psychology or the F I got in Art History.

After the summer term ended, I returned to Chicago. Luckily, I was home to intercept a pale yellow envelope from Western Union: "Regret having to notify you that the academic performance committee has declared you ineligible to return to Beloit because of academic deficiencies."

I knew it would be a bad scene when the official letter arrived. I waited at home for it every day and when the wrought iron gate clanged shut behind the mail carrier, I would crack the door open and pull the mail from the box. I would deal the envelopes out upon the dining room table, bills and letters, but there was nothing from Beloit.

One day, gnawing on my lower lip, I admitted to myself there was no way out. I couldn't bear waiting any longer; I would just get it over with. I did, and it was a bad scene that would have been worse if the Democratic Convention hadn't come to town and turned Chicago into a war zone.

The Way Out

In order to get out
I must go through.
                    There is no other way.
No other way?
But there must be another way,
                    an easier path, a well-lit road.
I cast about, scan the horizon—
                    No other way.
                              The way out is the way through.

The way through is the way hard.
Beset behind and before,
                    a heavy hand laid upon me.
Pass one trial, meet another,
                    leap one hurdle, run against another.
No turning back, no detours—
                              no other way.

Lord, how long?
As long as it takes to get me there.
                    Going down to go up,
                    Approaching heaven via hell,
No other way.
                    The only way out is through.

                              —Kathy Fuson Hurt, *Quest*

On August 26–29, 1968, the Democratic Convention was taking place in Chicago, much to Mayor Richard Daley's delight. On the convention floor, Senator Eugene McCarthy's antiwar forces were fighting a losing battle against Vice President Hubert Humphrey's supporters, while on the streets police battled the Yippies, members of the Youth International Party.

I joined in an antiwar protest rally on the downtown Chicago lakefront. Next to me stood Michael, the longhaired, bearded Marxist grad student who had berated me about going into the ministry. Attending was his idea. The mid-afternoon sun glowed hot and red through my closed eyelids, as heat radiated from everywhere: the sun, the people, the air. The only relief was the noise that filled my head—the chanting of thousands of anti-Vietnam War protesters. Alan Ginsberg, the dark-maned beat poet, stood before us on the Grant Park band shell. He intoned the primal sound of the universe and we repeated it: "Om."

Michael scorned this sort of bullshit. I could sense his scowl, even with my eyes shut. Om was still reverberating through me when I heard popping noises, and then yelling. My eyes snapped open. Turning, I saw a blue wall moving toward us—Chicago's finest. The newspapers called it a police riot. The popping sound was tear gas. I took off, heading north. Over my shoulder, I saw Michael do likewise.

This was the same route I had marched three years earlier when my Dad, brother, and I joined a protest against segregation in the Chicago public schools. As I ran my eyes smarted and I sucked air through the handkerchief covering my mouth and nose. Behind me hung a pungent white fog, but no sign of Michael. I ran harder. A block farther north, I spied the Southern Christian Leadership Conference Mule Train. They were also protesting—black men in overalls, some mules, and a wagon carrying an empty coffin in memory of Dr. King. He was dead, but his comrades, his moral migrant workers, were keeping the faith. Heading west, their protest was allowed to move toward the site of the Democratic Convention, the International Amphitheater.

If only I could reach them. But ahead another police blockade
cut me off. I turned south and found myself in the middle of the
Battle of Michigan Avenue.

All hell was breaking loose. Michigan Avenue churned with
people, predominantly young and white. Surrounded, I joined in.
"Peace now" and "Hell no, we won't go," we roared as the throng
surged toward the Hilton Hotel, where many convention delegates
were staying. As we approached Balbo Drive, I heard people take
up a different chant—not the Om of cosmic unity but a chorus of
discord that felt more natural. "Fuck you, Daley. Fuck you, Daley,"
they shouted, and so did I.

Suddenly a policeman blocking the sidewalk in front of us
stuck out his arm and sprayed mace in the face of the white kid
standing to my right. His knees buckled. I lurched back. My eyes
stung and nose burned. I bolted. I hadn't come downtown to battle
with police. I was getting my butt out of there.

As I reached the middle of Michigan Avenue, a long-haired
white guy grabbed my arm and asked, "Man, you wanna help us
flip a squad car?"

My mouth fell open. *Is this motherfucker crazy?* "Thanks, but
no thanks," I stuttered, and ran for a subway entrance. I was neither a revolutionary nor a radical, just a timid, terrified guy who
would've rather been at home watching it on TV.

August is always hot and muggy in Chicago, and the coolest place
was our basement, but retreating there didn't save me from the
heat Mother and Dad applied to get me back in school. September came and I gave in. I enrolled in Central Loop Community
College but never attended a single class, and then dropped out.
Then a letter arrived, classifying me 1-A and eligible for the draft.
I, too, began to worry; the next notice would tell me to report for
a physical. My childhood friend, gung-ho Eugene, whose father
had been an army sergeant, had enlisted. Everyone else I knew was
seeking ways out. I began putting together my case as a conscien-
tious objector and thinking about fleeing to Canada.

Sunday mornings were the only bright spot in my weeks. I taught kindergarten at First Unitarian, and the kids boosted my spirits. Slowly, Sunday after Sunday, as they hung on me, my self-esteem made a small comeback. With it, my trust in myself and others grew; and with that, although I could not have named it then, my faith. And ministry? It never occurred to me.

Meanwhile, Mother found me employment as a shipping clerk for Afro-Am Publishing Company. The work was boring, and I slept whenever I could, both on and off the job. At 225 pounds and climbing, I was beginning to look like Fat Albert. Realizing I was depressed, Mother sent me to one of the few black psychiatrists in Chicago.

Theodore Reid had an office on the Magnificent Mile, the most upscale shopping area in Chicago. As I headed toward our first session the bus crossed the Chicago River, passed the gleaming white Wrigley Building and the Water Tower which every Chicago school child knew was one of the few buildings to survive the Great Chicago Fire of 1871. Worrying about what to say if accosted by the doorman, I entered the building lobby, trying to appear as though I belonged. Dr. Reid's wood-paneled office contained bookshelves, west-facing windows, and leather-upholstered chairs. I sat in an armchair by the side of his desk and talked.

I told him what had happened to me at Beloit— that I hadn't wanted to go at all, how Mike Young had throttled and humiliated me, and how afterward the other black students had shunned me.

He listened.

I talked about Switzerland and watching the civil rights movement from afar, about U-High and the other opportunities I had been given and how I concealed all this from other black folks. It all led to one feeling—guilt. I had so much and others had so little. I had to do my part, had to share in the struggle, had to go south to work with poor people.

He nodded.

I revealed something even more humiliating—while my high-school girl friend had been Chinese American, I had never dated a black woman. I felt I should, but found myself tongue-tied around black women of my own age. Terror was not too strong a word to name what paralyzed me.

He queried.

I voiced my fear that I would be rejected because I didn't act black enough, and my consternation that I didn't know how to be different from who I was.

He challenged.

What I didn't express but he heard was self-hatred. For over four months, he comforted, coaxed, and affirmed me. I heard what he was saying, knew he was right, but still couldn't accept myself.

Driven by idealism minus common sense, I envisioned working in the Beloit College tutoring center in Cleveland, Mississippi. That was where my nemesis Mike Young had spent his field term, the experience that had radicalized him. But Mrs. Hudson, our other mother and a Mississippian herself, was positive that I would get myself killed down there, just like Emmett Till. All I knew was that I had to give my life to the cause. Mrs. Hudson and I fought about it, and in the end, my long-held dread of the South prevailed. Instead of going to Mississippi, I joined the Volunteers in Service to America (VISTA).

"Ask not what your country can do for you; ask what you can do for your country," President Kennedy said in his inaugural address. VISTA, along with the Peace Corps, embodied this challenge, and I was eager to take it up and serve my country, just not to kill or be killed for it. Full of nineteen-year-old idealism, I set forth to do good, help poor people, and save the world. Conveniently, it also saved me from the draft, for serving in VISTA included a II-A Selective Service classification, an occupational deferment. Most importantly, however, it was a chance to salvage my self-esteem.

VISTA promoted itself with a slogan adapted from the words of Black Panther revolutionary Eldridge Cleaver: If you're not part of the solution, you're part of the problem. As part of the solution, VISTA sent me to the South Side Settlement House (SSS) in a black and Appalachian neighborhood of Columbus, Ohio. The

Parsons Avenue corridor ran south from the gritty air enveloping the Federal Glass factory and the poverty of the Lincoln Park project to the belching smokestacks of the Buckeye Steel plant. While serving there, I came close to the hard edge of poverty, close to what I had once stared at from the window of the B train as it rocked and clattered through Chicago's South Side.

Being as naïve as I was idealistic, I proved to be as much of a problem to the people at SSS as I was a solution.

I got stopped by cops twice. The first time, my car was chock-full with an interracial crowd, and in 1969 there wasn't a cop who wouldn't have found that suspicious—must be Communists, Weathermen, or some other sort of subversives. The second time we asked for it. It was after midnight when four of us—me and another volunteer named Ed, plus Rev. Don Huey and his wife, Alicia—broke up a bull session to find an all-night convenience store. I drove. We found one, and as Ed went in, a black couple came out and walked to their car. A squad car pulled up, and a cop got out to question them. Don, who was white, jumped out of my car. *Man, are you brilliant or what?* I thought. I heard him say, "Hello, I'm the Reverend Don Huey. May I be of service?" I couldn't hear the cop's reply but I knew he was telling Don to mind his own fucking business. Don returned and I was more than ready to get out of there, but he insisted we wait until the black couple drove away. *Jesus, Don just doesn't get it.* It was enough that the cops knew we were watching them, but now I knew they'd be watching me. If it was possible to ticket me, they would, and if it wasn't possible, they'd find a way. With friends like this who needs . . . Everything proceeded in slow motion. I pulled away from the curb, stopped at the light, switched on my turn signal, turned left. *Please, God.* The siren hailed, the cherries flashed, and a spotlight filled my rearview mirror. I pulled over. Totally paranoid, I placed my hands on the steering wheel so they'd be visible, then waited. The cop ambled up. I looked out my window at his protruding belly, then up to his scowling face. "Yes, Officer?" "Get out. Give me your license." Then, pointing to the back of the car: "Come here." My heart raced. *Oh shit! Maybe I'm going to get more than a ticket.* "Your rear license-plate light is burned out." My relief had turned to anger by the time he wrote out a twenty-five-dollar ticket, but I smiled and said, "Sorry" to the officer—and "Damn you" to Don Huey.

During that year I had a run-in with the executive director of SSS, Bernie Wohl. He had an accent and attitude that had never left Noo Yawk and which he used to excoriate me for denouncing the war on a radio talk show. He wasn't pro-war but pointed out that many of the families SSS worked with had sons in Vietnam, who hadn't finagled their way out of military service as I had, and some of them wouldn't survive.

But I survived, even when I stepped between two homeboys who were ready to get down. As one pointed a switchblade at the other, I lamely suggested it might be better to talk it over. Thank goodness, they did.

I grieved over Jesse, a bright, baby-faced fifteen-year-old who got blown away. Jesse was small for his age and sassy, and managed all right as long as his older brother was around. But after his brother enlisted, people started going after badmouth Jesse. He vamoosed, and the next I heard he had hooked up with Afro-Set, a black nationalist organization. They made him the assistant leader of its youth group, then elevated him to the elite corps. That meant carrying a handgun to defend himself and the black community, a symbol of his position, power, and the manhood he yearned for. And that gun killed him. One day I had just left the Lincoln Park projects when Jesse showed up. With his black Afro-Set beret cocked on his head, he had come to strut his stuff. Showoff that he was, he handed his gun to a nine-year-old who, thinking it a toy, shot Jesse in the chest, and thought he was faking when he fell. Looking at Jesse's sweet, freckled face in that casket, I wondered whether I could have stopped it if I'd still been there or just gotten myself killed. But he was dead, and once again I had survived.

Somehow, during that year I began to feel that I belonged. This happened gradually, between celebrating Passover with the interracial SSS staff and learning to love the hog maws my neighbor cooked up in her vermin-infested home. It happened between role-playing an escape on the underground railroad with seven-year-olds and wiping their runny noses, between hanging out shooting pool and teaching my group of street toughs to water ski. It took place, as I took teens to Chicago to see Operation Breadbasket and hear Jesse Jackson exhort an audience that knew to respond "I am somebody" to Jackson's prompting. It happened while I convinced the brothers to participate in the local Mass Sole Walk for Hunger. I began to believe that, just maybe, I too was somebody.

Eventually I forsook the frayed austerity of my denim uniform for knit shirts and pleated pants. I stopped preaching asceticism and pushing my antiwar agenda, and learned to listen to the guys' desires to make some money and travel, their dreams of manhood and jobs, and their yearning to outdistance poverty. These young men came to accept me and so did others.

One day Ollie's mother asked me to accompany her when she met with Ollie's third-grade teacher to discuss his acting out. On many other days Harold's mother, Connie, whose heart was as large as her belly, treated me as one of her own, letting me watch her TV and feeding me, but also telling me when to straighten up the house—and my act.

I remember a late-night conversation with Luddie Hatten Jr. about what it meant to be a man, after I told him how much I admired his father. The Hattens lived across the street and his father was a quiet, rail-thin, dark-chocolate-colored man, who worked swing shift at Federal Glass and served as a deacon in his church. He kept his yard tidy, his car shiny, and his furniture encased in clear plastic; and he raised his son to have high aspirations. Luddie wrote to me before I left Columbus to return to Beloit College:

August 17, 1970

Dear Mark,

    I appreciate the things we have gone through together and the experience we have gained through loving and caring about our fellow man. I have grown and matured.

I remember last Friday night when you and I talked about Shade [a member of the youth group] and his search for manhood. You asked me what qualities I thought would make a man, and I told you some. Then you gave me your view of what a man consisted of and said I had an excellent example in my father. Well to cut this long story short, I feel you possess the same qualities.

You weren't the only one in the group who was looking for growth in others. I looked for it in you. I found it, and I am happy and satisfied. If a group leader doesn't grow with his group, then everyone doesn't receive the benefit of the experience. . . .

I must end now, for the lump in my throat and the tears in my eyes will allow me to continue no further. May the Lord bless you and keep you and yours, my friend.

Luddie Hatten Jr.

I shed a few tears, too. I had gone to be part of the solution but what I received saved my life. The people around SSS saw my failings and still respected me, indeed, even depended on me. Their acceptance healed my soul in a way no shrink could.

My service in VISTA convinced Beloit to readmit me, and with three friends, including my old high school girlfriend, Sharon Wang, I rented a house on Park Avenue. It was a restless time, full of weed, hash, and magic mushrooms; rock concerts, communes, and sex; Black Power, anti-war protest, and not much fidelity; and not one of us would graduate. The Selective Service had classified me 1-S, which was only good for that academic year; then I would be draft bait again. But at that moment I was happy to be back in school and living next door to my buddy Art Perkins.

Soon after the trimester began, he and I jumped in his '56 Chevy and drove to his parents' home in Sandwich, Illinois. On the way, Art mused vaguely about ministry. It was a real stretch for me to imagine aw-shucks-gee-whiz Perkins in a pulpit, and I think it was equally hard for him. His youngest sister, a future organist, serenaded us; his mother stuffed us; and his father took me on a tour of his church. Art's parents, still slightly plump but now white-haired, seemed as ageless to me as when I first met them. Ordinary, gracious, midwestern, God-loving folks, they had taught their children to sing "Jesus loves the little children/All the children of the world/ Red and yellow, Black and white/ All are precious in his sight." More importantly, they taught them to believe it. At the Perkins', I always felt at home and I'm certain that their Afro-Cherokee son-in-law felt the same a decade later.

The danger of accompanying white friends home was that you never knew what would happen when a "brother" walked through the door. I can understand why lots of black folks say, "I don't want to cope with this mess and for sure don't need the hassle." Playing "Guess Who's Coming to Dinner" was like taking your chances with Russian roulette. Welcome. Welcome. Slam!

One day a friend Katie and I were headed to Chicago for an antiwar rally and decided to spend the night at her home in St. Charles, a distant western suburb. Perhaps I should have anticipated trouble, but Katie was so confident and the context was so different that the incident with Sheila never crossed my mind. Besides, Katie had a copper cast to her skin, a husky voice, and straight dark hair that made me wonder if she had Native American blood, though I never asked. We were expected at her house, but my color wasn't. We walked in and said hello, and I was invited into the living room. Katie disappeared into the kitchen with her mother. I waited, hearing muffled voices. I waited longer, and still no one appeared. Finally Katie came back—we would have to go, she said. We're out the door. We're in the car. Then she tells me: Elderly Aunt Edie is visiting, and the family couldn't possibly expect her to deal with me. Embarrassed, she asked if I was all right. I lied. "No big deal," I said, faking resignation rather than confessing to a grotesque truth—I felt at fault.

Mortified and perplexed, Katie sped toward Chicago. Her mother had always talked a good liberal line about equality and all, but now it turned out to have been bullshit hypocrisy. I sympathized. "So sorry," she repeated. Again I lied, not telling her that my solar plexus was a black hole that let no feelings escape. Meanwhile she spewed forth her fury at a world of pretense. If I let loose with my anger as well, she would only feel worse about the ugliness and racism that she had never guessed resided in the middle of her life. I couldn't do that because above all I was a nice guy, so terrified of my own anger that it usually remained hidden, even from me. Katie, however, couldn't hide; I sat right next to her as she grieved a loss. Her family was not what she believed it to be. Already numb, I listened to what I didn't want to hear. The distance between Katie's image of her mother and reality only widened when we arrived at my house—where my mother, ever the social worker, welcomed her, fed her, listened to her, tried to assuage her guilt, and gave her a place to sleep.

College was different the second time around. I still didn't know what I wanted to become but at least I was engaged. My parents had agreed to pay my tuition. I was to cover all other expenses, and to do that I found employment as a security guard. I worked the graveyard shift, watching an abandoned hospital. Spooky, but it sure left time to study.

More intact than when I left, and emboldened by my new sense of self—I was black enough—I determined to confront my adversaries. I started with Walter, with whom I had argued hard and long following King's assassination. Catching him near the Indian burial mounds, I offered him a seemingly offhand invitation to chat. We found a classroom. I sat on a desktop, took a deep breath, and asked him if he remembered what had happened the night the black students met in Bushnell Lounge. He stopped, looking at me strangely, and denied that anything had happened. "Don't you remember what Mike Young did to me?" I asked. He didn't know what I was talking about. I pressed on. Shaking his head, Walter paced back and forth in front of the blackboard, insisting he had no memory of the incident. Finally he shrugged and walked away.

I sat there alone and in that silence all the hurt and hatred I had felt two years earlier returned.

After the encounter with Walter, I felt reluctant to approach Mike Young. After I flunked out, Mike had led a campus protest called Black Demands, and consequently his class selected him to give the commencement speech. In return, he inflicted his revolutionary rant on them. Following a year of graduate school, he returned to help implement the protest's demands, which were granted by the Beloit administration.

Mistaking venting for veracity and hyperbole for strategy, I obviously had misunderstood his motivation that hot July evening when he throttled me. Perhaps it was rage at black impotence more than white hatred, or an infatuation with the language of revolution more than its reality. Perhaps he was fending off hopelessness. Perhaps he needed to take his despair and direct it outward—riot, plan a revolution, pick on a skinny black hippie who won't sit where he's supposed to sit or say what he's supposed to say.

I never spoke to him and now I know why. In part, I feared he would scoff at me. But frankly, I didn't want to reconcile with him. I wanted to hate rather than to understand. I didn't want to see—indeed, refused to see—that it had never really been about me but about the checkerboard I symbolized. In trying to create a space for myself where I could live in both the black and white worlds, I represented the failed path. Grief stricken, many blacks rejected the path of interracial solidarity that had ended in King's death, and there was no better example than me—the honkified, folk-dancing, Negro fool. Mike used me for his ends, and then I used him. Holding on to my righteous indignation at being victimized kept me on a moral high. I was good. He was bad. I didn't care that he had returned to help implement the administration's response to the demands. All I saw was rank opportunism. No redemption for him; and for me, no need to forgive.

In the fall of 1971, Art began his final trimester at Beloit; Walter entered a PhD program en route to becoming a professor; and Mike, who would haunt me for years to come, continued on to what would become a career in college administration. Meanwhile, freed by the number 324—a draft lottery number so high the Selective Service would never call me up—and enticed by an opportunity I couldn't resist, I dropped out. I was going to sail around the world.

Return to the Alps

*I abandoned myself to the view and to the crisp air, trying to
assimilate the sight of this magic mountain. The Wetterhorn,
as it generously gave its beauty to all...*

—Max Knight, *Return to the Alps*

I sat in the apartment of Professor Nicholas Anim, a Ghanaian
who taught comparative education at Beloit, seeking help with a
huge decision—whether to remain in school or to sail around the
world. The voyage was a madcap project dreamt up by my school-
mate Stuart Dean, heir of a large Midwest dairy company, Dean
Food Products.

"You know," my mentor mused, "you can go to school any
time but such an opportunity to sail around the world is not
offered every day." That wasn't what I expected him to say, but it
was what I wanted to hear. Ten minutes later I called Stu. Next I
called home. Mother answered, but realizing where the conversation was headed, handed me off to Dad. He said no, of course. We
argued. I wouldn't budge. Later you would have thought the idea
had his blessing by the way he bragged, "You know what that boy
is up to now?"

Ten months after returning to Beloit, I requested a leave of
absence from the Academic Affairs Committee. They thought the
request unreasonable. I said, "Tough shit" and dropped out.

October came, and twelve of the crew flew to Ireland. Stu had rented a nineteenth-century mansion, Kilpeacon House, on a winding little lane outside Limerick, a city as bleak and gray as the countryside was green. There we waited while a broker sought a suitable schooner.

We were an odd crew. Eccentric Stu was on yet another quest. Years earlier, long before people had heard of biofeedback, he had taught himself to meditate using an electroencephalograph. Now he had this new idea and the money to implement it. The project was being managed by C. Michael Brown, a screenwriter. He almost got himself killed when a cow in the pasture next to the mansion head-butted him from behind and then trod on his face. The captain's nickname, Charlie Brown, didn't inspire confidence, and neither did his goofy laugh. Nonetheless, he had served as first mate on a ship in the Caribbean. The only nonwhite besides me was George Ikinaga, a Japanese Hawaiian who charmed his way out of every problem with a quizzical smile and innocent shrug. Of the bunch, maybe three had some sailing experience; I had none.

Since I was in Ireland, I decided to do like the Irish and joined a Limerick rugby club, the Rovers. They assigned me to the third string, which was good because most of the time I didn't know what the heck I was doing as I charged around the playing field. Eventually, though, I admitted to myself that I enjoyed the brutality of it—the straight arms and flying tackles, the scrums, the blood and mud, the mauls and mauling. I also loved the camaraderie and carousing, for afterward we always retired to a pub to guzzle foamy, brown, bittersweet Guinness stout and sing songs with lyrics so bawdy they made me blush.

One evening, the club showed a film of the team purported to be the best in the world—the New Zealand All Blacks. Made sense to me the best would be black. I arrived late with my date, slipped into a folding chair, looked at the screen, and saw deft passes, great open-field running, incredible dropkicks, but no black guys. I had figured the team was made up of Maori players native to New Zealand; in confusion I turned to the bloke next to me and whispered, "Which ones are the All Blacks?"

He looked at me as if I were daft. "The ones in black shorts and jerseys," he said.

My mouth fell open. I looked back at the screen—so much for my theory about racial superiority. I shook my head, then smiled, then chuckled, then erupted into laughter so loud that everyone turned and stared.

The longer I lived with Stu's motley crew, the more my misgivings mounted; I had been having concerns since we arrived. On the morning we landed at Shannon Airport I hurried down the ramp, and managed to separate myself from the hung-over, sweat-shirt-clad rabble I was traveling with. I had worn a corduroy sports coat for just this moment and proceeded to give the immigration officer the same spiel that I had used on my dad—that I was joining a research project on human behavior. I sailed through customs. Then, as I collected my luggage, I heard my name announced over the public address system. I looked across the hall and saw my shipmates pointing in my direction. Doofus Charlie Brown's mouth hung open in indignation, and he looked even dumber than usual. I returned to Immigrations and went through my routine again—yes, we were traveling together, yes, they were part of the same project. As soon as possible, I slipped away only to hear "Mark Reed" echo from a loudspeaker once again. Back I went and this time my passport was stamped with a six–month expiration date.

And the problems continued. Stu gave us the use of a zippy little Morris Minor, an allowance, and time off as perks to be earned by completing prescribed chores. I painted rooms. I cooked and washed. I tended the horses in the stable and assembled first-aid supplies for the voyage. Meanwhile my comrades lounged around and drank, dated local girls after I made the contacts, played touch football on Saturday afternoons, drank some more, watched the video of the game and drank still more, all the while grousing about how backward the Irish were.

Yet the more time I spent with the Irish, the less I liked the crew. Months passed, and I increasingly worried about putting my life in their hands. Fixing myself a room in the stable, I moved out of the mansion. Then, just as I wavered between loyalty to Stu and self-preservation, Stu's assets were frozen. His uncle—thank God—had gone to court, claiming Stu was mentally incompetent and incapable of handling his own financial affairs. Pending a hearing, the injunction was granted, and suddenly Stu had no money.

Four months after arriving in Ireland, we disbanded and everyone except me flew home. I went to Cleggan, a fishing village on Ireland's rocky, treeless west coast. Cleggan had one store that was also a pub, and a pub that was also the post office. My foolhardy plan was to go to sea with the fishermen, but it was February and the Atlantic rough, and luckily the fleet never left port while I was there. After living in the village for a month, a letter from Natalie Lüthi arrived with an invitation to work at the Ecole. Hallelujah!

Barns, fences, and trees flashed by my window, blurs upon the snow-blanketed meadows. As the train rushed along, I took it all in again. Somewhere between Giswil and Lungern, I became aware of my body: My breathing had slowed, my shoulders were no longer taut. It had been a long journey but this was not fatigue. To the contrary, every sense was alert. Something deep within shifted. My nose twitched with the sharp sensation that precedes tears, and it came to me—for the first time in the seven years since I had left Switzerland, I felt safe. As the train neared the Brünigpass, I sat back and sighed.

The staff was much the same as before: the pacifist Esperantist Herr Cool; the office manager, Frau Varga, whose scowl intimidated some but never left me doubting that she liked me; and Edith's pet Bengali Aurobindo, who still shuffled after her in his bathroom slippers, twittering "Edith, oh Edith." But the other of the so-called dwarves, Herr Horcher, had retired and moved to Luzern. I met him there once. I stepped off a train, walked down the platform, and there he was wearing a jacket rather than a blue smock and a hat with a brim rather than a skull cap. It didn't matter, I would have known him anywhere for the twinkle was still in his eye and his pipe in his mouth. Suppressing the urge to hug him I gripped his hand and pumped it up and down. Afterwards I was told everyone taking the train to and from the Ecole found him there, a one man welcoming committee.

Other things had changed as well. Three new buildings stood where I had once helped clear the woods. Herr Cool was married. He was Dutch; his wife, Florence, was French and their common language was Esperanto. The young American teachers I knew had returned to the U.S., but former Kameraden like myself replaced them.

Beyond the school, a fundamental social change had occurred. In 1971, Swiss men had finally given women the right to vote in federal elections, and by the time I returned a year afterward, ten women had been elected to the Lower House and one to the Upper.

Instead of facing the vicissitudes of the sea, I sat in faculty meetings as predictable and exciting as cows moving to their summer pasture. Edith Geheeb and Armin and Natalie Lüthi sat at the head of the table, and every seat was filled. To Armin's right against the wall sat Fräulein Petersen, who had directed me in the Christmas play. Next to her sat the ageless Frau Stein with the movie-star tan, and so on—I knew most of them from my years as a student. To Natalie's left was the mischievous Latin teacher, Herr Poeschel, who periodically contributed a sardonic remark. At the other end of the table sat Frau Varga, who dependably disagreed with Natalie. The crises were predictable as well—drugs, alcohol, sex, and the unpopularity of morning calisthenics and cold showers. Beneath the discussion was the constant click, click, click of a dozen pairs of knitting needles. Beneath the surface I sensed Armin's exasperation whenever Edith pulled rank by saying, "Paulus always said . . ." It meant the discussion was over.

I taught English. When the class read Richard Wright's *Black Boy*, we sang spirituals so heartily that other Kameraden drifted in when their classes were over. I also taught the beginning folk-dance class; assisted Herr Tentler, the new handyman; and reveled in being the Kameraden's friend and confidant.

One day, Art Perkins showed up. As I bounded down the stairs outside Turmhaus, I saw him strolling up the gravel road, carrying a duffel bag and wearing a smile. "Hey, Reed!" he said in his soft Midwest twang. "Hey, Perkins!" I yelled.

Unlike me, Art had actually graduated. Then, wary of the white-collar world and what he called "the conveyor belt of success," he moved to New York City, found an apartment in the Village, and worked as a laborer in an import-export firm. He was saving money to travel in Europe, but his plans were accelerated when he was seduced by his roommate, an older woman who was all of thirty-two, and he felt he had better get out of town. He had rambled across Europe for four months and now stood before me, nearly broke.

I found him a job as a laborer for a local construction company. He had no work permit, and hiring him was illegal, but routine. Illegal immigrants were paid under the table and called *Schwarzar-beiter*. It literally meant "black worker." When I translated it for him, he quipped that now he knew what it felt like to be black.

He didn't, but the Italian and Yugoslavian laborers who worked alongside him did. The Swiss call them *Gastarbeiter*, which means "guest workers." The misnomer added a special irony to Swiss-style apartheid, for the famed Swiss hospitality didn't extend to these laborers, who were treated like invaders rather than guests. Forbidden to bring their families along, the workers were crowded into dilapidated dormitories, shunned by the Swiss, and closely monitored by the authorities. Nevertheless the labor market was so tight that the number of foreigners in the population had nearly doubled to 27 percent since I had first arrived in Switzerland in 1962. This increase strengthened political movements that pro-posed limiting "guest workers" to 10 percent of the population, which would have meant expelling many of them.

Art and I drank too much and talked too late. I felt it every morning at 6:20 when the gong shattered my sleep. But the next evening I would reappear at the dark, spartan bunkhouse where

Art lived, with a couple of bottles of Eichenhof in hand. We would begin our lament about women and sex, and the appalling lack of the latter, until eventually our conversation, more entertaining than pressing, drifted toward reality, or didn't. And so we talked on into the night.

We were both twenty-three, both born on Chicago's South Side, both single, and neither of us knew where the hell we were headed. Art was philosophical. A bit bemused by life, he preferred ruminating to acting. He approached every option tentatively, certain only about what he didn't want. "I'm not interested," he said, "in holding down a series of better paying jobs that will addict me to the fruits of my disinterested labor." He would succeed, but at that point he had no notion how. He simply remained determined to make his decisions in an unhurried and unworried way. Life was what happened to Art while he applied himself to whatever the moment offered. As for me, perhaps teaching was my calling, and maybe I would stay at the Ecole.

That November was unendingly gray. Art and I wanted to get away from our routines, the gray peaks, and the overcast sky, so when Rhoda and Henry Isaac invited us to visit them over the American Thanksgiving weekend, we fled to civilization. Their home in Thalwil was just a twenty-minute train ride from Zurich.

We hitchhiked, and it was a miracle we got as far as we did. Who would pick up a six-foot, two-hundred-pound black dude with a scruffy beard and large Afro, wearing frayed bell-bottoms and an English bobby's cape, and a white guy with a long, dark ponytail, a drooping mustache hiding his mouth, and a U.S. Army surplus jacket protecting his gaunt body? We stood on the shoulder of the road as the day grew colder and the wait longer; only our conversation rambled on. I couldn't help but remember the night two years earlier when I had picked Art up outside Beloit. He had been returning from visiting the seminary his father had attended and was still wrestling with the question of ministry.

As majestic as the Swiss Alps appear, they're a nuisance when you are trying to get somewhere. There is no way to get anywhere without circling a lake, going over a pass, going through a tunnel, or traveling down one valley to go up another, and that's what Art and I did. One pass short of Thalwil, we looked up and saw the sky growing dark. Our thumbs throbbing, we gave up, walked into Zug, and took the train.

We arrived late, but they had waited up. I hadn't visited Henry and Rhoda since the preceding Passover, when they had invited me to their typically minimalist Seder. Henry, Art, and I plopped down in the living room and talked while Rhoda threw a snack together. When Henry put his feet up I noticed his legs were covered with small, curved, hairless patches and remembered his story: how he had been sent out of Germany at age sixteen; how his family escaped but lost everything; how he had joined the Army and been wounded. I had him tell Art.

It was late by the time we went to bed, and midday before Art and I got up and headed into Zurich's old town, a comfortable place of narrow, cobbled streets, stores to browse through, cafés to linger in, and few cars. We were going nowhere, looking for nothing—sort of suspended in time, sojourners in a foreign land on the margin of adulthood, romantically unattached, without children, mortgage, or profession. We were liberated from convention—liberated and lost.

Remembering the conversations we had had about ministry, I asked, "Art, when are you going to get around to going to seminary?"

Art stopped. He knew I was referring to the night I had picked him up outside Beloit after he had visited his father's seminary. More than once we'd talked about him becoming a minister. Finding it impossible to say yes and difficult to say no, he was stuck, and I wondered whether he was just putting off the inevitable.

"I'm not," he replied, "but you should!"

"Man, get off it," I said with a toss of my head.

"No. This is for real," he shot back.

I stopped, looked at him, and said, "You're not kidding?"

He shook his head and took my arm. "Come on, Reed," he said, guiding me into a nearby café.

Like Art, I had grown up in a church. I had been a compliant Sunday school student, a nearly angelic choirboy, and in my senior year, not just the youth-group president, but also the assistant janitor and Sunday office manager. I had been so involved with church that I almost didn't graduate from high school. It wasn't the church itself, but the idea of being a minister that surprised me.

But that thought wasn't actually new, just forgotten. After the disparaging reactions I'd received five years earlier, I had never thought about ministry again.

Over cups of tea grown cold, Art and I talked on into the afternoon. I couldn't imagine preaching every Sunday. He conceded that preaching so exhausted his father that he took a nap every Sunday afternoon. But ministry was much more than preaching, he insisted, and launched into a description of his father's life: the hospital calls, counseling sessions, marriage ceremonies, and funerals that consumed a minister's time. Then he began to describe how engaged I was with the Kameraden, and how accessible to them. He talked about how he himself had experienced my support and caring. But, most important, in his eyes, I was already doing ministry—he had been raised to it and knew that quality of presence when he saw it. A moment of silence came. No more questions from me. No more explanations from him. A sensation of peace settled upon me that was more sober than jubilant. I looked at Art and he at me, and I offered a half smile and a nod, before pushing my chair away from the table.

I stepped into the street, breathed in, and looked around. To my left, I caught a glimpse of blue sky above the overhanging eaves that lined the dark, narrow cobbled street, and a voice from within said: *Remember. Remember this moment.* My life had changed, and while this dream wouldn't save me from the calamity that lay ahead, it nonetheless sustained me.

Art departed after the snow had masked the gray mountains, in time to get home for Christmas. His future was still uncharted, but mine seemed clear. I missed him, and I missed being home for Christmas. I hadn't noticed it until after the Kameraden left and

stillness settled on the school. A little loneliness—a sort of aching
—colored my mood when I thought of Dad's extended family
gathering in D.C. The feeling would have been more intense except
for my excitement at finally having a chance to experience Christmas Eve at the Ecole.

The ritual leading up to Christmas was the same as in my
adolescence: the trip up the mountain to collect pine boughs and
mistletoe, the wreaths, the Sunday night feasts, and the Advent services. Sitting in the dark, listening to Armin read the traditional
Christmas stories, it was as if one year had passed, not eight.

On Christmas Eve, we gathered at dusk—teachers and their
families, some Kameraden, and a few folks from the village.
Twenty-five of us huddled in groups of two and three. We started
up the steep trail then veered left and went deeper into the forest.
We walked single file, the light fading, the forest growing dark and
darker, but ahead the path was lit. Burning candles, set out earlier,
sat in little hollows in the snow, and these little glowing lights led
us still deeper into the woods. We walked on the snow, each step
crunching as we followed in one another's tracks. In the distance,
there was a faint glow, and we approached, drawn to it. All eyes
lifted and fixed on a candle-adorned evergreen tree, not much
taller than a person.

Whispers drifted on the night air, but we fell silent as we encir-
cled the tree. Around us the air was cold and the silence unbroken;
there was nothing to say. Beyond the circle of light, the darkness
seemed endless, but in the circle we stood close, shoulder-to-
shoulder, our faces illumined by a little shining tree.

Armin cleared his throat, and from across the circle I saw him
move toward the tree. He opened the Bible and, bathed in the light,
he began to read. "And it came to pass in those days, that there
went out a decree from Caesar Augustus . . ." After he closed the
book we sang carols, our voices filling the vast sanctuary. We ended
with *Stille Nacht*, and all was still when Armin stepped forward
again and took a candle from the tree. Each of us did likewise, leaving the tree as it had been.

Candles in hand, we made our way home, the line of candles stretching out before me holding the world's darkness at bay. Flames snuffed out by the wind were lit again by friends, and I savored the wax that dripped warmly on my cold skin as we moved cautiously yet joyfully through the night.

Leaving the Ecole was difficult, and I might not have left at all if the decision hadn't been made for me: I was kicked out. Returning from the Easter vacation, I had caught the last train into Meiringen, and there was no way to reach Goldern except to walk. Night had fallen and I couldn't see far but it didn't matter; I knew the zigzag path. Halfway up, I passed the place where the frightened little Swiss boy had first seen me—I never went by that spot without remembering how he had turned and fled—and then the spot where his mother had slapped him across his face, but in the darkness all I could distinguish was the grayness of the path before me from the blackness beyond. There were no glints of snow—the fierce Föhn wind, the "snow-eater" it was called, had devoured it all. "The Föhn will dry the blood in the veins and feed upon the marrow of your bones" a fabled Hasli-dwarf long ago forewarned. The Föhn, you see, not only devours snow, uproots forest, and burns villages, but also destroys humans beings, for as the charge in the atmosphere rises so does the suicide rate.

It was an eerie climb. As I came around the next bend, I looked up and saw Edith Geheeb's visage hovering just above the trees. I knew it couldn't be, yet there it was. I closed my eyes. When I opened them it was gone, but in its place was the image of a skull and crossbones. I stopped, closed my eyes again, and opened them to blackness and a feeling of dread. I sped on, but it was after eleven by the time I arrived at the Ecole. All was dark. I slipped into bed, but hardly slept.

Edith was fine, but that afternoon Natalie telephoned. She, Edith, and Armin wanted to meet with me that evening. She was vague about why, and that left me agitated and concerned that they had found out about Lorelei.

Lori was almost nineteen, a Kamaradin. I was twenty-three, a teacher, and wrong to have allowed it to happen; I know that now and I knew it then, but differently. Now I know that it wasn't a question of consent. It was a matter of holding a position of authority and hijacking the trust inherent in that role to fulfill personal needs. But in 1973 the hippie in me regarded the prohibition as puritanical rubbish, remnant of a time before love had been liberated. I gave a lot of myself to the Kameraden—and in this case, too much. I gave, as people so often do, what I yearned to receive, and my own need for attention, affection, and affirmation was unremitting. I had seen it coming. "Where do you draw the line?" I wrote in my diary. "Be careful," I warned myself. But my need was stronger than my resolve, and passion had its way with caution.

Lori was a cool, pale-skinned, raven-haired German who, impatiently awaiting her escape from the confines of the Ecole, drew warmth from my consoling her. One night she slid into my room and between the sheets. I received the warmth of her skin, smelled the odor of cigarettes on her breath, and then . . .

I wish I could say we had wild sex, but the creaking bed, thin walls, and my conflicted feelings that vacillated between guilt and bliss, left me with a quick moment of passion but not much peace. I sought escape—to be embraced for who I was and engulfed in sensuality. Instead, I discovered that sex can be less about tender caressing than desperate clinging.

Then her roommate snitched. An American, she'd been caught getting it on with a local boy and spilled the beans about our liaison in an attempt to justify her own. When Lori left before Easter, I sat on a bench, looking at the Wetterhorn and crying. She was headed for a kibbutz in Israel, while I was headed for misery.

Sitting before Armin, Natalie, and Edith, all I could hear was Natalie's query echoing in my head: "Mark, how could you?"

"I love her."

"But you had to know it was wrong."

The only answer remained unuttered: *Dumb nigger, can't do anything right.*

"Mark, we trusted you," Natalie said.

I sniffled, and then she was crying, too. Armin's grave voice broke the teary silence. I would have to leave. They would give me a couple of days, but I'd have to go. My only consolation was that old Edith reached over, touched my hand, and assured me that someday, after I was married, I could return. And I would return, but at that moment I couldn't imagine how or when.

For days I couldn't stop crying. The tears were still flowing when Phipu, my old roommate, drove me to his apartment in the countryside near Reigoldswil. Spent, I lay in bed.

Eventually I drafted a letter to Lori. I told her I would follow her to Israel. But fearing that she would say no, I left the letter as a diary entry. Instead, I wrote home. I also wrote to Jack Bierschenk, who was directing an American junior college in Austria, and I wrote to Stuart Dean, my wealthy college friend who had financed the aborted sailing trip. My parents' responses were predictable. "We have applications for the University of Illinois (Circle Campus), Loop College, and Roosevelt. . . We strongly advise you to hurry," wrote Mother.

Given my goal of becoming a minister, going back to school made sense, but I couldn't get my head around it. In fact I didn't do anything except lay on the living-room couch, staring at the ceiling.

Weeks passed. When not staring at the ceiling, I took long walks through the countryside, talked to the cows in the pastures, and rambled in my diary: "My head spins. I don't want to go back to the States. I need time to collect myself, to figure out where I'm going." "Anger—what do you do with it? Where do you direct it?" "What do I do with the pain?" "What do I do? What should I do? What do I want to do? What can I do?" "How do I stay in touch with black folks?" "Why do I feel I have this duty to Humanity?" All these questions went unanswered.

One day Phipu dragged me along to the school where he taught to help him teach a lesson to his ninth-grade class about the United States and what it is like to be black there. Afterward he urged me to stay in Switzerland and go to teachers college. In the evenings, Phipu's friends would drop in, full of questions critical of the United States. "What about Vietnam?" Fritz asked. But since the last U.S. troops had been withdrawn a month earlier, it wasn't quite the pressing issue it once had been.

"And what about Watergate?" queried Heinz. "Your president is a crook." Revelations about the Watergate break-in and cover-up filled the newspapers throughout the spring of 1973.

Just before my life blew up, the *International Herald Tribune* ran an article with the headline: ELDRIDGE CLEAVER ASKS FRANCE TO GRANT HIM POLITICAL ASYLUM. The former Black Panther leader, who had fled the United States in 1968 after the revocation of his parole, sought, like other black Americans before him, a safe haven in France.

Phipu and his friends kept asking what it was like to be black in America and why I would go back to such an awful place. I had a strong desire to remain in Switzerland, but I also felt the pull to return home. I didn't know what to do.

"One ever feels his twoness," W.E.B. DuBois writes, "an American, a Negro; two souls, two thoughts, two unreconciled strivings, two warring ideals in one dark body." When years later I discovered this description of the American Negro, I saw that DuBois had spoken to my condition. My blackness included a feeling that I resisted: I was, indeed, an American, and I felt I had a duty that was best met there. Besides, I would never be Swiss—their insular society would never really let me be. No matter how hard I tried, I would remain a sideshow—perhaps no longer a freak to gawk at, but still a curiosity without any real consequence. With the rise of anti-immigration party leader James Schwarzenbach and his xenophobic ranting, I could feel Switzerland becoming less hospitable to people like me. I could not escape racism, but it seemed that I might make some difference in America. Besides, if I was serious about ministry, perhaps it made sense to go home.

I wrote in my diary, "If I finish college, then what? Where do I live? In Chicago with Art, in Denver with my brother?" After grad-

uating from Hyde Park High in 1968, Philip had enrolled at More-
house College in Atlanta, but by the end of 1969 had dropped out.
The next year, he became a research assistant to Dad's colleague
Mitsunobo Tatsumoto at the U.S. Geological Survey in Denver.
Following in our father's footsteps, Philip became engrossed in
analyzing lunar soil samples.

Another letter arrived, this one from eccentric Stu, an invitation to join the remnant of the sailing crew in Portland, Oregon.
They were embarking on a new venture: excavating their emotional pasts and screaming their way toward wholeness using primal therapy. Hell, why not go? Such inner work, at least, would
address my pain and sense of being trapped within self-destructive
patterns of behavior. Something was wrong, something that college wouldn't solve. Perhaps before I could help anyone else, I'd
have to save myself.

Left to right: Mark's "Grammy" (Eleanor Reed), Great-aunt Irene Hawkins, Mark as an infant, and Mark's mother Selina Reed in Chicago, 1949.

The Reed family. Clockwise from top left: Mark's father George Reed, mother Selina Reed, brother Philip (7), sister Carole (4) and Mark (8). In the backyard of their home on Calumet Ave. in Chicago, 1957.

The Ecole d'Humanité, School of Humanity, the boarding school in Goldern, Switzerland, where Mark was a student and then later a teacher. This is how it looked a few years before Mark first arrived.

Mark, age 17, a senior at University Laboratory High School in Chicago, 1967.

Mark's family at his parents' home in Chicago, 1984. Clockwise from top left: Mark's sister Lauren, his son Elliot, Mark, his brother Philip, his daughter Charlotte, his sister Carole and his nephew Jordan.

The Morrison-Reeds at the First Universalist Church of Rochester, New York, 1986. Left to right: Donna, Charlotte, Elliot and Mark.

Mark giving presentation at Unitarian Universalist General Assembly in the mid-1990s.

I'd Leave Town If I Were You

Faith in God is an opening, a letting go, a deep trust, a free act of love—but sometimes it was so hard to love. Sometimes my heart was sinking so fast with anger, desolation and weariness, I was afraid it would sink to the bottom . . . and I would not be able to lift it back up.

—Yann Martel, *Life of Pi*

I flew home and announced I was heading west.

"Absolutely not," said Dad.

What else is new? He wasn't finished either. "And I want the money you owe me for the airplane ticket. Now."

I bounded upstairs to my bedroom. On the dresser were six hundred-dollar bills, all I had. I grabbed the three hundred I owed him, raced down the stairs, and slammed the bills on the table. "Here's your goddamn money," I yelled, and stormed out of the house. I knew what game he was playing—trying to keep me in Chicago, trying to force me to go to school. *Well, bugger you.*

Within days, I found a lift on a ride board, and three days after that I was in northern California, trying and failing to hitch a ride on Route 70 through a forlorn, rural scrubland. There were no cars in sight, just shimmering waves of heat rising from the asphalt. As the sun crept higher, I unstrapped a black umbrella from my backpack, opened it, and hid beneath its shade. Just then a highway patrol car cruised by. I stiffened. It made a U-turn. As it came back toward me, I remembered the times I'd been stopped by cops when I was a VISTA volunteer in Ohio. The car pulled up, and the officer leaned over. From behind mirrored sunglasses, he said, "You'll never get a ride here. Hop in and I'll drop you at a better spot." I offered a big smile as I slid in next to him and, just in case, memorized the name on his badge. When he let me out just south of Yuba City, he bought me a Coke, and after he drove away I laughed at myself and readjusted my view of the world—a little.

In Portland, I found a one-room basement apartment. Having no refrigerator, I survived on peanut butter sandwiches, fruit, water, and fast food. I bought a red notebook and started writing, dredging up my earliest memories. And every few days I went to Stu's, where I would go down to the basement, step into a padded room, and scream until I was hoarse, drenched, and exhausted. As I did so, old memories and words, echoes of my childhood, returned. Sometimes after screaming I would go back to my apartment, curl up in the closet, and cry as I never had before that calamitous spring, cry until my sinuses ached, as tears of rejection vied with tears of outrage.

Crossing a bridge over Interstate 405 on my way to Stu's, I would grip the cold steel handrail, peer over, hear the roaring traffic beneath, and feel my stomach go queasy as I considered jumping. How easy. Just drop down in the path of a semi, and it would be over. Just a matter of seconds. Then I would envision that last instant—the agony, the trucker, his guilt, the mess, my family, their grief. Better to go on living with the pain. Every time I touched that cold railing, I had to decide again; sometimes I stuffed my hands in my pockets so I wouldn't have to. "It is more my fear of death than my will to live that keeps me going," I wrote in my diary.

The only contacts I made were of necessity; needing money I'd show up at the Industrial Employment Center around 5:00 a.m. and take my place in line. Didn't chat, just sat on an old folding chair, listening and waiting. That's how I learned where to sell my blood. Anything for easy cash.

There was the employment center and my room; there was screaming and silence; there was my diary, the bridge, and sleep. I slept so I didn't have to face it all, slept until my back ached, tossed until no position felt comfortable. Then I walked until my feet throbbed. Returning to my little room, I wrote in my journal, always hoping to find myself among the words. I wrote a few letters too, and Dad wrote this in response to one:

August 4, 1973

Dear Mark,

I am very pleased with what you're experiencing. I guess that's what I really wanted for you, namely, to find yourself in yourself. We do need people, but we need ourselves also and the balance between the outer and inner [person] will be different for each of us . . .

We didn't talk about you and the Ecole. I wanted to but you seemed to be so much on the go that there wasn't really any time. I wasn't quite up to waiting, as your mother did, until you got in at 1 or 2 a.m. But I figured there'd be an opportunity later when you got back from Portland.

It's certainly true we've come along in different worlds. I'm not enamored with mine and can see and empathize with yours. What concerns me is that what your world has to offer will get lost because youth doesn't take its head out of the clouds long enough to deal with the real world effectively . . . Dealing with the world as it is is a tough and a life-time job. The challenge is to be successful enough (in the sense of being self-sufficient and independent) to have an impact and to keep up the fight . . . But all of this takes time; it's a long journey and we can progress only a step at a time.

By the way, rote learning was very difficult for me. In college I used to go to a vacant classroom at night and outline the material on the blackboard just to look at it and try to reinforce what I had in my notes . . . For us to make

it in this society each one of us has to discipline himself. This still does not mean succumbing.
Philip left last night and should be seeing you soon. We all enjoyed his visit. You may share this letter with him if you wish. Guess we can't know too much about one another.

Love,
Your Dad

Five weeks later my brother picked me up and we drove to San Francisco and an unanticipated test of my desire to become a minister.

Rev. Dr. Howard Thurman received me in his book-lined, shadow-filled study. During my parents' student days, he had been the dean of Rankin Chapel at Howard University, and Mother had mentioned him as soon as I talked about going to Meadville Lombard Theological School to prepare for the ministry. In 1944, he left Howard for San Francisco, to co-found the Church for the Fellowship of All Souls, the first intentionally integrated church in North America. Later still, he taught at Boston University. Regarded by many as one of the great spiritual figures of the twentieth century, he was a pastor more than a prophet, a worship innovator more than an organizer, and a writer of meditations that reflect the yearnings of the heart more than the machinations of theology. Mother insisted that I visit him.

We sat across from one another in high-back leather armchairs. I explained that ministry felt like the right fit for me, with its teaching, counseling, justice work, and community building. While I babbled on, his enormous, bald forehead rested in his hand as if it needed support; perhaps he was weary or perhaps he was just chuckling inside. How many times in his seventy-two years had he heard a similar story from a young, ultra-earnest, would-be-minister? When he finally spoke, his words flowed in deep, slow, measured tones. I hung on every syllable, and yet all he said was washed away by his final admonition: "If there is some other way you can do what you want with your life without entering the ministry, you should do it."

In that moment I was capable of hearing only half of his challenge—"if there is some other way." It took another twenty-five years before I understood the full import of his admonition. Until he cautioned me, I had thought I knew where my life was headed: I was going to be a minister. Following that morning's audience, doubts haunted me.

I left his study and entered the wilderness anew, wondering whether there was another path for me: Teaching? Community organizing? Social work? The day passed but I hardly noticed as, lost in thought, I wandered along the broad streets of Pacific Heights. The grass was lush, but through the fog I couldn't see much else.

Is there another way? I brooded. *No, not just working with children; not simply being an activist; not just helping those in distress.* I yearned for something more holistic.

Coming upon a small park, I strolled through it and as I passed out the gate on the other side, a soft voice said, *No.* It came from within, and it was louder the second time. *No, there is no other way.*

I didn't jump for joy, nor did this reaffirmation bring the peace it had that first time with Art. In the year following that decision, love's frailty and life's turmoil had left me emotionally frayed, my ego tattered, my weaknesses obvious, and the power of my own shadow too apparent. This time, that soft voice offered a moment of relief, but not release.

Throughout my life, friends have come through for me. This time it was Jack Bierschenk, my Ecole buddy with the Pinocchio nose and hyena laugh. He recommended I be hired as the assistant manager of the junior college he directed in Austria.

En route to Austria, I stopped in Chicago and found my parents at war. As usual Mother wanted to "share," so when I slipped in the back door, she was waiting for me. She had a way of cornering you with your back against the kitchen sink while she blocked the doorway into the rest of the house. A pro, she would begin coaxing information: "Where've you been?" "Who'd you see?" "How are you feeling?" Lauren once bowled Mother over while pushing her way past, but I sat on my angry feelings and "shared."

Professionally Dad's life had never been better. Following the Apollo 11 mission he had flown to Houston. There at the space center he was given a little vial holding a lunar soil sample. With it joggling around in his shirt pocket he flew back to Chicago with no one on the plane any the wiser. Who, after all, could imagine anyone carrying a piece of the moon worth tens of millions in his pocket, much less a black man?

However, on the home front life had never been worse and this time Dad was eager to talk as well. My parents had had little squabbles ever since I was a kid, but during the latter half of the sixties, inspired by Black Power and influenced by women's lib, Mother began asserting herself more and more often, and as she did the arguing escalated. She would announce she had an out-of-town workshop to attend, and leave. When Dad went away he would return to find the house remodeled, a wall-sized mirror in the dining room after he had expressly forbidden it. Three years earlier, during the fall of 1970, Mother had suffered a nervous breakdown; she was diagnosed with manic depression and prescribed lithium. Even so, she kept trying to wean herself from the medication, and each attempt led to wild mood swings between frenetic activism and despair. Now I wonder if Mother, an extreme extrovert, "empath," and world-saver, was simply overwhelmed, not just by her own life and her response to King's slaying, but unconsciously by the communal grief of Afro-Americans.

To avoid the onslaught, I retreated into the basement, but Mother pursued me. Cornered, I listened while she assailed me with her litany of grievances: your father this, your father that. Distilled down, it meant Dad was too rigid and emotionally inaccessible. She talked until all I could hear in my head was a voice from my past, screaming *Leave me alone*. I begged her to stop.

Ignoring my plea, she kept right on grousing until I exploded out of my chair, my arm pointing her toward the stairs.

The next evening Dad appeared, pacing the floor and complaining: your mother this, your mother that, which translated to her being angry and unreasonable.

Forgotten were the oft-used endearments; they seemed headed toward divorce. The childhood ache in my stomach returned. Driven as much by my own anxiety as theirs, I asked Dad if Mother had a therapist; I couldn't imagine that he'd ever been to one. He directed me to Dr. Wright. I found her telephone number in their address book, called, made an appointment, and then announced that the three of us were going.

At her office, I was left in the waiting room until the end of the session, when the white-haired, crone-like Dr. Wright ushered them out and beckoned me in. They had agreed to continue in counseling, she told me, and then bluntly advised, "I'd leave town if I were you."

"I'm going," I said.

I already had a plane ticket and was yearning to see Lori.

Two weeks later, I joined Jack Bierschenk and his British bride, Jill, in Austria. The International Community College was a small American junior college that used the Great Books series as its core curriculum. About thirty of us lived on an estate outside Salzburg.

I wrote to Lori as soon as I arrived and arranged to visit her in Germany. Her family's warmth went beyond cordiality, but not Lori's. As I prattled on about our making a life together, her eyes, which had once beckoned from behind her bangs, were cold and as impatient with me as they once had been with the Ecole. She chain-smoked her way through a long afternoon walk, while I pleaded with her to give our relationship a chance. "No," she answered.

"Deep inside something is turning me around and around," I wrote in my diary afterwards. "I didn't cry although I wish I had, perhaps I would have felt better. I drank instead . . . drank enough so I could go on without this terrible pain. That's why I drink, it numbs."

Since my responsibilities included shopping, the merchants often gave me gifts, including alcohol, and the half-drunk bottles cluttered my closet floor—Campari, Southern Comfort, vermouth, gin. My drinking accelerated. Meanwhile, life at the International Community College turned sour as its funding slowed and then stopped. We had barely enough to cover basic expenses and nothing for our salaries.

As this educational experiment went through its death throes, Jack became both more withdrawn and demanding. Slowly our decade-old friendship grew tense and distant, as the characteristics I had admired in him played out in ominous ways. An adopted child, Jack had an overwhelming need for control. Always organized, he now turned obsessive, asserting his will on the things he could—food and excursions, the flow of information, and decision making. Only Jill, his sympathetic but always protective bride, knew what dread weighed upon him, and Jack began to communicate with me through her.

As our connection dwindled, my sense of betrayal grew. My anger simmered until I started drinking in preparation for staff meetings. I drank before dinner and after, never enough to let loose with an expression of rage, just enough to anesthetize.

Nine in the morning, time for staff meeting. Hurriedly I poured a drink. Then suddenly—all at once—I felt my desperation and saw the tumbler, bottle, and booze as if for the first time. I turned around and looked at the liquor that had taken over the back of my closet. A chill ran through me; I knew what I had become. I put the bottle away and didn't drink again for years.

Numbing myself was a compulsion, but losing control to liquor was way too terrifying. Besides, there were other ways to deaden the pain—television, food, dope, depression, sleep, sex, and sexual fantasies (the latter being safer). I piled work upon work or procrastinated as long as possible, withdrawing into my head and over-intellectualizing. And, of course, being a super nice guy helped me avoid conflict and rejection. I embraced any means to put my problems off to another day, anything to keep me from living in the present painful moment, anything to help me avoid the anguish.

That's the way I had always dealt with pain—by fleeing from it. Retreat into closets and comic books, into drink, drugs, and depression; retreat from clouds of tear gas to the safety of home; retreat from the black community and hide out overseas. Best to avoid life's hard edge and sink into the numbing embrace of "a life which belongs to death." I'd be no Jesse. No bullet in the chest for me, nothing like the bloody end that society expects of young black men growing up in urban America. My death wouldn't be violent and brutal. Instead, until I found the courage to face my demons, I'd just keep dying a little each day.

Growing Up

The road to honor is paved with thorns; but on the path to truth, at every step you set your foot down on your own heart.

—Olive Schreiner, *The Story of an African Farm*

Chicago has a reputation for being a rough-and-tumble city, yet after my wanderings—the flop in Ireland, the fiasco in Switzerland, and the debacle in Austria—I was ready to return to the devil I knew.

Again August offered the typical Chicago swelter, best endured in my parents' basement. All the same I soon ventured forth to see Art. He was living on the north side so I caught the B train. We hung out and jawed and ruminated, as usual. But it was different now. I had made the decision to enter the ministry and so my doubt about my direction in life had receded. Art's, however, hadn't. Two years of indecision frittered away working in a day-care center had eroded his self-esteem until his despair turned into self-loathing.

We fell into a pattern. Art would give me a holler most Sunday evenings, then proceed to dump on himself. My half of the litany was to tout the good in him that he couldn't see, a ritual we repeated until I wearied of being his emotional cheerleader. One Sunday I insisted he hop on the El and come south. When he walked in, I stood him in front of a mirror, held him there, and made him affirm himself. After we stopped laughing, I wrung a commitment from him to go into counseling. With that settled— or so I thought—we went around the corner to the Woodlawn Tap and Grill. I drank ginger ale.

Despite a circuitous route through college that left me without a BA, when I enrolled in Meadville Lombard Theological School I was simultaneously admitted to the University of Chicago Divinity School. My parents were elated. At last I had returned to school. Mother babbled on about her son "the rabbi," and amid her enthusiasm little room was left for my own. Panic welled up and in my confusion I wondered: *For whom am I doing this—my crazy mother or myself?*

After King's assassination, Mother, wanting to become more deeply involved in the black community, accepted a position as assistant professor and chair of the Department of Social Work at Kennedy-King Community College. She also maintained a small counseling practice, not to mention the many causes to which she devoted herself—Urban Gateways, an organization that provided cultural opportunities for inner-city youth; the Chicago Center for the Society of Samaritans, a counseling hotline for the suicidal; and the Abraham Lincoln Center, a community center where she served as a social-work consultant. Mother inspired me. She also plagued me, for when she wasn't saving the world she was intruding into my life—except when she withdrew into a dark lethargy. "Mother, it will pass," I would coo in those moments. I felt like a yo-yo: fleeing, then comforting.

Mother was as manic as Dad was methodical and predictable. During the years I wandered about Europe, his letters always began with a plea for me to return to school, but now that I had matriculated he left me alone.

I had returned to the world of my youth. Meadville Lombard was kitty-corner to First Unitarian Church, while my parents lived just five blocks north. I lived in an apartment around the block from my parents' home. My life was the circuit I followed along 57th Street—studying at Regenstein Library, eating at Hutchinson Commons, working at church for the Chicago Children's Choir, shooting the breeze in the Meadville Lombard lounge, and browsing at O'Gara's bookstore on Fridays to check out the new acquisitions.

A large, faded sign hanging over the sidewalk read: "USED BOOKS—Bought and Sold." A fat, gray, longhaired cat lounged in the showcase window among the books. Inside, a library-like hush hung over O'Gara's, the only sounds a quiet conversation at the front desk, the ring of the cash register, the hum of the fluorescent lights. The wooden shelves along the wall reached to the ceiling and were accessed by ladders on runners. The white and black floor was laid out in checkerboard fashion, while the cracked and missing tiles revealed worn, warped hardwood planks.

I came to a shelf that was not quite chest high, where that week's additions to O'Gara's twenty thousand titles were lined up in two rows, spines upward. Starting at one end, I scanned them until I found one of interest. A book with gold background and black letters caught my attention: *Later Poems of Rabindranath Tagore. Worship material?* I wondered. I knew Tagore was a nineteenth-century Indian poet, educator, and Nobel laureate. I picked it up.

Skipping the introduction and the translator's note, I paged through the poems. Halfway through, I came upon a section entitled "Poems of Wonder." On the next page, instead of a poem there was a dedication: "To Edith, whose love has sustained me through life. Auro." *No, it can't be,* I thought and flipped back to find the translator's note. There, at the end of the note, was written "A.B., Ecole d'Humanité, Goldern, Switzerland, August, 1973." *My God, this is what he was doing?* All the years I had dismissed him as a fool, Auro had been translating these poems. He had been among the first to attend Tagore's school, and had gone on to become a nuclear physicist and then a translator of Tagore's poetry. This was his fourth book. Abruptly, the judgment I had passed on him turned back on me. My face burned. I looked around the room and, of course, no one was paying attention but I felt like hiding anyway. I pushed four dollars across the counter and, clutching the book, fled outside. Fleeing didn't lessen the intensity of my feeling—my cheeks glowed like embers. Retreating to my study carrel, I read until I came to this warning in the poem "Do Not Judge":

Do not judge—
Where you live is but a small corner of this earth.
So far as your eyes reach,
They encompass so little,
To the little you hear,
You add your own voice.
You keep good and bad, white and black,
Carefully apart.
In vain you make a line
To draw a limit.
Do not judge.
Alas, time flies by
And all debate is vain.
Look, the flowers blooming at the forest's edge,
Bring a message from the sky,
For she is a friend of the earth;
In July rains
The grass floods the earth with green,
And fills her cup to the brim.
Forgetting self,
Fill your heart with simple joy.

Before the fall term of my second year began, I headed west to visit Jeff Bordelon, a housemate from Beloit. Half Jewish, half Cajun, and another Beloit dropout, Jeff, ever the hustler, was getting established in his career. He had just purchased a ranch outside Sacramento, where he played at being a farmer but made his living as a lawyer.

One day just before lunchtime, a truck pulled into the yard of his ranch to deliver two adorable twenty-five-pound porkers. Guiding them into their pen, Jeff waxed eloquent about a future pig roast. Meanwhile, I headed toward the house.

"Mark!" Jeff bellowed. Whipping around, I saw that those two cute little pigs had set their snouts to rooting, and just like that had escaped his makeshift pen. Almost as quickly, Jeff, his dog, and I had them cornered. Jeff dove. He got one, but the other took off across the pasture. I was on his tail and closing in when he turned sharply to my right and plunged into an irrigation ditch. So did I. With water squishing from my sneakers, I was corralling him back toward the house when he stopped, turned, faced me, and charged. "Get his legs," Jeff yelled as that damn pig dashed through mine.

Seeing that no help was coming from Jeff, since he was doubled over laughing, I turned and sped after the pig. The darling darted under the fence. Stepping over the barbed wire, I snagged my jeans and ripped the crotch. By then the pig was scurrying down the road toward the next driveway. Again I cornered him, again he charged. Determined not to be tricked this time, I fell to my knees, only to have the delightful critter slip right through my hands. We hit the road once more, and as we did, a family in a station wagon drove by. The kids' faces were pressed up against the window, their eyes as big as golf balls. I waved. *God, I must be crazy.* The pig turned up another driveway. Confronted by a three-legged dog that ran away from the pig and after me, I hesitated for a moment, then hotfooted it right back down the driveway. Jeff could catch his own frickin' pig.

I wasn't afraid of that dog—even I could outrun a three-legged dog. But when it began to bark, I imagined some peckerwood looking up from his television. He's been watching the news. A race riot fills the screen—sirens, smoke, shattered glass, looters dashing away carrying TV sets, others posing with Black Power salutes. Hearing his dog bark, he glances out of his window, and jumpin' Jehoshaphat, Fido's chasing a stranger—one of them niggers, namely me. And I'm yelling "Get da pig," but there's no pig in sight since he's disappeared under a hedge. There's only one conclusion the redneck can come to: This juggle bunny is up to no good. Lickety-split this cracker grabs his shotgun, shoots me dead, and claims when questioned, "One of them black revolutionary fellas that wanna overthrow our country come trespassin' on my property. I just done my duty and I is proud of it."

Ridiculous, perhaps. But that was what flashed through my mind. As involved as I was in chasing that bodacious piglet, I never forgot that I was a black man in rural white America, because my survival depended on knowing it. It was just an everyday exercise in risk assessment. As I hightailed it down that driveway, running for my life, not for an instant did I feel paranoid—just relieved to be out of harm's way. Many white folks find this impossible to believe but being a black man in America is risky business—you never know when something bad is going to happen for no other reason than that you're black and you're there.

Several years earlier, it had happened to my brother, Philip. After he had moved to Denver he'd been riding his bicycle home from work when he found himself pinned spread-eagle against a squad car, and all he could do was pray that the cops didn't do anything even more idiotic. His crime was riding through Lakeview, a white neighborhood, just after a drugstore had been robbed, and he happened to be the first black man the police encountered. Philip was carrying his security clearance for the United States Geological Survey, but they just wanted to know how he'd gotten his hands on it. They kept him sitting on the curb until their supervisor arrived; then, opening his backpack, they found a geology textbook and a research paper. They eventually released him, but offered not a word of apology, and it took the threat of legal action by the director of the Geological Survey to force them to expunge Philip's arrest record.

Donna arrived at Meadville Lombard in the beginning of my second year. Today more than half the settled Unitarian Universalist ministers are female, but that wasn't the case in 1975; she was the only woman in that year's class and one of only three in the school. I had arranged to receive credit from Meadville Lombard for teaching Sunday school and needed a co-teacher. It had to be a woman, and Donna Morrison was the only viable candidate. Finding her sitting in the school lounge, I asked, "Would you like to teach Sunday school with me?" Some say it's the best come-on they've ever heard, but I was serious. I didn't need another romance. I needed help, and from our collaboration a friendship evolved.

She was tall, dirty-blond, with an athletic build and the best legs at the school. A tough-minded white Canadian, she was dispassionate unless trying to persuade you to do something, and self-controlled except when she got angry—and she could get angry. When one little seven-year-old white boy poured a bucketful of crayons on the floor and proceeded to roller-skate over them she grabbed his dashiki and jerked him off the floor. I soon found her wrath could be directed at me, too.

Ours began as a straightforward relationship. Co-teaching worked well. She was energetic and decisive, I was flexible and warm, and we had both grown up in Unitarian Sunday schools. Together we created an atmosphere that, unbelievably, made the kids eager to attend.

Neither of us was looking for a romantic relationship, but something happened as we taught, struggled together through a course on Paul Tillich's *Systematic Theology*, and drove together to Toronto. We became friends and then drifted reluctantly into a turbulent courtship.

We would have a major blowup one day and have dinner together the next. She would gnash her teeth and tear my shirt, I would pound the bed and spew profanity, and then we would make up and go square dancing. We fought regularly because, besides being more direct than most people, Donna couldn't stand my victim litany: "couldn't help it," "wasn't my fault," "it's not fair," "I'm not good enough," "I never do anything right." My passive, pouting, poor-me behavior made her eyes bulge. Feeling misunderstood and attacked, I fought back, and in the process learned how to stay in a relationship, rather than retreat. I also learned I could survive the acrimony.

As the fall of her second year and my third progressed, planning for internships dominated our conversations. One afternoon we were in Regenstein Library, talking it over. I was set on Eugene, Oregon. Donna thought going to Eugene was nonsense, since she would be on the other side of the continent in Mount Vernon, Virginia. So in an offhand, just-for-the-sake-of-discussion kind of way she said, "We could get married and both do our internships in the Washington area."

"Really?" I said, and silently began figuring out how to make it work.

When I saw Donna the next day I asked the obvious question: "What day?"

"What day?" she said, looking puzzled.

"Yeah. What day are we getting married?"

Donna was glad and miffed at the same time. She had put the idea out as a discussion starter and I, coward that I was, ducked proposing to her by acting as if the matter was settled.

While spending the Christmas holiday with my family in D.C., I told them about our engagement. Meanwhile, Donna told her sister and brother, but withheld the news from her parents. Instead, the Morrisons received the announcement over the telephone, an exchange that ended abruptly when Donna slammed down the receiver. Then the letters came. Her parents assured us it was nothing personal; indeed they found me "personable, alert, and friendly." However, while an interracial relationship might be fine in an "isolated university community," we must ask ourselves whether integration was "a possible or even desirable situation for the whole world." We hadn't been thinking about the whole world. Passions being as they are, we weren't thinking far beyond ourselves. One of the letters read:

January 20, 1977

Dear Donna,

. . . I believe the proposed marriage between you and Mark to be a prescription for disaster. The first and most obvious reason for an objection is the racial difference . . . Toronto is a multicultural city, but like other such cities it has Greek neighborhoods, Chinese neighborhoods, Portuguese neighborhoods. These people are not forced to group themselves, but choose to live together because they feel happier and more comfortable with people like themselves. Do you think that these people should be encouraged or even coerced into spreading out and mixing up? I used to believe that universal love and brotherhood could be achieved by eliminating human differences and by all of us becoming the same shade of tan, but I don't believe that anymore . . .

Love,

Mom

Back and forth went the letters. In one round, Donna's mother cited her Jewish and Japanese friends' opinions on the perils of mixed marriages; she apparently missed the irony of achieving such parental solidarity across ethnic lines.

After the letters came the invasion—first her father, then her mother. A redhead with a Scottish temper that fit the stereotype, he roared into an already "Windy City," returning to the U of C campus where he and Katherine had met and wed twenty-eight years earlier, to stop us from doing likewise. Intimidated but determined to maintain control of the discussion, we insisted on having a mediator.

The encounter took place at Meadville Lombard in a formal, wood-paneled meeting room, a setting that matched the tone of the discussion. Indeed, prior to Mr. Morrison's arrival, when I sat next to Donna, she reassigned me to a chair on the opposite side of the room. This was war, not a social get-together. Donna and I marshaled our arguments in defense of our position and our responses were so well reasoned that halfway through the interview Mr. Morrison blurted out, in his customarily obtuse fashion, "Where are the hormones?" Hormones? I didn't get it until later when he repeated for my parents this "good one" he'd gotten off. He was wondering where the passion was.

The conversation continued at my parents' townhouse, and included Mother, Dad, Mr. Morrison, Donna, myself, and my sister

Carole, who had by then returned to Chicago after graduating from Boston College. When Mr. Morrison asked their opinions on interracial marriage, Mother jumped right in. "My son is a proud black man," she said. "And I'd hoped Mark would marry a black woman."

Shock struck, then anger. I had come home expecting support, and instead Mother offers a treacherous confession. *Shut the fuck up* a voice within me screamed, but I just set my jaw and sat in seething silence.

Why would Mother—who had friends of every hue and who lived by the mantra "to thine own self be true"—choose that moment to express her benighted hope? Maybe if the phrase *woman of color* had been part of the racial vocabulary in 1977 Mother might have used it instead of *black*. It would have reflected the truth my whole family already knew—she had wanted me to marry my high-school sweetheart, Sharon Wang. In her typical way, my mother had insinuated herself into my love life. The fact that I was still in high school hadn't kept her from musing about what lovely, exotic children Sharon, the offspring of a mixed Anglo-Chinese marriage, and I would produce. The nadir had been the mock engagement party Mother and Sharon had orchestrated. Now Mother was messing around with my life again.

What the fuck was up with her? I didn't have a clue and didn't care. I just wanted her to cram it!

"Then again," Mother continued, "given how Mark was raised and where he's lived and all, I accepted long ago that was unlikely to happen." This was not support; it was resignation. Mother might as well have sided with the Morrisons.

This shit was worse than what I got on the street. Step out with a white chick and I'd get tried and convicted. Some soul sister was sure to cop an attitude and shoot me a look as sharp as Tabasco that said, "How dare you! You sorry-ass Negro. You Tom. You traitor." The message was unmistakable, and I would feel the urge to pretend I didn't know the white woman standing next to me. Lots of sisters expected racial fidelity from black men. Intraracial dating and mating was our duty to the race, because there weren't enough eligible, employed, straight, unincarcerated brothers to go around. Seeing so few of us, panicky sisters adopted a survivalist mentality that demanded exclusive rights.

What perplexed me was how exclusivity could possibly solve the problem. Racial isolation serves as a barrier; cultural differences are challenging. Fear, distrust, and discomfort cause many to live parochial lives. Using this fear to stigmatize interracial love, both white supremacists and black separatists portray it as repulsive and an act of betrayal. But those of goodwill—and romantic inclination—always have and always will cross racial and cultural boundaries. My entire family history from Senōra Doll and Thomas Corker Jr. to Betsy Reed and Joe Gregory testifies to the fact that whites and blacks are not competing teams or warring clans; they are not the Hatfields and McCoys or the Capulets and Montagues. We are not different species. In fact, humankind shares a common African ancestry, and racial mixing is as old as human history.

Individuals fall in love, not racial groups. I couldn't understand why anyone would embrace a draconian rubric that ruled out romantic relationships with people based on the color of their skin rather than the content of their characters. And I was not prepared to do what my sister Carole had done. After King's assassination, she felt compelled to withdraw from all her white friends. The exception was her boyfriend, Jeff Blumenthal, who, in her mind, was acceptable because he was Jewish. They maintained their relationship through her first year of college but she finally dropped him, too, and never again dated a white guy.

If state statutes hadn't stopped my ancestors from loving and raising children across racial lines, why should the opinions of black zealots keep me from doing so in the 1970s? I couldn't fathom why my choices should be limited by the narrowness of other people's lives. To appease others' bigotry? To promote a racial purity that doesn't exist? A cultural identity that from the beginning has melded with and been transformed by the American experience? I just didn't get it. But I did know that I was expected to date black women.

If someone was waiting for me to make a move, to sidle up and say, "What's up, sister? You're sure fine," it was not about to happen. I was not a sweet-talker, and the obligation was doubly daunting because there were so few black female contemporaries in my social circles—graduate school, church, and international folk dancing. Nonetheless about a year before my relationship with Donna became serious, I had made an effort. Her name was Flo. We met while folk dancing. I saw her often, but didn't know her well. She was thin and poised, her movements lithe, her skin honey colored, her hair rolled up in a bun. She had never shown any interest in me, but had grown up in Hyde Park and we had enough in common that I thought our first date might work. I was wrong. Over dinner I was at my empathetic best, which prompted a quick confession from her: She was in love with the tall, blond, ponytailed folk-dance leader. What a date killer. Unfortunately, he was in love with someone else. Once again, I was the confidant rather than the chosen.

Asking anyone out was difficult. But the threat of disaster loomed behind affirmative action dating. Beneath my reluctance and behind the awkwardness I was scared of being measured and rejected by a black woman. I knew about rejection—every guy does—and had been rejected often enough by white women. That hurt, but it didn't terrify me. I could always say, "She rejected me because I'm black," an excuse that had the power to soothe even when it wasn't true. With a sister, that defense was gone and the rejection cut to the core of my insecurity—not *good* enough, not *man* enough, not *black* enough. So, given the emotional risks, the dearth of opportunity, and lack of a compelling reason, the possibility of my marrying a black woman, as my mother said, was unlikely.

Over time, however, I've come to see that my shock at Mother's imprudent confession was misplaced. Mother was trying to defend if not support me, and I completely missed it. It was a put-down. Smiling the whole time, she was saying: "Mr. Morrison, you sanctimonious bigot, you come into my house to say my black son isn't good enough to marry your white daughter. You've got it backward. Your daughter isn't good enough for my son." Of course, the message was veiled since she was battling her always-be-polite dictate. But what mother wouldn't want to rip his throat out? Plus, there was another coded, and probably unconscious, message. Rather than passing judgment on my choice, her declaration "I'd hoped Mark would marry a black woman" simply reflected, yet again, the fragility of black self-esteem. Mother didn't see our engagement as me choosing Donna, an individual who happened to be white, but rather as my rejection of black women, and by extension, herself. Of course, it all went right by Mr. Morrison. All he heard was her affirmation of his belief in cultural apartheid.

The conversation with Mr. Morrison went on, but I had withdrawn. Dad finally broke in. "Listen!" he said, "Ultimately it doesn't matter what we think. The decision is theirs, and our role is to support them." That brought the visit to an end.

Before Donna's mother, Katherine, arrived for a visit that was less dramatic but no more conciliatory, we received a letter from Mr. Morrison:

April 10, 1977

Dear Donna, Mark and Professor and Mrs. Reed:

We have been having much anguish in the three months since learning of Mark's and Donna's decision to marry. We regret the anxiety that this has caused you . . .

Only last night did it dawn on me that words normally imply communication and enhancement of understanding, but in this case they seem to have obfuscated . . .

If Mark means by "working with the black community" that he works with those that seek integration and equate this with the desirability of, or indifference to, intermarriage, then he is consistent. If he means that he has a hope of being effective with the rapidly growing majority of blacks that believe otherwise, then I believe that Mark is mistaken. For them, he "becomes" a white when he marries one. I believe that Mark and Donna could "go over big" in most white communities, but not with blacks who are sensitive to this matter. They are rapidly becoming more numerous.

Mark's insistence in denying the above theme with words means, for us, that his words do not constitute the message. His actions constitute the message and they contradict the words. If they are flexible and intelligent, Donna and Mark may be able to "make it" if, denying Mark's words, both of them act as if they were white. We rather expect that they will act this way. Indeed, they are acting this way, now.

[We] cannot endorse the marriage of Donna and Mark, but we are prepared to attend the ceremony. Naturally, we will be as supportive as we can bring ourselves to be, after the event.

Sincerely,
Russell Morrison

"Becomes a white"? What was he talking about? Was I white because my birth certificate said so or because of the company I kept—guilt by association like a contagion? Maybe it was the blood of my white ancestors coursing through my veins that made me "white" in a reversal of the bizarre "one drop rule."

And his suggestion that we might make it if we act white? What urbane bigotry. I associated acting white with the imperious sense of entitlement that seemingly self-assured white men like Russell Morrison brought to every interaction and with the bravado displayed by my three chain-smoking, American embassy-brat schoolmates at Villa St. Jean. But to a white person, the phrase *act white* normally meant behaving in an honest and upright manner. To a black person, it meant the opposite—you are either double-dealing, selling out, or both. Since he seemed oblivious to the phrase's multiple and contradictory meanings, it was unclear what he meant. Was I to give up watermelon or was he simply referring to our working in a predominantly white context? There were no other options for Unitarian Universalist parish ministers.

The word *integration* was another loaded term that seemed to have multiple meanings. Used by white people imprisoned within a Eurocentric worldview, integration was synonymous with assimilation. White hubris assumed blacks would adjust, conform, and act more like them—becoming WASPs with pigment. Given their cultural preeminence, whites took it for granted that after integration they themselves would carry on merrily as before. The changes they awaited were in appearance, not substance. This is why many black Americans distrusted the process of integration and mocked those who succeeded in the white world for being Oreos.

Mr. Morrison seemed unable to understand that true integration entails genuine change: the bringing together of our cultural parts—and our lives—to form a new whole, a melding rather than the subjugation of one by another. Understood in this way, integration transcends the legal battles of the civil rights era and is relocated in the commonplace and mundane. In its ordinary everyday context, integration requires courage, for our relatedness can be fraught with apprehension and awkward moments. But these moments—these "oopses" and "ah-hahs"—foster growth and new creation. A static culture is a dying one. The rough-and-tumble synthesis of integration is the lifeblood of tomorrow's culture, which will emerge from unforeseen relations and fusions, just as rock-and-roll emerged from the fusion of blues, gospel, and country music.

The ultimate goal is a society in which every individual is treated with respect and given an opportunity to be a full participant. The issue was never really integration, but racial justice. Legislated integration was only a means to that end.

Donna's father meant I would have to give up my identity as an Afro-American if we were to "make it big." He expected me to assimilate into white culture and jettison my black self. But it was my sense of self as a black person that called me to find a way to work with and for, if not from within, the black community. I first heard this calling to help change the world while marching up the mountain behind a Swiss boy fleeing in terror from my dark skin. The same sense of duty led me to forsake the expatriate life and return to the United States. Another need drove me as well. Given that I had spent so much time on the fringe of the black community, I yearned to reaffirm that connection. I had served the black community before, as a VISTA volunteer in Columbus, and I intended to do so again. The choice to serve was mine to make. But I had no control over how others would perceive me, and in this regard Mr. Morrison's prediction would prove painfully true.

On June 10, 1977, the eve of our wedding, as the carillon tower cast its long shadow eastward along the wide, green Midway, both families gathered beneath Rockefeller Chapel. Halfway through our training to become Unitarian Universalist ministers, Donna and I were about to receive the degree of master of arts in divinity from the University of Chicago. Twenty-five years earlier I had watched my father receive his PhD there. Since then, Philip, Carole, Lauren, and I had performed in its chancel with the Chicago Children's Choir dozens of times. Ten tumultuous years had passed since I had sat there for my high-school graduation, and nine years had gone by since my mother had eulogized Martin Luther King Jr. from its pulpit.

There I was again, the sanctuary flooded with light, the faculty robed, many in the school's maroon and black colors. Donna's name was read first and a little later my own. I strode across the chancel, and Dean Greenfield placed the diploma in my hand. What a long road. I knew how many courses and how many qualifying exams it had taken; I knew how many failures and how much work. Yet I didn't really understand. Acquiring an education had once seemed more a familial edict than a choice, an ultimatum rather than an opportunity. Progressing as far as I had without appreciating the significance my family invested in education required a studied blindness. Wed to this willful ignorance, the challenges I confronted on my way through school, unlike my father, were not from obstructions others placed before me, but from within.

It was one thing for Dad, in 1944, to be naïve about the obstacles and lack of opportunities facing Afro-Americans. My naïveté in 1977 consisted of thinking I could walk away from my family's values and ignore the early conditioning embedded in the psychic crevices where the "Captain," the "General," and the "Senator" still lived. The expectations placed on me by my heritage and the Negro race had been established long before my conception. They were then modeled and unrelentingly imparted by my parents. Life demanded education, duty, hard work, and service. Every college graduate was a credit to the race, a repudiation of all who disparage black intelligence—proof of something that shouldn't have to be proven.

I didn't consciously intend to prove myself because I was black or to redeem my race, but even at such a proud moment, the myth lingered. I cannot tell how much of my drive and self-doubt reflected this perspective, which was so old, so often reinforced, and so deeply internalized. Only one thing could have changed the situation—if my birth certificate had been correct and I had, in fact, been white. Then my graduation would not have been about forwarding the race, but about celebrating my achievement, as it was for Donna.

I had been loyal to my parents' espoused values rather than their fears. I had to find myself within myself, which required that I seek my own excruciating way through to what, in hindsight, seemed inevitable. My waywardness transformed an academic education into more than a credential or the fulfillment of others' expectations. When I was ready, the path toward ministry became a means of self-discovery that, in the end, reconciled others' hopes with my own desires.

Likewise, getting married symbolized more than the commitment Donna and I were making to each other. Our marriage was possible because I had forged upon an anvil of adversity a strong enough sense of identity and a clear enough idea of where I was headed to enter into a relationship without losing myself.

Donna and I moved to Mount Vernon, Virginia, where she was to serve as intern minister while I commuted to an internship in Bethesda, Maryland. It was a homecoming for us both. We lived an hour's drive from the Reed homestead in Westmoreland County. Donna's maternal family, the Longs, distant kin of both George Washington and Thomas Jefferson, also had its roots in Virginia. Soon after arriving, we drove down to visit Washington's estate. "Wouldn't it have been nice to live here?" Donna said, while strolling through the mansion, its grounds, and the slave quarters. "No way," I snapped. "Where the hell do you think I'd be sleeping?" Her ancestors could have owned mine, a history we couldn't escape.

I had never lived in the South before, much less traveled around it with a white woman. That alone made me anxious, but the Morrisons' letters implying that we would find the world outside the University to be hostile stirred up that old black paranoia. I remained vigilant. I wondered how people down here would react to a mixed marriage. But nothing much happened: a few stares, no catcalls. It seemed that in the world beyond our families an interracial relationship wasn't worth noticing.

Still, it felt peculiar to live in Virginia, a state where miscegenation had remained illegal until so recently. One hundred years earlier, Betsy Reed and Joe Gregory, my great-great-grandparents who had six children together, used to walk down the road holding hands, but they couldn't marry because she was black and he was white. Indeed, until the 1967 Supreme Court decision *Loving v. Virginia*, declaring a 1924 Virginia statute and similar laws in sixteen other southern states unconstitutional, I would have been fined for performing a marriage like my own and perhaps driven from the state as the Lovings had been.

Our marriage gave Great-aunt Irene cause to reminisce about the Canadians she had known. "Mr. Pinter was from Canada and he fell in love with me, just watching me," she said, with the smile of a twenty-year-old. Nonetheless she had declined his marriage proposal. And she told me again of her older brother, Stacy: "He was gone over thirty years before we saw him again. He was married to a colored girl out in California for a while, then moved to Canada. Of course, I didn't know nothin' about that because we didn't hear from him until he was living in Connecticut married to a girl from Nova Scotia." I found comfort in her stories. We weren't crazy; it had been done before, and in less propitious times.

After the wedding, the Morrisons made overtures and the waters seemed to calm. But that fall, Donna's mother began calling every Sunday, pleading with her not to have children. It would kill her, she said. And every Monday, Donna would have a cold. It took a month for Donna to put two and two together and tell her mother to stop calling unless she had something pleasant to say. The pleading calls ceased, which led to a miraculous healing. When Donna called home the following fall to deliver our happy news—she was pregnant—the telephone on the other end not only fell silent, it fell to the floor.

In need of moral support in our ongoing skirmishes with the Morrisons, we would retreat to the home of our friends Karen and David Yano. An interracial couple with three children, they had weathered the assaults of Karen's parents. Why her parents, themselves a mixed marriage between a German Jew and an American of Scandinavian descent, never welcomed David, a Japanese American, was not clear. Karen and I had attended the Ecole d'Humanité together, and she and David were members of the Cedar Lane Unitarian Church, where I served as intern minister. But what really drew the four of us together was the opportunity to grouse about our parents ad nauseam.

My D.C. family also supported us. Grammy welcomed Donna and Great-aunt Irene would throw open her arms and gather her in, although the Canadian in Donna would have preferred a handshake. Surrounded by my large, black extended family, with our Sunday dinners and holiday gatherings and hugs, Donna found her parents' drivel a little easier to endure.

Whenever Donna and I came to Sunday dinner at 114 S Street, all my good feelings from childhood returned. The house looked so much like all the other tall, narrow brick row houses on S Street that I had to look carefully for the gilded numerals on the glass arch above the door. Half a flight up was the passage to Great-uncle Lloyd's basement office. A brass plaque Philip and I had loved to polish read: Dr. L.H. Newman. The front door was up another half flight. Great-aunt Irene would answer the door, saying, "Oh, my precious child." I would reach down and hug her, remembering that once my head would have been pressed into her bosom, my cheeks covered with kisses.

Our Virginia suburb felt alien, but not Washington, D.C. It was the center of the world, not because it was the capital of the country but because 114 S Street was the center of *my* world. It felt as though this was where we came from—this was the house that Mary Elizabeth's children had purchased for her around 1918 and where my great-grandmother lived with Great-aunt Irene and Great-uncle Lloyd until she died. Her casket had been placed between the bay windows in the parlor, and the visitation took place right there. Dad had literally been born around the corner, and during my childhood this is where we returned in the summer and every other Christmas.

On Christmas Day, upwards of twenty of our multicolored family would converge upon that narrow old house which held us all without a problem, as long as we stayed out of Great-aunt Irene's kitchen. My first and second cousins poured into Great-uncle Lloyd's mystery-filled basement office, reveling in the artifacts from his travels, the ten-foot long bar, the refrigerator full of Coca Cola, and the spiked eggnog that made us even giddier than we already were. Great-aunt Irene wrote in her diary:

> Xmas 1967
> . . . We had a most delightful time. Everyone went downstairs to dance. Of course you know I had danced enough around the kitchen all day so I did not go.

This was Christmas: Great-aunt Irene in perpetual motion, rarely sitting, always shuffling out to the kitchen to prepare or orchestrate—warming this, serving that—corn pudding, tangy greens, Smithfield ham, mashed sweet potatoes covered with melted marshmallows, rich brown gravy—then up again to refill the platters, and get the plum pudding ready for its grand entrance.

The little lie, one of many, was that Great-uncle Lloyd had cooked it, which he did in a manner of speaking. Great-aunt Irene would do all the preparation and then, like a surgeon, her brother would make his entrance and do all the mixing, leaving her to the cooking and cleaning. On Christmas Day, Great-uncle Lloyd again played the central role. We would gather in the dining room, the lights switched off. The plum pudding was carried from the kitchen, ablaze, to a chorus of "aahs," then presented to Great-uncle Lloyd, who would spoon up the burning brandy from the platter, letting the blue flame cascade down over the pudding until the fire died out. When the lights went on, we scarfed it down. Meanwhile Great-aunt Irene, who had disappeared upstairs, would reappear with a Christmas envelope for each of us. And we all knew what was inside—a newly-minted, crisp twenty-dollar bill.

There was another side to Christmas. Loud arguments between Grammy and Great-aunt Irene would be punctuated with one snapping, "Girl, you don't know what you're talking about," and the other responding, "Well, who made you the Queen?" When they weren't going after one another, they targeted Leona, their dark-skinned cousin, who received many a cutting comment. The skin-color issue always lurked in the background, and I occupied the darker end of the color spectrum, surpassed only by the darker men who had married into the family. I heard these and other disturbing undercurrents but didn't always understand the old battles and unnamed tensions.

Christmas at 114 was more than a child's delight, however, for I could also see that it marked the passage of time and the cycles of life—marriages and births, divorces and deaths—near-constant change in something I hoped would never change.

During the Second World War when Little Lloyd was serving with the U.S. Army in Italy, Great-aunt Irene wrote:

> Xmas 1943
> On Tuesday, December 21, Grace and I put new linoleum
> on the kitchen floor and Lloyd painted the kitchen. We
> had a hard time getting a turkey for Xmas but Lloyd got
> one. [This is] the first time baby Lloyd has been away for
> Xmas.

Dad's clan was expected to be there, and my mother resented it. In 1947 Dad had insisted they go to D.C. for Christmas rather than Wilkes-Barre. Then, six months later her mother, Naomi, had died and Mother never ceased fuming over it.

Christmas at 114 was a touchstone, and as much as I wanted it to be changeless, it was also a way of measuring how I had grown and changed. Only my memory imperfectly preserves a reality that kept altering.

Change never ceased. In 1977, Donna and I couldn't make it to D.C. for the traditional Christmas Eve dinner at Great-uncle Harry's and Aunt Ethel's house because we were participating in the services at our congregations. Early the next morning we arrived at Grammy's house. When breakfast had been cleared away, Donna called her family in Toronto, and afterward sat in the rear parlor, weeping—her first Christmas away from home. Sitting beside her, I looked around. It dawned on me that given a minister's responsibilities I would never spend another Christmas in D.C. and sadness misted my eyes, as well.

The changes continued, and in her last Christmas entry before she died, Great-aunt Irene wrote:

> Dec. 1983 Xmas
> All alone with my thoughts, thinking of days gone by and
> of all the wonderful Xmases we have had the pleasure of
> spending together. We have had a big family. When we chil-
> dren came along we had to make trimmings for the tree,
> string popcorn, cut out paper ornaments, make candy canes
> and different things. Now everything is so different . . .

Christmas has grown more bittersweet with the passage of time. The season now stands as a milestone marking life's transitions. Quiet reflection has replaced frenetic motion as memory has taken the place of anticipation—memories that I treasure more than gifts, memories of what was and can never be again.

The Call

It seems as if I have completed some mysterious cycle which does not measure itself by years but relates to some cosmic mechanism centered in time cycles of the universe, reminding me that we are already "out there" and that heaven, the place from which we came and also the place to which we must go, is not necessarily far out in space but also right across the room.

—George M. Solomon, letter, March 21, 1986

Between 1974 and 1979 I was the only black student at Meadville Lombard, the first since 1968. Driven by curiosity and fueled by the need to know what I was up against, I had set out to track down my black ministerial predecessors. It took years, but one by one I found nearly all of them.

I began with Marshall Grigsby. That was easy; he was the assistant minister of my home church. A couple of years older than myself and, like me, raised Unitarian Universalist, he was the closest thing I had to a peer. Yet my advances never elicited more than an indifferent response. He was neither interested in mentoring me nor in parish ministry, an impression confirmed when a year later he took an administrative path that eventually led to being president of Benedict College.

During my third year of theological school, while spending the Christmas holiday in Washington, D.C., I made an appointment to see David Eaton. The most prominent black minister in the Unitarian Universalist Association (UUA), he served the large and historic All Souls Unitarian Church and was also chair of the Washington, D.C., Board of Education. I was anxious, but that faded when David threw his arms wide, said, "Mark!" with his mid-Atlantic drawl, and drew me into his wood-paneled study. "Man, let me tell you how it is," he said. This was what I wanted.

Nine months later, after Donna and I had begun our internships in the greater Washington area, I interviewed Lewis McGee. Thirty years earlier, he had been the founding minister of the Free Religious Fellowship (FRF), a small interracial congregation on Chicago's South Side. Now retired, he was genteel, fair-skinned, and more circumspect than David. The following June, big, brooding Thom Payne gave us a tour of the First Church of Roxbury, Massachusetts. It seated fifteen hundred and had a membership of forty. That same week I reunited with Renford Gaines— he had not only preceded me at Meadville Lombard, he had also been the youth advisor when I was president of the youth group at my home church. In 1969 he had preached a sermon entitled "Blacks, Get Your Guns" to his lily-white, southern Illinois congregation, and within a year had moved to Boston. Subsequently he changed his name to Mwalimu Imara and was now working in Boston as a minister-at-large for the Benevolent Fraternity of Unitarian Churches. After seeing his nose flare and jaw clench as he offered his fiery memories of the UUA's retreat from the Black Power agenda of the sixties, I realized how difficult it would be to focus my thesis on that era and abandoned the plan.

In an old woman's home in Jamaica, New York, I got down on my hands and knees and pulled a clothing box from under her bed. It was filled with sermons handwritten by her father, Egbert Ethelred Brown, a turn-of-the-century Jamaican Unitarian minister. When I returned to Chicago, Ben Richardson, a professor of history at DePaul University who had been McGee's succes-

sor at FRF, was reluctant to meet. Over lunch, he remained evasive about his experience with the denomination. Donna and I
trekked north to pay homage to Jeff Campbell. A part-time minister in Brattleboro and full-time teacher at the rustic, ramshackle
Putney School in Vermont, he regaled us with colorful yarns and
old labor union songs. So it was that I came to know my remark-
ably perseverant predecessors, whose spirits shone, often through
bitter stories.

Out of this pilgrimage came my action plan for serving in
the ministry, a doctoral thesis entitled "Black Pioneers in a White
Denomination." It posed two questions: Given my chosen voca-
tion as a minister in a white denomination, how can I serve the
black community? And, second, how can I inform the Unitarian
Universalist tradition through the black experience? Answering
these questions helped prepare me to serve in a religious movement that was 97.5 percent white, as the eighteenth black minister
since 1888, and only the second regularly settled Afro-American
reared within the faith.

Donna, in typical punctual fashion, had finished and defended
her dissertation before the end of March; was ordained by the
Mount Vernon Unitarian Church on April 1; gave birth to our
daughter, Charlotte, a month later; and six days after that participated in my ordination by the First Unitarian Society of Chicago.
Not surprisingly, since she had recently spent thirty-six hours in
labor and given birth at 3:00 a.m., she felt faint during the ordination, and in the middle of the invocation randomly chose a sentence, spoke it with finality, and sat down.

We were anxious to get settled and move on with our life, but it
had been nearly ten years since Mwalimu Imara had gone through
the settlement process, and no one knew how long it would take,
or even if an oddity like us could be settled. The UUA submitted
our names to a half dozen congregations. One in Woodstock, Vermont, was interested, but we heard not a word from three other
New England congregations. A fellow seminarian whose name,
like ours, had been sent to the First Unitarian Society of Exeter,

New Hampshire, returned exasperated. "They couldn't deal with me as a woman. You two better forget it," she said.

In May we flew to Evansville, Indiana, to interview for a position. Evansville lies across the Ohio River from Union County, Kentucky, where Donna's mother's family, the Longs, had settled in 1837. A black couple to whom we were introduced counseled that if we had a sense of humor and didn't mind being seated at the rear of the restaurant, we would do fine in "River City," a town that had been a hotbed of Ku Klux Klan activities in the twenties. This was a lot to ask for a halftime position. The visit went well and they wanted us. Fortunately, the First Universalist Church of Rochester, New York, wanted us as well—a hundred-fifty-member congregation that included four black members, an Anglo/Hispanic couple and their two children, and one white family that had adopted a black child.

Universalism was founded in the eighteenth century and, like Unitarianism, was a reaction against the Puritan portrayal of God as angry, righteous, and ready to assign all but the elect to eternal damnation. Universalism offered instead a God of Love, who, as one preacher proclaimed, would "drag the last sinner kicking and screaming into heaven." However, by the time the Universalists merged with the Unitarians in 1961 to form the Unitarian Universalist Association, they had become a religion focused less on God and more on the global family of humanity, the inherent worth and dignity of each person, and social justice.

On Friday, August 13, we left behind Hyde Park: the hospital where I was born, the church I grew up in, my parents' townhouse, U-High, the U of C Divinity School, Meadville Lombard, and O'Gara's, where I had stalked used books. We drove south down Stony Island and up onto the Skyway that arches over Chicago, and then east toward Rochester. The faulty Ryder truck was filled with boxes of books, hand-me-down furniture, and, between us in her car seat, our well-traveled three-month-old, Charlotte.

As I lugged another box of books through the side door of First Universalist, quirky George Solomon, the church member whose bulk was holding the door open, mused "You know, if the church doesn't make it, it won't be your fault." Mr. Porridge—that's what George called himself—must have surmised from my reaction that he had been too obtuse. He elaborated. The congregation's future was the members' responsibility. Donna and I were not called to save them from a declining membership and dwindling endowment, or to rescue their historic building with its leaking roofs, crumbling mortar, sagging Tiffany windows, and wheezing organ. We weren't called to succeed, but rather to serve to the best of our ability. Offered midway through the first hour of our first day as their ministers, this wise counsel from a rabbi's grandson was wasted on me.

Inauspiciously, we had arrived four hours late, after the transmission in our rental truck seized up in Jamestown, New York, but the congregation was still there waiting to help us unload. We were untested yet eager; they were desperate enough to call us right out of school, something the congregation had never done before. Nor had they ever hired a woman, a black, or a couple. Now they had all three. They were taking a risk. We were relieved to be employed.

When our books were finally stacked in our office and our belongings stored in the basement, we retired to our studio apartment at the Chestnut Arms Hotel—our home for the next three months. We had unpacked our suitcases, eaten, gotten Charlotte to sleep, and were reassembling her playpen when the phone rang. Who would call us at 10:30 on our first night in Rochester? It was the president of the congregation. My mother had called, wanting to wish Donna a happy birthday. We were shocked. How had Mother gotten hold of his number? Then it came to me that I had left it with her during our first visit three months earlier. It was typical of Mother—cute, thoughtful, and intrusive. As usual, I wanted to pass the incident off; Donna, however, was incensed.

Donna and Mother had never gotten along and never would. The first battlefield had been our wedding. While Donna's parents were threatening to boycott, Mother first cajoled, then argued with us over how many friends she could invite. Since she knew half of

Chicago, she couldn't live with the twenty-five invitations we had allocated. We had wanted a small wedding and ended up inviting hundreds. Moving to D.C. provided a year's respite from Mother's intrusiveness, but when we returned, it started again. Sunday dinners were tolerable, but on our second wedding anniversary Mother had called seven times to invite us to celebrate it *with her*. She was out of control, and it was wearing.

Our first day in Rochester was the wrong day for Mother's zealous caring. What a nightmare—Mother calling our church members. Even six hundred miles didn't faze her. What would be her next excuse? Donna told me that there was no way my mother was going to insinuate herself in our congregation. "Call her right now."

I called. Mother asked for Donna. "No! Donna ... does ... not ... want ... to ... talk ... to ... you," I said.

"Tell her," Donna mouthed from across the room. With Donna glaring at me, my demand stuttered forth: Never ever again call one of our church members for any reason whatsoever. Then, with Mother's anxious apologies filling my ear, I hung up.

Since I was a rank coward, the situation between Mother and Donna reached an impasse. The harder Mother tried, the more intrusive Donna found her. The angrier and more distant Donna grew, the harder Mother tried. As one member of First Unitarian in Chicago said, "There wasn't a person that could get away from Lee." But that was before Mother's controlling style ran into Donna's battle-honed defense. What a volatile mixture. Donna responded to Mother's invasion with confrontation. This was the strength that had attracted me to her in the first place. Now I found it impossible. And as clash followed clash, my anxiety soared. I knew what both my wife and my mother wanted but I couldn't figure out where I stood. "To thine own self be true" was Mother's mantra, and she had repeated it to us hundreds of times. This line from *Hamlet* seemed to embody both her lifelong struggle and my own. I agonized over what being true to myself might mean, but in this circumstance I could not find an answer. When it became clear that their mutual desires were incompatible, instead of taking charge, I equivocated. Unable to accommodate or flee, I became evasive.

We started our ministry in Rochester estranged from my meddlesome mother. And though we lived only sixty miles as the crow flies from Toronto, the emotional distance between Donna and her parents soon grew into a chasm. In the summer of 1980, at the end of our first year of ministry, we happened to be visiting the Morrison's when Donna's sister Leslie called and told their mother she was engaged. Delivering the happy news to us, Katherine's eyes danced and her face radiated joy. Seeing how enraptured she was, we couldn't help but remember her response to our engagement— the hue and cry, the letters, the visits. The contrast was more than we could endure; we packed and left, and before the end of the year had reason to cut them off completely.

The truth was, Donna's parents would have been happy if our relationship had ended—later they would confess this outright. Intent on helping it dissolve, they invited Donna to visit Toronto without me. She refused. They made apocalyptic predictions: Our children would never be accepted by whites or blacks. Donna stopped communicating. They sent Christmas presents to Charlotte. Donna returned them unopened.

Meanwhile my mother's health deteriorated. As her illness progressed, the acrimony between her and Dad decreased, but my relationship with my family worsened. Mother shared with Philip and Carole her unhappiness over our alienation. They responded by attacking me. Philip phoned in a pugnacious mood, calling me a hypocrite, and threatening to expose my callousness to my congregation. Carole called as well, assailing me with an aggressiveness honed in law school. Calling me a racist, she interpreted our setting limits on Mother's behavior as cutting her off. "You're choosing white ways over black," she charged. "Black people always pull together in a crisis," she said. "We have to pull together because the world out there is hostile."

They couldn't see that the issue involved neither my lack of caring nor racism, that handy indictment. The situation was actually a rerun of our family history of weak, absent, or broken men unable to fend off powerful, domineering matriarchs—a remnant of historic necessity. Strong wandering providers like the Captain and John Thomas Newman had chosen strong wives like Sarah and Mary Elizabeth, who bound the family together, directing and protecting it. The boys, raised by these commanding women in their husbands' absences, became dutiful providers like my grandfathers. "Grandmother was a stickler who ran a tight ship and you had better toe the mark or you'd get slapped," Dad said of Sarah. Regarding his other grandmother, Mary Elizabeth, he said, "She was a tough cookie and nobody crossed her." These women, like a runaway slave mother suffocating her fretting infant to keep the band of fugitives from being captured, slew their sons' gumption. The accommodating, quiescent men they bred worked for the federal government, one as a clerk, the other as a postal worker, surviving in an era when an overly assertive black man wouldn't have. These sons, in turn, married strong women who were driven to see their families prosper. The big lie was that these men were in charge, when to the contrary they simply became compliant husbands. This then left two generations of women reared to rule and expecting to be obeyed, vying for power over their sons and husbands.

Great-uncle Harry told me that my great-grandmother Sarah "was bossy and so was your grandmother and they didn't get on none too well. That's for sure." I had surmised as much from one of Grammy's oft-told stories. Sarah had written to her son, my grandfather, pressuring him to send her some money, but with three children he and Grammy barely had enough to get by. He was unwilling to say no to his mother and unable to say yes, and the stress was tearing him apart. Grammy didn't know about the letter, but sensing something was wrong, pressed until he told of his mother's appeal. Grammy wrote to Sarah immediately and laid down the law: "Don't you ever ask George for money again." The steel in Grammy's eyes whenever she repeated that story reminded me of Donna.

I had done the same thing my father and his father had done. Granddad moved to D.C. and married a woman strong-willed enough to protect him. Dad, another eldest son, married a woman skilled enough to fend off his mother, and moved from D.C. to New York City and then Chicago, where he withdrew into unlocking the secrets of the universe. I, yet another eldest son, married a woman assertive enough to keep my mother at bay, and moved away. Faced with emotionally domineering mothers we fled, and thus fed a rivalry between mother and daughter-in-law that is as old as marriage itself—a feud desperately needed and slyly encouraged by men who lacked the courage to say no to their mothers. Yet all my siblings could see through their own anxiety was malice and racism.

During the last years of Mother's life, paralysis beset me. My dual desires to flee conflict and yet be close, rendered me powerless. Naturally, Grammy intervened. Her observation was the obvious one. "Mark," she said, "you won't be able to live with yourself if your mother dies and you aren't on speaking terms." I came to a compromise that I would never talk to Donna about conversations with Mother, nor to Mother about Donna, to travel to Chicago on my own or with the children, to make sure my parents' stays in Rochester were fleeting, and to accept that Mother and Donna would never have a comfortable relationship. As it turned out, it mattered less and less as Mother's cancer progressed.

Mother lived with cancer for twenty-one years. At her memorial service in 1985, the Chicago Children's Choir sang and 1 Corinthians 13 was read. Her friends offered tributes, and so did the mayor of Chicago, Harold Washington. An imposing black man in both girth and presence, he recalled how Mother had hounded him when he was a member of the Illinois State Legislature, until Martin Luther King Jr.'s birthday was declared a state holiday; then she began working to make it national. The hundreds who attended the memorial made up as diverse a group as you could imagine—young and old, black, white, yellow, and brown—and, in accordance with her instructions, we wore nametags, talked, and drank cases of wine as we celebrated her life.

After the service we arrived back in Rochester the day before our Thanksgiving Sunday service. In a daze, I sat through it and, fortunately, my only responsibility was to deliver the prayer. Right before I rose to step into the pulpit, I scribbled down a few words, then stood, and said something not particularly coherent. I was headed for trouble.

Just before Christmas, I conducted a funeral for a man I didn't know—a suicide. He was father of three and black.

Winter came.

Spring was only days away when Gwen, a young single mother, the granddaughter of one of First Universalist's few black church members, slipped while taking a shower in the tub, hit her head, and drowned. As I sat at my desk composing Gwen's eulogy, the phone rang. It was George Solomon's wife, Joan. Over the six years we had been in Rochester, Mr. Porridge had become one of my best friends in the congregation. She told me he had had an epileptic seizure during the night and died of a heart attack.

I forced myself through Gwen's memorial service, then rushed across town to comfort Joan. I came in the back door, turned a corner, and seeing her in the front vestibule, I spread my arms and collapsed, sobbing, into hers.

Joan held the wake in their home. George was laid out in the living room by the east window. His brother Ray, who like George had a weird and wonderful sense of humor, gave me a bear hug when Donna and I arrived. Then he and I went over to the coffin and somberly knelt. I stared. George didn't look right, and it wasn't because he was dead. His dark hair had been combed straight, his perpetual five-o'clock shadow was missing, his shirt collar buttoned, his tie in a neat knot, and he was wearing a three-piece suit—I didn't know he had one. I had never seen George look so sharp.

"Ray," I said, "this is too strange. George never looked this slick before."

Ray was on my wavelength. Quick as a flash, he nudged me and whispered, "You're right. You hold him down. I'll undo his tie."

We laughed so hard we would have toppled off the kneeling bench if we hadn't had our arms wrapped around one another.

That moment of levity was an exception. Somehow I made it through George's memorial service, but I didn't know if I could make it through another. I couldn't cope with any more death and didn't see how I could offer others comfort when I needed so much consoling myself. The question couldn't be avoided: Could I remain in the ministry?

A minister might be expected to pray for fortitude, and I did, but I also entered therapy, and as I talked it wasn't long before we came upon my first great loss—the death of my maternal grandfather, George Edwards.

He was a slight man, kind and quiet with long, straight but thinning white hair. He lived nearby at the Wabash YMCA in Chicago. He was retired and available to take care of me, which he did. As he grew older, he became confused and frail—more and more often Mother would whisper to me as she was leaving that I was to look out for him. Late in the fall of 1957, when I was eight, he was admitted to Michael Reese Hospital. Their regulations prevented me from visiting, but my parents would point to his window when we drove past.

He died in December and the funeral took place in Wilkes-Barre. Our parents went, leaving us in Chicago. Soon afterward, as we prepared for our Christmas visit to D.C., we drove past the hospital and I asked, "Isn't Granddad coming to Washington with us?"

In therapy I started crying again and haven't stopped.

A month after George Solomon's death, Donna, Charlotte, Elliot—our second child, now three years old—and I drove to D.C. to celebrate Charlotte's seventh birthday. We had been spending May Day, her birthday, in D.C. since she turned four. Great-aunt Irene would be turning ninety-seven on May 7, and Grammy would reach eighty-nine on May 19.

As usual, anticipation filled me as we wound south through the Appalachian Mountains, along the Susquehanna River, past Gettysburg, onto the beltway, and down Georgia Avenue. We did what we always did—visited the Smithsonian museums, saw cousins, had a big birthday party—and I, as I loved to do, listened to Great-aunt Irene tell her tales. She loved to tell them as much as I loved to hear them; some she had written down in her diaries and she had shown me where these were hidden.

During this last visit, Great-aunt Irene spoke about my mother. "Child," she said, "Your mother was such a lovely girl we were glad to have her in the family, and you know, I told her mama that I'd look after Lee. Yes, I did, and the Lord knows I tried." She spoke with compassion, a feeling, which until then, I had resisted. If anything, I felt ambivalent about Mother's death, for my grief was entwined with relief—Mother was released from her pain and I from her incursions into my life, or so I thought.

Mother's health had never been good. She had tuberculosis in 1953 when Carole was born and remained in the hospital for several months thereafter. Other health problems included a chronically infected kidney, the cancer, a hysterectomy, and the manic depression. Besides having four children to raise, she had her failing father to look after, and poor uncle Max, whom she had tried so hard to help. Great-aunt Irene shook her head. "Yes siree, the good Lord knows I did the best I could by her," she said, sounding like she had completed yet another duty.

The morning we left D.C., I gave Great-aunt Irene a hug and a kiss, then walked down the stairs, crossed S Street, and opened the car door. I looked back. She was standing on the top landing waving good-bye, while 114 loomed behind her frail, bent figure. I waved back.

This might be the last time, a voice within said.

I left Donna and the kids sitting in the car, walked back across the street, bounded up the stairs two at a time, and hugged her again. Instead of my head being buried in her bosom, as it had been so long ago, I felt hers resting on my chest. I held her with a firm tenderness, trying to hold on for all eternity.

Early that autumn, Great-aunt Irene fell while coming downstairs from the second floor, and after remaining in a coma for over a month, she died on October 19, 1986. "Ask her how she was," Donna said in her eulogy, "and you would always hear the same answer: 'I have no just right to complain. The Lord has been good to me. He surely has.'"

Our home on Crosman Terrace faced Pinnacle Hill, a wooded moraine, and as fall progressed I watched the colorful collage through our picture window—shimmering orange and vibrant yellows translucent in the sun's rays, crimson and mauve, and purple dark as shade. I watched as each day the range of color lessened, until brown, bent, and arthritic, the leaves barely held on; then I watched their merciful release and zigzag descent. When the wind stirred I would hear the sound of those still clinging—a sort of death rattle—and see the fallen fly up, giving substance to the air. And when only the shriveled remnants remained, my rake made crisp, crackling mounds along the curb.

Who watches leaves in autumn after their peak has passed and their color gone? I did. I couldn't keep myself from watching, and staring at the bare branches and silent, dark trunks, I thought about death. Every fresh loss tapped into earlier losses, every pang a reminder, until grief turned into a source of strength and tears became the companion of loving and letting go.

Although grief at first threatened my ministry, in the end it saved it. Living with loss reminded me that the church was a place that I had repeatedly turned to in pain; where, having gone, I was cared for; where cared for, I could heal and move on. Grief led me to reaffirm my calling. I had chosen ministry in order to help sustain religious community—a place made holy by what people experience there—the seasons of their lives and the healing of their souls.

Whenever I return to Chicago to visit Dad, I make time for Art Perkins, my college compatriot. Art lives in the moment—unencumbered by ambition, without interest in status, untouched by angst about tomorrow. A life very different from my own, his is uncomplicated, almost monastic, a situation neither of us imagined when, ruminating night after night in Switzerland, we envisioned our futures.

If Art has a suit, I've never seen it—not at my wedding, nor my ordination, nor my mother's memorial service. He really has no use for anything more than an old sports jacket and the bolo tie he puts on to dress up. Beyond his harmonicas, tools, and bicycle, he doesn't seem to need material things. He is self-employed as a restorer and refinisher of antique furniture. He works for enough to pay the rent, feed himself, and put a little away for retirement. His pleasures are simple: He attends church, hunts for arrowheads, and plays in a blues band. Without guile or pretense, he welcomes the world with a wry smile and soft chuckle. He's living the life he set out to find when he graduated from Beloit. And yet his semi-ascetic path has sometimes left him feeling deficient. Only after nearly dying did he come to accept himself, and I to realize how much I love him.

"It was Christmas Eve," Art said, recounting what happened. Late as usual, he stuffed a backpack full of the wooden toys he had made for children at church. He hopped on his bike and started off. There was no wind or traffic, just a light dusting of snow. He saw his reflection in a shop window and felt like Santa Claus. The next thing he remembered, it was morning. As he faded in and out of consciousness, he heard his sister speaking to him. He was in a hospital bed. She sat beside him. His shoulder was dislocated. He had several broken ribs, a missing eyebrow, a concussion, and a ruptured artery in his head that could have killed him. "Yeah, I would have gone to sleep big time," he said and chuckled. He thought it was a hit-and-run, but the memory has been lost. What he did discover is how much he is loved; people's outpouring surprised him, but not me.

I always find it difficult to say good-bye to Art. One time I felt flushed, as if I had fallen in love. Maybe I had, because when we hugged as I was leaving my eyes brimmed with tears. The time I visited him after the accident it was more difficult to leave than ever before. I saw that to lose him would be to lose part of myself. That evening I didn't hug, I clung.

Art has been there when I needed him. The day I delivered my first sermon, he drove me from Chicago to Peoria, while I anxiously tinkered with the text. He was there the day Donna and I got married—I saw him slip in after the service had begun. Two years later, he participated in my ordination at the First Unitarian Society of Chicago, offering his version of how I came to enter the ministry. Art was there for Mother's memorial service, and he wore his sports coat. The miles between us are many, but they mean nothing, and while he is white and I am black, between us that means nothing either.

Bright banners bearing symbols of the world's religions signaled First Universalist's effort to be inclusive, while the worn green carpet, eggshell blue walls, and wooden pews gave the domed sanctuary a warm, earthy ambience. I would scan those pews every Sunday searching for black faces and counting them—I couldn't help it. I did this everywhere. I had to know how many. Spy even one person of color and I relaxed a little, although I couldn't have told you why.

Looking out from the pulpit I saw two black families. Actually, I could hear Mattie, the matriarch of the Lawson clan, long before she swept into the second row with her sister, daughter, and grandchildren. They had been attending since the sixties, before urban renewal had forced them out of a nearby tenement. And there was mellow, chain-smoking Bob, a high-school guidance counselor whose family accompanied him only on Christmas Eve. He was sweet, independent and, as a black Republican, a rare breed in 1979.

First Universalist was not nearly as integrated as my home church. Knowing how few black Unitarian Universalists there are I didn't expect it to be, but I hoped we could move in that direction. So it was a good omen when in August 1982 Ryan and Elliot were born. Elliot was our second child, and Ryan, days older, arrived second since he was flown in from Korea. Ryan's parents, Ron and Tikki, were church members for whom we had submitted a reference letter and been interviewed by a social worker. UU congregations, already a home for many mixed religious marriages and interracial couples, also became a natural haven for cultural mavericks who adopt transracially.

Having gone through this experience with Ron and Tikki, I figured I knew about international adoption. So, two years later, after months of attending the toddler swim class at the YMCA with Dave Ferguson and his daughter Emiko, my patience ran out. I had waited and waited, hoping Dave would offer an opportunity for me to ask about Emiko's adoption. He hadn't.

"Hey, how old was Emiko when she arrived?" I queried, when he and Emiko came wet and naked out of the shower.

"Seconds," he replied. My open mouth and cocked head told him I had missed his point. "My wife is Japanese." I blushed. "How old was Elliot when you adopted him?" he asked.

"Well, my wife is white," I said.

Once the laughter subsided, we began trading locker-room stories. Dave said that all the months I had been looking at Emiko and him, he had been wondering about Elliot and me. In Dave's eyes, blond Elliot and I looked so completely different that he had figured he didn't need to ask, because Elliot was clearly adopted. Besides, he knew what it was like. People were always asking about Emiko. One co-worker had blurted out, "How much did she cost?" He thought, *Well, I had to sleep with her mother.* But he said, "free" and left it at that. Not wanting to offend me, he hadn't said anything, since the most obvious and important thing was that we were father and son. Anyway, in the back of his mind, he knew that one day I would broach the topic of Emiko's adoption.

I told him about our friends Karen and David Yano, and the time Donna and I experimented with parenting by taking their four-year-old daughter, Kay, home with us. Everywhere we went that weekend, I noticed people who looked first at this cute Asian child, then at Donna, then at me; then with quizzical looks, they started all over again. "Dave," I said, "it was as if a program in their brain was saying 'Does not compute.'"

Dave told me about people's incredible preoccupation with what mixed children look like. I told him about my visit to Como, Italy, where the villagers mistook my Swedish friend's white infant for our baby, and kept strolling across the piazza to steal a peek. He told me that even his own parents kept remarking on how Asian Emiko looked, while his wife's parents couldn't get over how Caucasian she looked. "All I cared about," he sighed, "was that she was a happy, healthy baby."

I knew exactly what he meant. "Why does your child look so white?" someone had asked, following Charlotte's birth. Flabbergasted, I had shrugged and mumbled something about my mother being fair-skinned. But after that first time I was prepared: "Guess I have weak genes," or "You know Donna. Her super-strong genes must have overpowered mine." A few times I quipped, "Guess I'm an Oreo." But white folks never got it. And what no one dared to suggest but some must have thought was that Charlotte wasn't really my child. A few baffled souls even thought it appropriate to express their condolences: "Too bad your baby doesn't look more like you." Actually Charlotte and Elliot look very much like me if you ignore the color of their skin. But obviously that's what people noticed. "It's all in the genes. Maybe next time?" I'd muse. Of course, everyone stopped commenting when Elliot came out looking pretty much like his sister Charlotte.

People who saw me with my children simply couldn't make sense of it, and when they tried to make us fit their take on the world, they found no category to put us in. They knew some categories: a white woman with a beige-skinned child equals mixed marriage, a dark-complexioned woman tending a white child equals nanny, a white man with Asian child equals adoption, and the last could be stretched to include a white man and a black child. But there was no niche in anyone's mind for a black man walking around carrying a blond, white-looking child. When I took either one of them to the mall other people's perceptions inevitably accosted us. When Charlotte or Elliot weren't holding my hand, people simply couldn't conceive of our being related. If I let them experiment

with independence and walk a little ahead of me, even if only a
few feet, some well-intentioned white lady would invariably swoop
down upon these poor, lost toddlers. In the early eighties, it was
not yet a common sight to see men looking after toddlers in the
middle of the day, and black men never have white children, so
there could be only one conclusion. There was no context in which
this relationship could exist. During outings I actually came to rel-
ish counting how many "do-gooders" I would have to fend off with
a strong "Thank you very much; the child is mine."

I suppose if the kids had been a shade darker than a summer tan
it would have spared me some awkward moments, but for them I
simply hoped that with enough love, and the security of a supportive community, they would do fine. If anything, I was more curious
than anxious about the kinds of identities they would develop in a
post-"black is beautiful" era, when integration, at least tacitly, had
become the norm. Charlotte, Elliot, Emiko, Ryan, and Art's multiracial niece Becky were growing up outside the old well-defined
racial categories—artificial labels that were beginning to collapse.
Whatever they might face, I was certain their struggles would be
different from my own.

Following the announcement of Donna's sister's engagement,
the Morrisons quickly added insult to injury by vetoing Leslie's
wish that Donna perform her wedding ceremony. Not wanting
to damage our relationship to her sister, we showed up, sat stoi-
cally through the ceremony, then cut her parents out of our life.
A year and a half passed, and Donna was pregnant with Elliot
when an unanticipated intervention arranged by Leslie brought
Donna's family together. No one really wanted to be sitting in a
psychiatrist's office—not her petulant, opinion-spewing father or
her long-suffering mother, not her indignant sister who'd arrived
with a pouting husband in tow or her twitching brother—but the
alternative was complete estrangement. Stone-faced Donna, ever
wary of her parents' motives, expected the intervention to fail. I
was uptight. And knowing my tendency to turn into a chatterbox,

Donna cautioned me not to talk too much. So instead, I sat there grinning like Stepin Fetchit. The psychiatrist urged us to tell our stories. The Morrisons confessed that they would have been pleased if our marriage had failed and had done their best to sabotage it. We confirmed that we wouldn't have anything to do with them if they continued to attack our relationship—in other words, no contact with the grandchildren. Leslie was peeved that her wedding had been dragged into the feud. Listening, it dawned on me that her wedding fiasco hadn't been about race, but about the control these pigheaded parents were trying to exert on their adult children's lives. I had stumbled into a well-established family drama; race was the excuse, not the reason. Donna and I hadn't seen this because we had naïvely latched on to the obvious explanation, the one they kept repeating—race, race, race. Having allowed the issue to be reduced to race, we missed the truth.

The go-around continued, and when my turn came, I expressed frustration and confusion. I explained that Katherine—always cordial, warm, and motherly when she visited—had conveyed an unspoken expectation that I would reciprocate. And I, craving acceptance, did so. She would leave appearing reassured, but soon the phone conversations would grow awkward again, then downright weird and full of increasingly frantic warnings about interracial relationships, as if her visit hadn't taken place. As the intervention continued, I became more convinced that race wasn't the primary issue; it was only the focus of displaced anxiety.

Then Katherine, in an attempt to prove she wasn't prejudiced, told about the most significant Afro-American in her life—her family's housekeeper, a woman of particular importance due to Katherine's past. She was an only child whose upbringing had included being shut in a closet when the truant officer came to make her mother's "baby" go to school. She would lie curled up in bed listening to her schizophrenic mother and alcoholic father tear into each other; and hear the siren of the ambulance taking her mother away in the night. How easy to imagine this little girl sitting on their black housekeeper's lap, soaking up all the maternal affection and emotional stability no one else was able to offer. As Katherine ended with her customary melancholy sigh, it struck me that some of the positive feelings she felt for this black woman had been transferred to me. This explained the mixed messages. For she also spoke as someone raised in the twenties and thirties, an era when Jim Crow reigned and segregation was the norm. She spoke as someone who had invited an Afro-American friend to her wedding—an invitation she withdrew when her Kentucky-bred father threatened not to attend if her friend did. She spoke as someone who moved to Canada in 1951, three years prior to the U.S. Supreme Court ruling that ended legal school segregation and four years before the Montgomery bus boycott. She had departed the U.S. when the civil rights movement was nascent and integration a distant dream. Overwhelmed with feelings of dread that made her impervious to our reality, she had written to us, "If only I felt that you knew what you were up against. . . ."

Many would call Katherine racist, and dismissing her as such, would care little about the wounds that fed her attitude. But racism is too pat an answer. She was someone fending off unbearable feelings, feelings of shame and, above all, terror. Shame about how she had treated her girlfriend and how she was treating us. And terror of a taboo deep-rooted in her Southern heritage, amplified by the neediness of someone whose lonely childhood was spent with a truly crazy, often institutionalized, mother. Projecting her abiding fear and early loneliness onto her children and grandchildren, she wanted to spare them and, unconsciously, herself, from intense anxiety. She longed for normalcy—a compulsion that wouldn't accommodate an Afro-American son-in-law. Rather than face the truth about her own life and deal with feelings that were emotionally threatening, she made race the problem. And the solution was to get rid of me.

That afternoon, when the incongruity finally began to make sense, I felt some of my apprehension drain away. Reconciliation requires truth, for truth-telling creates a relational foundation that people can rely on, while denial, falsehood, and avoidance undermine authentic connection. Exposing our wounds to one another, which is what we do when we share our stories, evokes compassion and builds trust. When we trust, we become more willing to risk, and one cannot love without risking, for love asks that you enter into another's experience.

Toward the end of the session, Donna's father offered that the day had only been a beginning and that the hard work lay ahead. Whether it would succeed we didn't know.

Sometimes my race means everything, and sometimes it means nothing. And sometimes I delude myself.

I believe that when one soul encounters another, race is a tissue, a thin rather than substantive barrier. The dying don't care about the color of my skin when I hold their hand. The suicidal don't reject my counsel because I am black. My bleary-eyed jogging partners couldn't care less as we groan about our aches and pains, our children and spouses. Days go by when the thought I am a black man never crosses my mind. Sometimes I am allowed to be simply me—beyond categories and characterization. Still, serving in the ministry, I never knew when one of my white parishioners, someone I had known for years, would surprise me. Suddenly something hidden would grab me by the collar yet again.

One evening, having skipped dinner, I was lying in bed with a fever when a call came from a church member. "Mark? Please come. There's been a fight. Peter's in his room and won't come out. Hurry, please!"

Five minutes later I was in my car, ten minutes after that at their front door. I knocked. It opened. There was a fist-sized hole in the stairwell wall.

I talked to the parents. I talked to Peter. I comforted his sobbing sister. I coaxed him downstairs. We all talked. I got them to listen to one another. We worked out a plan of action. I forgot I was burning up.

When it was time to go I hugged the wife and she confessed, "I could never have imagined being held by a black man before."

Suddenly I was not there; I had shifted out of my body. I was looking down on this white woman and black man standing in the middle of the living room. *What the hell is going on?* I had not thought of my skin color or theirs for one instant. *What does my being black have to do with anything?*

I half heard her explain something about her childhood, some story about her father's extreme prejudice, a story she needed to tell. But at that moment, I was unable to listen. *Why now? What is she really saying?*

She had broken through some barrier, some barrier I hadn't realized existed. She called me, trusted me, and the emotional dissonance had educated her—and me.

I mouthed a quiet thank-you, offered a sad smile, said an awkward farewell, and stepped out the door. Settling into my car, I shook my head more at the absurdity of it all than in bitterness. As I backed down the driveway, I glanced at the clock. It was nearly midnight. Abruptly aware that I was in a white suburb, I kept an eye out for the police as I drove home.

Who Was Alicia McCuller?

This above all: to thine own self be true.

—William Shakespeare, *Hamlet*

Being black meant everything and nothing, and more in others' eyes than in my own. It meant everything because I brought my black experience and perspective to every encounter. It meant nothing in moments of human intimacy. Therefore it meant more in my community work than it did in the routine of everyday church life.

Living out my faith in the world at large was important to me and I was committed to finding ways to be relevant to the black community. True to my upbringing in a home where my parents were perpetually attending meetings, I jumped into the Rochester political scene. Good works to prove to myself that I was really okay and really black.

The United Church Ministries (UCM), a coalition of more than fifty predominantly black Rochester churches, met in the basement of New Bethel C.M.E. Zion Church. The chief of the Rochester Police Department (RPD), Delmar Leach, had requested this particular meeting, and brought the former chief, Bob Hastings, along. They were white; everyone else was black. The turnout was better than normal, but as usual, none of the town's black female ministers appeared at this male enclave. Rev. Raymond Graves, pastor of New Bethel and president of UCM, called us to order.

Chief Leach had come seeking support for the consolidation of the local police departments into a countywide force. The atmosphere was cordial, and consensus easily reached on two points: that the RPD had significantly improved since implementing the recommendations of a task force established in 1975 after a police officer had fatally shot a young black woman; and that consolidation would improve the city's financial situation. However, there was one major reservation—the prospect of having suburban police officers, from forces known to harass blacks, patrolling the city was a non-starter. Shifting them into our neighborhoods was unacceptable. On this we were unanimous, and only after Chief Leach pledged that this wouldn't happen did UCM endorsed the plan.

Hovering on its margins, I yearned to be more connected to the black community. So when Bill Johnson, who had attended Howard University with my UU colleague Thom Payne, befriended me, I was thankful. Bill was well respected, outspoken, and in the middle of political action in Rochester. As the executive director of the Rochester Urban League, the man who would be future mayor of Rochester knew what was happening. One day as we walked back to First Universalist after sharing a meal together I asked the question that scared me most: "Hey! What do you think the UCM ministers make of me?" "Man," Bill said, "they look at you leading a bunch of white non-Christians with your white wife to boot, and they don't know what to make of you. You might as well be from the moon." I had known it in my heart, and I could have grieved over it, but there was nothing I could do about it except face reality and find a way to be supportive of the black mainstream while remaining on its fringe.

A way presented itself when Robert France, chair of the Monroe County Human Relations Commission, invited me to join the group. Among the commissioners were ex-pro basketball player Dick Ricketts, director of personnel at Kodak, and Will Sprattling, a vice president at Xerox. I grabbed at the chance, only to find the old hippie in me nearly as ill at ease among these corporate types as I had been with UCM.

Willie Davis, the commission's executive director, had walnut-brown skin. This only registered with me because the contrast between he and both Sprattling and Ricketts was stark. Sprattling was so fair that Donna, who doesn't notice that sort of thing, didn't realize he was black—and both he and Ricketts would have passed the brown paper bag test.

Reading the nuances of skin color was something I had learned to do long before I understood its roots in slavery. White masters had to determine whom to trust, and chose those with light skin and white blood—often their own. In addition, white masters would sometimes grant both freedom and land to their mulatto offspring. Being thus favored and given access to the house was advantageous for the few, but created a barrier of distrust between them and the slaves laboring in the fields. Great-aunt Irene told us that her mother wasn't allowed to associate with what they called the field hands. "To her they were just ordinary, common people," Great-aunt Irene said. "And when anyone black came around, well, Mama was very prejudiced." Perpetuated by attitudes like my great-grandmother's, a fair-skinned Afro-American middle class emerged and fostered a color phobia that too often affected blacks' relationships with one another. This dynamic still plays out: Insiders, those with access to the white establishment, are more often than not light skinned, like Sprattling and Ricketts. Nor is it surprising, given my own upbringing, that I eventually came to fit into the commission in a way I didn't at UCM. Those outside the establishment were often darker, less middle class, and freer in their condemnation of the status quo. In Rochester, foremost among these was Jim McCuller, the executive director of Action for a Better Community (ABC).

Barely a week after the referendum on police consolidation was defeated by the suburban voters, another shooting brought the rapprochement of the United Church Ministries and the Rochester Police Department to an abrupt end.

Following a night spent partying at an after-hours club, Alicia McCuller had returned home, where she had a violent argument with her boyfriend, who'd been babysitting her six-year-old son. She sent her son out to phone 911. As the police arrived, her boyfriend was backing out the front door. She followed, hunting knife in hand. He fled. She gave chase. They yelled at her to drop the knife. One officer, trying to knock the knife loose with his nightstick, slipped on the icy street and fell. Then the boyfriend slipped and fell, but her headlong charge after him continued until, when she was barely two feet away, the second officer fired twice. Alicia died instantly, and her son, having witnessed it all, sat on the curb crying, "I want my mommy."

My jogging partner, Alan, a cynical white liberal, was the first to tell me. "Couldn't stop a ninety-eight-pound woman without killing her," he snarled. Ready to be outraged, I listened. Instead, the plain facts described a tragedy, and I felt more despair than anger—until I heard that she was Jim McCuller's daughter. Dread gripped me. Shit was going to hit the fan. I knew there would be a call to action, and the call came: a rally at the Central Church of Christ. Alarms went off, warning me to stay away, but I had to go. I wrestled with the decision as I had on the day I'd been throttled by Mike Young at Beloit. This time, however, I persuaded myself that other matters were more pressing. I stayed away—any excuse would have done, any reason to help me avoid the truth that I was terrified that one of the UCM ministers would call me to the pulpit. Addressing that emotionally charged sanctuary, what would I say?

Let us pray to the God who dwells within, among and beyond us all. Let us take all those who this tragedy has touched into our hearts. Let us ask the questions we do not dare ask. What of Alicia and the pain and despair that fueled her rage? What of Robert Ralph, her boyfriend, whose life hung in the balance? What of Officer Whitmore, who certainly responded to the call hoping to do good? And what of Alicia's son, Ryan, whose loss is beyond imagining, but we hope, with God's mercy, not beyond healing? O Solomon, guide us toward justice. O Jesus, fill us with your love. O Lord, let the healing of a community torn asunder begin. Help us to mourn our loss rather than rush to judgment. Alicia is dead, and tonight it is grief that unites us. Amen.

Had I dared to utter such an honestly worded, circumspect prayer, they would have spurned me afterward. No way. Any pretext to stay away would have done; anything to keep from being unmasked because I refused to condemn the sacrificial villain. "No more Whitmore" became the rallying cry, but I wasn't going near it. Better to be silenced by my fear and insecurity than reviled; anything to avoid having my blackness called into question again.

The next morning, as usual, my running partner appeared. Right away, he began regurgitating yesterday's rant. "She was only ninety-eight pounds. Just a woman and they couldn't stop her. Had to kill her," he said as we shuffled along.

I had had it. "Give it a break, will you? It's bullshit! Can't you smell it? It doesn't hold up. Two months ago, I sat in a room with Graves [the UCM president] and the rest of them, and what did they tell Chief Leach? Everything's hunky-dory. But last night they're condemning the RPD as racist and terrible. It's like that meeting never happened, like they didn't say things have gotten better, like solidarity around police consolidation didn't exist. But I was there and it did happen and this uproar doesn't make sense unless this isn't about yesterday."

As we continued, my finger jabbed the air. "Try this. What's Jim McCuller feeling? Terrible. He's grief stricken. He's enraged, and if he doesn't find someone to blame, he's gonna have to look at his daughter's life and his role in it. So who is Alicia? A single mother who's been out partying all night. She's drunk, got a knife, and sure as hell is gonna stick it in her boyfriend. Show me the facts, man, cuz it don't add up. They're supposed to let her slice and dice the dude? If she'd killed him, these same folks would be yellin' they didn't stop her because he's black, and the cops don't give two shits what niggers do to one another. So, suppose they're white. How's it play out differently? 'I beg your pardon, ma'am. Mind putting the knife down, please?' Come on!"

As words flew out of my mouth, my usually plodding pace sped up. "You know what's coming down. McCuller's got to be mad at himself. He failed her, but ain't nobody gonna throw that in his face. They're lookin' for someone to blame. Someone has to be at fault and putting the finger on Whitmore does the trick. It feeds right into the black view of the world. Black life is less valued. The police hassle us every day. Injustice is everywhere, and this racist system is meant to keep it that way. And since we all have experienced this reality we substitute a generalization for the truth and disregard the facts. We choose solidarity. No middle ground. No questions. We're all supposed to line up behind the motherfuckers and chant 'No More Whitmore.' Well, no goddamn way!"

Whenever I fell into a rant like that, something else was going on inside me. I had an intense reaction to social action bullies—justice-seekers who would run over others, moralists who got high on being righteous, activists who couldn't be bothered to treat people with respect. Better get out of the way because the cause is all that matters—I had been abused by that type.

There it was: the emotional trail that led back to the night Mike Young humiliated me. Over fifteen years had passed, yet the fear and rage remained. The morning I heard of Alicia's death, all the feelings associated with that hot July evening returned. So did the disgust that came years later, when I learned that my nemesis was both a Beloit trustee and university vice chancellor. Rage, disgust, and, yes, fear. I refused to be unmasked again—not black but an Oreo, not a brother but a traitor. I detested the arrogance of radicals and saw them all as self-serving. Press my button and I would deliver a diatribe. It was a bitterness that took me a long time to move through and get beyond.

After telling the story of Mike Young over and over, always feeling sorry for myself, it has come to sound like a comic routine—my beloved victim role, as comfortable as an old sneaker, and just as smelly. Returning to that moment with the distance I've gained, I marvel at the power it had over me. Eventually a day came when I re-told my moralistic epic only to find that I no longer enjoyed the rush that comes with righteous indignation. Instead, Mike appeared in a new light; indeed, I had never seen him at all until that instant.

Finally I saw that Mike was just a Chicago boy like myself, not much older. I remembered the strength coiled within the muscular frame of a man-child. I saw that the assassination of Dr. King had grabbed him—as he had grabbed me—by the throat. Rage and buried grief had overwhelmed him. Possessed by the cause, Mike had cast away Negro-ness in order to become black and powerful. He had committed himself to bringing about change, wresting it if necessary. And eventually I came to accept, with some bitterness toward him but even more dismay at my own egocentrism, that he probably never thought about me again, much less disliked me. What happened hadn't been about me. I wasn't a real adversary, but a scapegoat—the despised symbol of a failed path.

As for me, it was the memory of that moment, and nothing else, that I had hated and ranted about all those years. He was the personification of my edgy relationship with the black community, not its cause. My adversary was not Mike, but the bitterness I carried in my heart.

Like Mike, I was committed to changing the world and even feeling rejected and shunned had not stopped me from trying. But it had taken many more years to turn that memory into a blessing; it took blood, sweat, and tears, to wring meaning from it. And although too often I felt like a victim, that moment helped make me a man who is not as timid as he once was, and who uses his affability to carry on the dogged day-to-day work of building the institutions that make a difference. Ironically Mike Young and I made the same choice—to work within white institutions to change them. When I saw the truth about his life and my own, relief flooded over me and the hatred dissolved.

A few days after Alicia's death, I received an invitation to another meeting. This one at the First Baptist Church of Rochester, a large white congregation in Pittsford, Rochester's most affluent suburb. About forty gathered, mostly clergy from mainstream congregations, including a synagogue. I felt at home in this group—mixed faith, gender, and race engaged in a more dispassionate search for a response. Not that I didn't understand why Rochester's black community was so volatile. The anger wasn't just about Alicia; it was about every black who had been pulled over, harassed, arrested, or killed for no reason other than the color of their skin.

Sitting in that meeting, the image of my brother being stopped by cops in Denver kept forcing itself on me. Joining the steering committee of this ad hoc clergy group was my effort to make my ministry relevant to the black community.

Winter arrived, the Christmas shopping season mounted, and the "No More Whitmore" marches continued. While Jim McCuller, and the McCuller Committee formed in response to the shooting, stood vigil in the cold, other parents nearly rioted in the frenzy to buy Cabbage Patch Dolls for their darlings. The work of our clergy group also continued. By spring we had organized the Police Community Relations Conference, and by 1985, I had become the chair of its successor, the Community-Police Relations Task Force of the Monroe County Human Relations Commission.

This task force culminated in June 1988 with the Report on Community-Police Relations. Released shortly after yet another black, Calvin Green, was shot and killed by yet another white police officer, the report addressed his death, saying: "When the condemnations, protest, and mourning have ceased, the work of change must continue. Yet the changes that will help avoid other deaths and improve policing in this community are not sweeping ones, but rather modest ones that take time: quality officers, recruiting more minority officers, better training and supervision, improved communications between citizens and police, and more confidence in the Citizens' Complaint Process. Tragedies like the death of Calvin Green move us to act."

I was astonished to find that as our years in Rochester accumulated, I had become one of those leaders newspapers called. A reporter phoned to get a reaction to Rochester mayor Thomas Ryan's charge that "clergy have created an environment that makes it very difficult for the people who have the responsibility to solve the problem . . ." Concurrently, the commission's work was dismissed by the McCuller Committee as too moderate and centrist. Being attacked by both sides was a good sign. I knew the task-force report would never receive support from the most vocal elements in the black community, but I couldn't keep myself from yearning for it. However, what I really wanted—affirmation of my blackness—they could never give.

Being a Unitarian Universalist, I understand that one's religious identity must begin with one's own direct experience of life. Yet when it came to blackness, instead of looking within myself at the one experience that mattered most, I looked to others. It began with my mother's commandments; later, as a young man, I went to a black psychiatrist who reassured me but couldn't repair my self-esteem. At the South Side Settlement House, I found redemption in good deeds and others' acceptance. I left Meadville Lombard inspired by the lives of my black UU predecessors. In all of this I failed to lay claim to my own blackness—blackness defined by *my* past, *my* conscience, and *my* choices.

My own heritage as an Afro-American is rich. I am the amalgamation of all my ancestors: Universalist and Unitarian; Mende and Bolum, English and Scottish, Native American, French Huguenot, perhaps Fijian and whatever else. I am the progeny of plantation owners, slave traders, and slaves, of those who fought for the Confederacy and for the Union, a state senator and a seafarer, strong matriarchs and dutiful men. I am, in fact, a descendant of all who came together in this ethnic cauldron, and no one has a stronger claim on being Afro-American or All-American than I. I am what I am. I refuse to disown white Confederate Joe Gregory, or to pick and choose among my ancestors. My Afro-Americanness is not a politically correct ideology; it is an experience, a legacy with its own intrinsic authenticity. The pain of being excluded led me to conclude that blackness as an ideology narrows its meaning. Those who use blackness as a litmus test to discredit some Afro-American voices while sanctioning others abuse it; they turn blackness into a political artifice meant to consolidate power. They racialize every issue to divide rather than unify, and usurp rather than empower.

Being an Afro-American is a diverse experience that resists simple characterizations. Every time I sit and listen with an open heart to the stories of my black sisters and brothers, the meaning of blackness gains new richness, depth, and breadth. And when I am reminded that there is no one way or right way of being black, the ache of my loneliness retreats and my sense of belonging grows.

As disheartening as it was to watch Rochester's black ensemble reenact the old hurts, anger, and distrust, I developed an equanimity about it—a Zen-like acceptance of my role as chair of the Community-Police Relations Task Force. They applied the pressure; I got in the door. And so we spiraled between hope and despair, lashing out and then collaborating. They protested; I negotiated. That's the way it was, and I chuckled to myself as each of us acted predictably, for the dismissals and criticism were no more about me than the protest was about Alicia McCuller's death.

Confirmation of my sellout status came months after the report was released, when I was among those designated Citizen of the Year by the Monroe County district attorney, Howard Relin. The affirmation I had hoped would come from the black community came instead from the Establishment, and I accepted it with a sense of satisfaction for playing the role in which I was cast.

A Unitarian Universalist standing at the pearly gates sees two signs: one, "This way to heaven," the other, "This way to a discussion about heaven." The UU, of course, heads for the discussion. There are many jokes about the UU proclivity to make a sacrament of discussion. Donna, however, could tolerate only so much discussion. I knew the signs. Too much kvetching, pedantry, or indecision would cause her eyes to bulge. I am convinced she became a home renovator as an antidote. No meetings required. She could see progress. Hammers neither argue nor walk away, they do what they are told. And wielding a Sawz-All during the demolition phase is therapeutic in its own cathartic way.

One summer, she renovated our kitchen. In the midst of the Lebanese War, we called it the Beirut Room. The gutted room had four ceilings, one lurking beneath another; dust and lath lay everywhere, and all we could do about the gaping hole in the back of the house was to cover it with a plastic tarp. If the job was too high, tedious, or dirty, I got to do it; I also cooked on an electric skillet on the floor, did the dishes in the bathtub, and tried to keep Elliot from putting nails in his mouth. It is a miracle we all survived.

It was also a miracle Rochester Universalist survived. When Donna and I arrived in Rochester in 1979, we noticed on the cover of the quarterly financial statement a column of numbers that ran down the left margin. Each time the statement came before the church board, several more numbers were crossed off. When one of us finally asked Walt, the curmudgeonly treasurer, what this meant he told us, "That's the number of months before the endowment is used up." And then there was our beautiful, ramshackle 1907 building. With its belfry full of dead pigeons, it was slowly collapsing around us. The pointing between the bricks was gone. When it rained, the flat roof became a wading pool and water poured down the inside wall of the sanctuary. We prayed that the brick corbelling wouldn't land on a passerby's head.

Seven years into our ministry in Rochester, the congregation had stopped deficit spending. We experienced modest growth and added one black family. But, sadly, we had also lost one: Sweet, chain-smoking, Republican Bob had died. We had celebrated the congregation's 150th anniversary and mounted two capital campaigns to restore our historic landmark church building and its one-of-a-kind pipe organ. In the process, Donna blossomed into a first-rate fund-raiser, and at the end of our second capital campaign, the congregation bestowed upon her a Smurf figurine holding a drum in one hand and a whip in the other.

In 1987, the congregation granted us a sabbatical. At long last, the opportunity I had awaited—we would go to Switzerland. For me it meant a return to the Ecole, for Donna a return to the country that her persecuted Mennonite ancestors fled from more than 260 years before.

Föhn Within

I have come to believe over and over again that what is most important to me must be spoken, made verbal and shared, even at the risk of having it bruised and misunderstood.

Audre Lorde, "The Transformation of
Silence into Language and Action"

The flight from Toronto to Frankfurt departed late and felt long. Yet, standing in the aisle waiting to disembark, my exhaustion vanished. I was back. Thirteen years had passed since I had forsaken Europe, and nearly twenty-five since I had first arrived. That first time, when I exuberantly strode down the gangplank after the SS *France* docked in Le Havre, I was ready for whatever the world offered. How easy it had been.

Now I was returning to Switzerland with my own family, and the scene unfolding before me seemed familiar—déjà vu with a twist. I was my father. Filled with a quiet satisfaction, I surveyed Donna and the kids lined up in front of me, anticipating the adventure before us. Then I noticed myself, rumpled after a sleepless night and loaded down with a knapsack on my back, a briefcase, and a couple of jackets in one hand and two children's violin cases in the other. I felt like a packhorse and chuckled in recognition. I was also my mother in all her disarray.

Confinement in an airplane hadn't suited Charlotte, age seven,

or Elliot, age four. They barreled down the jetway and past a security guard with a submachine gun strapped across his chest. Trying
to keep up, Donna hurried past him as well. But as I approached,
the guard's eyes fixed on me and he leaned in my direction. There
was something about me. The violin cases? The color of my skin?
Instinctively I fumbled for my passport. Catching a glimpse of its
blue jacket that said American, the guard nodded and in an instant
the incident was over. Amazed at being taken for a terrorist, a smile
formed on my lips, only to dissolve as it struck me—Europe was
not the safe haven I remembered.

Neither was the Hasliberg. The narrowest section of the only
road that traversed the mountainside was being widened. Throughout that spring, they blasted away the cliff above and hauled off the
rocks. On either side of the construction site the road seemed like
a highway compared to the narrow lane that had once wound from
village to village. The villages themselves seemed larger, too. The
route was lined with new stores and cafés. Just above the villages,
clusters of chalets had sprouted. And high up toward the mountain peaks, thin black lines bisected the ski trails—lifts whizzing up
slopes I had struggled a half day to ascend.

Across the valley, the Wetterhorn captured my attention as
always. So high are its peaks that clouds get stuck behind them and
when mountain guides observe this they know it's time to return
to the hut or descend into the valley because bad weather is on the
way. This magnificent mountain had not changed, but the Ecole
d'Humanité had. The student mix was different—a handful of
Asians, fewer Americans, and many more Swiss—making it less a
school of humanity and more a Swiss school. Likewise, two of the
older buildings had been torn down. In their place stood a large
new one and the faculty met in its conference room. Filling in for
two teachers on leave, Donna and I sat among them. The knitting
needles were still clicking away and that familiar sound brought a
smile to my lips, as did the many well-known faces. The staff had
aged. Armin and Natalie Lüthi were grayer. Herr Cool was about to
retire. Herr Poeschel remained as plump and quick-witted as ever,

but Fräulein Petersen was more deaf than before and crankier. The tan, ageless Frau Stein could still beat all comers at ping-pong, but the robust and tenacious Frau Varga was in a hospital, recovering from back surgery. Gentle old Edith had died five years earlier, and Aurobindo had passed away as well; I regretted that I couldn't thank her or make amends with him. Then one day, during the teachers' conference, it was announced that Frau Horcher, the handyman's widow, had died. Hearing the word *widow*, I realized that Herr Horcher was dead, and a sadness came over me.

I slipped smoothly back into the rhythm of the Ecole. The day still began with a workout followed by a cold shower. One morning soon after we arrived, I looked out upon dismal gray mountains, saw the sky was overcast and threatening, and set out on my daily jog anyway.

The chilly mountain air chafed my skin and made my ears tingle as I shuffled along. Turning left at the gravel pit, I plodded and panted up the steep path until suddenly I was accosted by a voice.

"Good morning."

"Morning," I shouted up at a stooped, little white-haired woman leaning over the balcony of a chalet.

"How are you?" she yelled across the space.

"Fine," I replied.

"And your wife and child?"

She had the number of children wrong, but she seemed to know me, so I didn't bother correcting her. "Great," I said. "They're practicing violin right now."

"We should talk. Come for breakfast."

"O . . . okay?"

"You must first call," she added.

"Su . . . sure. See you later." And with a wave I trudged on.

How odd! An invitation to breakfast from a complete stranger. Didn't have a clue who she was, yet she knew me. Then it came to me. Ruth Cohn, the psychoanalyst. She had developed a psychodynamic method of group process and trained a number of Ecole teachers in its use. One of them must have told her I was visiting.

The next day I phoned and introduced myself. A long pause followed.

"Oh, excuse me," she said, her voice wavering as she began a contrite explanation. She had mistaken me for James Branch. James, the only other black man on the mountain, had begun his studies at the Jungian Institute in Zurich, and she wanted to know how it was going. Now she filled the phone with apologies.

What a presumptuous fool I'd been. I was speechless, and nothing she said eased my chagrin. If she had shut up, the rest of it wouldn't have happened, but her monologue continued until, as she groped about, she stumbled on the idea of inviting me to tea, and I accepted. Thus we struck our crooked deal—you flatter me and I'll forgive you. Donna just snorted.

The next day, I marched back up the mountain to have our conversation. I asked about her psychodynamic approach, but that was not on her agenda. She launched into a recitation of her experiences with blacks in New York City—how she had remained when blacks moved into her neighborhood, and how black men had called her racist if she wouldn't sleep with them on the first date, which led into a too-detailed description of her black lover. As her pitiful attempt to prove to herself and me that she wasn't prejudiced dragged on, I remembered other unwelcome confessions. Retreating behind a hard smile and automated nod, I played the sympathetic listener. I had grown to hate these white recitations, all of their experiences with and feelings about blacks revealed to me as if I were a therapist who specialized in race. I was expected to absolve her, and I fulfilled the role perfectly: "Oh yeah, bet it was hard." "Sounds like you really tried." "If only there were more people like you."

Motherfucking bitch. Stupid nigger. I growled to myself on my way down the mountain. I disliked her and was disgusted with myself.

Years earlier, after I had returned to the United States, James Branch had been hired to teach math at the Ecole. Later he married Christine Hirsig, a local whose family owned a hotel just up the road from the Ecole. Long before we first met, James and I had heard about one another. Now I climbed the hill to arrange a get-together, and as I walked I reflected on all that James and I had in common: Chicago, where we both grew up; Rodney, a mutual friend; and of course, the Ecole. But the most compelling bond was being black veterans of cross-cultural, interracial marriages that had withstood the furious objections of our spouses' parents.

As the front door of the hotel swung shut behind me, a teetering old man pointed at me and proclaimed, *"Ich war auch mal Mathematiker wie Du!"* ("I was once a mathematician like you.") I stared in bewilderment as the hotel's matron, Frau Hirsig, who was Christine's mother, put a firm hand beneath the codger's elbow and gently led him away. Then it came to me and I chuckled. The old man had mistaken me for James.

I found James and set a date. This was just our second meeting. The first had occurred in Rochester, New York, in 1983 when en route to Chicago to introduce Christine to his family, the two of them had stopped by to confer with us. The consultation had been brief but earnest. They sat, wincing and nodding, as Donna and I, interrupting each other to add details, had described the turmoil our marriage caused in her liberal Canadian family. That had been four years earlier and I was anxious to hear what had happened to James and Christine.

Charlotte and I were with the rest of the school at a concert in Meiringen when the bells began to ring. Donna had stayed with Elliot in a nearly empty campus, put him to bed, and happily curled up with a book. Just then a strange, far away, rhythmic tolling began, as if the mountain had a pulse.

It was like thunder in the distance, except it had a beat. It was like a thousand men marching, except it had a ring.

Rousing Elliot, she scurried outside. Way down the road in the half-dark a phalanx of Swiss farmers approached. Three across and about ten deep, the aberration marched in Donna's and Elliot's direction. Each man gripped a large, black, unwieldy bell. Swaying back and forth in the fading light, the bell ringers loomed as though they were corpses escaped from the horror movie *Night of the Living Dead.*

With each sway they slid a foot forward, then followed with the other, making the bell swing from thigh to thigh. They came up the street, closer and closer. Their bells thundered in unison and as the men drew nearer, the bells thundered louder.

Then they were upon them in a deafening roar.

Ignoring Donna's and Elliot's presence, the phalanx continued past. Without a word or a nod to one another, the bell ringers left the road at a village farmhouse, the bells thundering as they swayed around the building.

Rock 'n' ring.

Rock 'n' ring.

Then heading back whence they came, they passed Donna and Elliot again, without a glance. Marching on, they disappeared into the dark and slowly the thunderous ringing died away.

When I arrived home and the strange happening was described in detail, it left me a little confused. I only heard farmers ring the bells in preparation for New Year's Eve, but the next day we discovered that the marchers had circled the house of a bridegroom to drive off the evil spirits, just as they drove the evil spirits away at the beginning of the New Year.

The farmers came again in late June, toward the end of our stay at the Ecole. As the ringing thunder filled the air we all ran to look. Standing on the roadside by the water trough in the middle of the village, I was transfixed by ringing so loud it left no room for thought—just the sight and the sound and the desire to be among them.

I wanted a bell in my hands. I wanted to be part of the procession. I wanted to be one with the sound.

But constrained by the lack of a bell, I just rocked back and forth with the rhythm until eventually the thunder passed and the passion ebbed.

As the ringing returned in echoes off the mountains, I recalled a story told by Swiss psychoanalyst C.G. Jung. He had been heading through Uganda toward Sudan when he found himself among the "blackest Negroes" he had ever seen. The Chief called for a dance and a huge fire was built. An inner circle of women and children and an outer circle of men swayed in dance upon the waves of heat and the beat of the drums. The tempo built until Jung sprang into the dance, mingling with the warriors, waving his rhinoceros whip as the heat intensified and the rhythm of the drumming mounted. He could see in their faces that they approved. As night deepened and their excitement grew Jung, remembering that a countryman had been struck by a spear in the course of such a dance, began to worry. Fearing for his party's safety Jung managed to pull the tribe's frenzy back from the edge. But he writes elsewhere of Europeans "going black under the skin," and later during this same journey he describes himself as coming "all too close to 'going black.'"

The paradox of a Swiss man "going black," and myself, a black man "acting white" made me smile. How ironic. The euphemism act white means "in a civilized manner." But for me, among those Swiss peasants, "acting white" would have meant having a bell in my hand and getting swept up into the unconscious, the same sense of being overwhelmed that Jung associated with "going black," a state in which the "vitality" of the unconscious—that which "rationality" is always struggling against—gains control.

On the African Savannah the dance goes on, while in the Swiss Alps the bells still thunder. These ancient and powerful rituals are still capable of penetrating our modern psychic veneer. We may have to travel far from home to become aware of the domination of the unconscious, but in fact it is always immediately at hand. And throughout our time in Switzerland, such unexpected incidents kept hammering at my psychic façade.

No clanging cacophony of bells circled round the Hotel Gletscherblick warding off evil spirits prior to James' and Christine's wedding. Both were outsiders. He was black and the Hirsigs, having only lived on the Hasliberg since 1906, were newcomers.

When Christine, James, Donna, and I finally sat down together one evening in a quiet booth in a corner of the hotel's dining room, their story unfolded. Donna and I already knew that Herr Hirsig had rebuffed James when this soft-spoken man asked for his daughter's hand. The rejection made no sense. Not one of Hirsig's five children had married someone Swiss. With German and Austrian sons-in-law, and English and Chinese daughters-in-law, an Afro-American was just what was needed to round out this international clan. Nonetheless, after James and Christine married, a civil silence marked the relationship between James and his father-in-law. James's pleasant and kind manner didn't change Herr Hirsig's attitude, nor did the fact that they worked side by side and lived under the same roof. The arrival of baby Viola finally ended the silence. Her curly locks, beige skin, and big brown eyes swept away his resistance, and Herr Hirsig had delighted in his granddaughter until a heart attack silenced him forever. Now twins were on the way, and as we revisited the absurdities that had turned our lives into soap operas, laughter kept erupting from our corner of the room.

The evening passed, pregnant Christine retired, and we talked on. Night came and Donna walked back down to the Ecole, and still the conversation continued. James explained the Jungian concept of the shadow—the way the unconscious manifests the elements of our personalities that we strive to repress. These disowned aspects of ourselves are projected onto other people; they also appear in our dreams. He shared his observation that the shadow sometimes surfaces in dreams as a black man. One of his teachers had speculated that the shadow blacks project might be white. I didn't know, but I did recall reading that when Africans first saw Europeans they mistook whites for ghosts and devil spirits from the beyond. I could see how fear of the stranger (an embodiment of the unknown) works in tandem with our projections. We have to start somewhere in understanding what is totally new. Projecting something we already know upon the foreign is the natural first step; it also makes distortion inevitable.

I knew firsthand. People found it difficult to see *me*, yet rarely overlooked my blackness. The phrase "But that was before I knew you" was a sure sign that a white church member was about to make a contrite confession. Likewise the Morrisons' inability to see beyond their own anxieties about my color meant they didn't notice how well-matched Donna and I were. A similar dynamic played out regularly in public with white women. I could be jogging in the early morning or walking home at night when some white woman's deer-like alertness, sideways glance, and quickened pace would tell me I had been spotted and force me to be aware of my color.

Give me a break. Think I don't know what you're up to? Making a mugger out of me. You and a whole goddamn world that dreads and demonizes black men. You don't know or care or see who I really am or what you're doing. You fucking bitch. That's it, retreat. Leave me with my fury, cuz now, God help me, I do feel like . . .

In the end, I did turn into a psychic assailant—the monster she believed me to be in the beginning. Lurking just beneath the surface, white fear and black rage make for a volatile mixture, one that can obliterate the other person—and oneself.

I pondered this all-too-human power of distortion: No one is born racist, but the combination of our natural wariness toward strangers and the phenomenon of projection make prejudice nearly unavoidable. The implication challenged my most fundamental beliefs: that each individual is due respect—indeed, reverence— as a unique manifestation of God's creation; and that, beneath everyone's skin color and cultural fascia, we are first and foremost human, sisters and brothers belonging to one human family.

These truths were affirmed by the two institutions that had most profoundly shaped me—the Ecole, a school of human- ity, and Unitarian Universalism, a humanitarian faith. Given this upbringing, racial integration had always made sense. Yet, my con- versation with James forced me to consider that humans may be emotionally constructed in a way contrary to this belief. Was racial prejudice inevitable and my hope naïve? That night, my mood was as dark as the path I descended.

These questions wouldn't leave me alone. I observed people more carefully and listened more discerningly: A conversation, a memory, a chance observation would seize my attention. A dark-skinned person had been a rarity and a curiosity in Switzerland when I first arrived in 1962, and while there were many more when I returned in 1971, I couldn't help but notice how dramatically it had changed by 1987. Now there were people of color everywhere I looked. In Basel and Bern I saw Turkish laborers and African students; in Zurich I came across street musicians from Central America and Tamil refugees from Sri Lanka. When I mentioned the Tamils to Robi, a Swiss charge of mine who was in perpetual trouble, he told me his buddies went out evenings and beat up refugees for the fun of it. When I expressed skepticism he insisted it was true. When I asked why, he only shrugged.

The Ecole reflected Switzerland's shifting demographics. The percentage of Swiss Kameraden had increased by half. Yet, at the same time there were many more not of European origin, over a dozen altogether, and three of them were Swiss: an indigenous person from Ecuador and two Koreans. One of the Koreans, a plucky adolescent who was adopted as a little girl, felt certain that when she finally found a place to call home it would not be Switzerland. I pondered what life was like for her and the many children like her that had caught my eye. I wondered if it could work in this conservative little land. I hoped it would.

It struck me that I was no longer the oddity I once had been. Yet if I was no longer what James Baldwin called a "living wonder," what was I?

Swiss Vote To Tighten Refugee Law read one of the headlines in the Monday, April 6 edition of the *International Herald Tribune*. The vote had approved a federal referendum that would enable the Swiss Bundesrat to tighten restrictions on refugees and make political asylum even more difficult to obtain; and although both the Roman Catholic and Protestant churches opposed it, it passed by a margin of 2 to 1. Was asylum being abused as the government claimed? Or, as its opponents argued, was "the issue skin color and race [since most] of the recent refugees come from the Middle East, Asia and Africa and are not white." I wondered if the vote just reflected the natural mind-set of a people used to being hemmed in by mountain peaks and deep, remote valleys—terrain that had long protected them from the world beyond. Was this the Swiss reaction to a world which could no longer be kept out? Or was something new emerging—provincialism evolving into racism?

The morning after Donna and I talked with Christine and James, he called to say he had an article for me. Written by Jungian analyst James Hillman, it was entitled "Notes on White Supremacy." Hillman's writing was dense, but his point was clear: "The supremacy of white depends on oppositional imagining." Over against "the supremacy of white" was black. Images and words cascaded upon me: cowboys in white hats and villainous black knights; expressions like black sheep, black market, and black magic, all unsavory and all bearing the same connotation in either English or German. Art Perkins, because he worked illegally, was a *Schwarzarbeiter* (black worker). Meanwhile I—a University of Chicago graduate, minister of a Unitarian Universalist congregation, and member of the Monroe County Human Relations Commission, all mainline institutions—was "acting white."

How misleading to refer to people as black or white—words that are oppositional, that set one group against the other and implicitly establish a hierarchy that bolsters the self-esteem of one. Embedded in this false dichotomy is a preposterous oversimplification of cultural and racial variations. To pretend that the words *black* and *white* can capture the essence of a group is ludicrous since as categories they reduce something that is inherently complex, nuanced, and evolving into something that does not exist. Given the festering divide this fiction promotes, it becomes natural to distrust and easy to demonize one another. Perhaps it is better to never use these racial misnomers again.

Clasping the Hillman article, I stepped out the front door. A car pulled up and the driver jumped out. I turned right and continued toward the path. "Don't you recognize me, stranger?" the man asked.

I stopped, looked over my shoulder, and wondered, *Is he talking to me?* No question he was looking straight at me, smiling. My mind shifted into overdrive. *This bloke thinks he knows me. He's British, okay. How do I know him? Where could I know him from?* I must have looked dumbfounded because the next thing he offered was, "It's only been two years."

It came to me: *James.* I thought, *We all look alike, eh?* Edited, it came out as, "Oh, you must be looking for James. Just saw him. He's inside."

The man's cheery smile disappeared. Sighing, I consoled him, "Don't worry, you're not the first." I walked away, feeling disgust toward him and anger with myself for being so understanding. James, with his lanky build, long face, and receding hairline looked nothing like me—husky, round-faced, bespectacled, and button-nosed.

How long? O Lord, how long? The sarcasm turned bitter in my mouth as I headed down the path, digging my feet into the gravel and sending it flying. More troubling thoughts arose. *This is human nature—blindness and inattention, projection and distortion. These white people see nothing but my skin color; it seems they don't see me at all. I'm a goddamn magnet attracting all the notions, good and bad, about blackness that lurk within them.*

Looking up, I saw a little Swiss boy peering at me from between the slats of a fence. I couldn't help but remember yet again the nightmarish scene of another little Swiss boy frantically running up the mountain shrieking, "*Mutti! Mutti! Ein Schwarze kommt*" ("Mother, a black is coming"). This little boy only stared as I passed, but all I saw was the boy from the past, fleeing in terror.

Terror! My thoughts shifted with my emotions. I saw my brother, Philip, spread-eagled with an officer's revolver sticking in his back. A second time, but now in Ventura, California, and like before he had done nothing except to be born black. People's reactions—reactions which in Switzerland had created awkward situations—could be fatal in the United States, where authorities sanctioned police terrorism in the name of public safety. That's why rage surfaced in Rochester. Alicia McCuller's death instantly evoked memories of a thousand other incidents. You're minding your own business when you are stopped for no reason except that police officers have been conditioned to see a black-assed, drug-pushing pimp who has done something criminal, or will, as soon as the opportunity arises.

In the days that followed, I became obsessed with the idea that white supremacy and black inferiority are embedded in the language, symbol, and mythology that all of us use, regardless of race, to describe the world. We describe the world to define and control it. We define blackness and dark-skinned people as nocturnal, mysterious, and above all negatively. As bleaching cream lightens dark skin, these layers of language colonize and whiten the mind, relentlessly structuring our worldview so that Afro-Americans are always seeing ourselves through others' fearful eyes. We are forced to adopt ways of thinking that foster the cultural deceit that misrepresents who we really are. This distortion is made worse by the projection of the shadow side of lighter people upon darker ones—a shadow that Caucasians cannot admit to casting, because white supposedly has no shadow. I couldn't stop brooding, nor stop picking at scabbed-over memories. And I couldn't prevent this thought process from resurfacing in my dreams.

The Föhn, because of the way it affects people's moods, is sometimes called the "Witches' Wind" and when it blew, I slept fitfully and remembered more of my dreams than usual. One night I had the following dream:

My fingers are cramped but my mind is flying. I haven't finished writing the last words, but people are already arriving. I look around and feel panicky. The hall is in disarray, the chairs turned every which way, the podium not in place. I wrestle it into position. Then, weaving through the crowd, I retrieve my manuscript. The pages aren't in order. Quickly I reorganize them and count—there are nine—they're all there.

"Silence," I yell. Then, pausing, I scan their faces. They are all white and I am black. I begin, but before I have completed one sen-

*tence, I hear a coarse, booming voice coming from an adjacent room
to my left. Through the wall I see another black man gleefully singing
and strumming his guitar. He is taunting me.*

*He has appeared in my dreams before. "Stop," I yell, but he just
shows me his teeth. "Throw him out," I shout. No one moves. I go
after him myself and grab him by the collar. He twists and struggles
as I walk him to the front door and heave. Landing hard, he curses
me.*

*"Fuck you, nigger," he shrieks. His words strike home, and sud-
denly my annoyance turns to shame. I waver. I want to speak with
him. I need to explain. I want him to understand, but tell myself,
"Later, later." I turn away and walk back toward the sanctuary, but
when I look around the room is empty. The people have vanished.
Tears well up.*

My own whimper awakened me. I touched my cheek to wipe
away tears, but I was surprised to find it dry. Awake, I looked
around. It was still dark, not even a hint of dawn.

The dream began like every minister's nightmare, because we
ministers are haunted by fears. Our lives are chaotic, the demands
overwhelming, and we simply are not and never will be prepared
for this weighty calling. We worry that the sermon won't be finished
on time, or that suddenly in the middle of preaching we'll find that
a page is missing, or that something unexpected will disrupt the
service or, worst of all, everyone will walk out. For me, however,
that anxiety overlays something deeper. I work in a largely white
religious movement and when my Common-Negro-Self, the black
minstrel hidden inside me, tries to get through to me, I throw him
out. I have spent a lifetime struggling with the "common Negro,"
for that scorned being my mother forbade me to act like has simply tagged along as my shadow. So when Common-Negro-Self
raises his voice, I say throw him out. When he laughs defiantly, I
seize him. And when I do throw him out, his curse brands me nigger. There is no escaping who I am—a nigger just like him—and
my anger turns to shame as my fake "white" civility is unmasked.
I feel ashamed of what I've done and who I pretend to be. I know

I am connected to him, but that connection scares me. Paradoxically, in throwing out my Common-Negro-Self, my lifelong companion and shadow, I throw out the possibility of being whole. I betray myself and empty the sanctuary of my being. If my self is dismembered then I, who deliver the message, am not wholly present. Being false to myself, I am also false to the congregation, and aware of the pretense, they leave. Thus my annoyance turns to shame, then guilt, then grief at my loss.

This dream left me searching for the self I had thrown out. And while I knew where to look, I feared what might come from integrating this rowdy other into myself, rather than continuing this psychological apartheid.

Then I had a dream in which the message was unmistakable:

I am marching through lightly forested, rolling hills. I am in front of a group of people, and it is a pleasant, warm day. The sun is shining, and we are moving along when I hear a low growl from behind a knoll. My heart races wildly and I look around, yet no one else seems to have noticed. But I know what it is. A grizzly bear, a part of me. "Oh, shit," I whisper between gritted teeth. I know it's there, I know it's coming, and I know that I don't want to face it. I turn to run, but everyone else is marching along toward the knoll as if nothing has happened. I'm getting nowhere running against the flow, when suddenly a huge grizzly looms up behind the knoll and covers the sky. Now there are loud cries and pandemonium. Everyone starts to run, but there is no place to go because black bears and gray gorillas have surrounded us. We look like the Keystone Cops as we careen off one another, tripping, yelling, running with our hands above our heads, diving under bushes. Amidst this chaos I slip through the line, and running as fast and far as I can, I keep going until I collapse from exhaustion.

"Lightly forested, rolling hills" captured the setting of my life at that moment. I had returned to the Alps, a place of comfort, nurture, safety. My leading the group made sense because I had been doing a lot of that in the life I left behind in Rochester. So I am in front when I hear the bear. I had come to accept the bear as my totem. People, always Caucasian, seeing me as big, brown, and cuddly have been known to call me a teddy bear. But I had seen glimpses of another bear—a grizzly that was violent, angry, and out of control. It was my shadow—the enraged Mike Young within me, calling for a revolution, the manifestation of the rejected "common Negro" of my unconscious. I know that anger, like the bear, is nearby and as usual I want to flee. Normally I hide my anger so well that people, including me, don't notice it. Panic-stricken, I run from my anger faster than anyone else, only to be surrounded and penned in by black bears, my lesser fear and anger, and gray gorillas, the primitive, instinctual man within. The chaos—my fear and everyone else's—allows me, once again, to escape dealing with my anger, but in retreating I forsake the challenge of pressing ahead, the one thing that would lead to growth. Instead I run until I can run no further. A life spent fleeing from this anger had exhausted me.

I'd known rage in my mother's eyes and drunk it with her milk, even as she trained me to sit on it. Well-behaved, middle-class Negro children don't let it show. Encouraged to deny, I became expert at dissociating, remaining there yet not being there, pretending everything is okay. Oblivious to my own feelings, I smiled. It was all automatic now. And the guilt I had felt about my extraordinary opportunities made it even easier to discount my anger. What, after all, did I have to be angry about?

But mostly fear kept my anger at bay. Let it erupt and I would turn into the "common Negro" Mother scorned. Because this rage was unacceptable I split it off from my everyday identity. Otherwise I might become Mike Young, and I would scare away all the white folks that filled my life. Unleash my Common-Negro-Self and rejection was certain.

Ultimately both these dreams convey a sense of two personas—one vying for expression, the other feeling its control slipping away. Mother had delivered contradictory messages: "To thine own self be true," and "Don't act like a common Negro." The former encouraged me to find my truth within myself. The latter was the secret, passed from generation to generation, of how to survive in a world dominated by Euro-Americans. Poor Uncle Max had been trained to be "the least objectionable to prejudiced people of any colored man," as the dean of Bucknell had described him, and so had I. It meant bifurcating myself, a division that left me acting like a caricature. A fabricated self created in juxtaposition to my Common-Negro-Self. The former began by learning never to say nigger and ended up knowing a hundred different ways to help people feel at ease and get over their fear of black men—eye contact that beckons, a wink, a smile, a softening of the voice into a hush. I disarmed them with nuance. The "common Negro," however, was lively—or is that loud? Spontaneous—or out of control? Demonstrative—or overly emotional? Too happy, too angry, too sensual? It seemed that personal fragmentation was the price of racial integration.

As I continue on my journey toward wholeness I keep returning to *The Souls of Black Folk*. W.E.B. DuBois's book is the primer for every discussion of Afro-American identity. In it he depicts this sense of two-ness as a double consciousness: "One ever feels his two-ness,—an American, a Negro; two souls, two thoughts, two unreconciled strivings, two warring ideals in one dark body, whose dogged strength alone keeps it from being torn asunder." I had felt this war and responded by returning to America in 1974, but DuBois goes on to elaborate on a deeper struggle: "The history of the American Negro is the history of this strife—this longing to attain self-conscious manhood, to merge his double self into a better and truer self. He would not Africanize America, for America has too much to teach the world and Africa. He would not bleach his Negro soul in a flood of white Americanism for he knows that Negro blood has a message for the world. He simply wishes to make it possible for a man to be both an American and a *Negro* . . ."

The struggle with this double identity is the paradox lived out in every Afro-American life. The common response has been to embrace one and expel the other. We'll never know how many pass;

but some who can't pass ape whiteness instead. Others reject and attack all things white. Many romanticize Africa, but few return to her. Being "blacker than thou" is enough for others, while the "Black Bourgeoisie" imagine they are above it all.

The reality is that we are Africa's infants and America's children, and there is no way to disentangle this past. Rather than suppress or reject parts of myself, I yearn to be integrated—self-integrated. I want to amalgamate all that I am, the full scope of my personality and heritage, into myself and thus become whole.

The gong shattered the silence of another early morning at the Ecole. Pulling on my sweats, I looked out the window at patches of white left behind by an unusually late snowfall. When the Föhn would appear to claim the last of it was anyone's guess. But it would come, and come as it always does—from Africa. Heated above the hot sands of the Sahara, loaded with moisture from the Mediterranean Sea, it gathers on the south side of the Alps where it cools, condenses, and its rain pours down. Now dry, the air is squeezed over the mountain ridges as it flows from the high pressure south of the Alps to the low on the north. This compression increases the temperature and then this African wind roars as it cascades down the northern slope. Warming further as it rushes down the wind-tunnel valleys, this stream of air melts the snow, makes trees sway, houses moan, lakes churn, and rivers swell with rampaging waters. Some can predict when the Föhn will arrive. They know to look for the *Föhn Mauer*—*Mauer* meaning "wall" in German—the ominous, impenetrable mass of clouds that swells up behind the Alps as the wind approaches. A barometer will, of course, tell you. Others know when the Föhn will arrive because they feel it. As I set forth, there was a slight breeze and a little whistle. Perhaps the Föhn had arrived.

"Salut, James," a voice rang out as I passed one of the houses in the bend between the hotel and the village. I glanced over my shoulder. A silhouette by a door. Didn't know who.

"Ciao," I shouted without breaking stride.

Once this misdirected salutation would have brought forth a chuckle. But I couldn't laugh at their willful naïveté any longer. I couldn't stand the neighborliness of these blind innocents. Their greetings, however well meant, felt like camouflaged attacks. Why not yell "Nigger?" Just another way of saying, "can't be bothered to notice the difference between one Negro and another." James didn't jog. Yet Caucasians—whether from one hundred meters or ten—kept mistaking me for him. *There's something with brown skin and two legs—must be James.* Once flabbergasted, I now felt assaulted. But my anger was held in check by childhood training and by their helpless shrugs and hapless smiles, and when this was not enough to stop it from erupting, I thought about James, who would still be here after I departed.

The mountain scenery no longer held my attention. Feeling as raw as a cold morning, I ran hard. And as I ran, words from the prologue to Ralph Ellison's novel, *The Invisible Man*, beat within my head: "I am invisible; understand, simply because people refuse to see me. Like the bodiless heads you see sometimes in circus sideshows, it is as though I have been surrounded by mirrors of distorting glass. When they approach me they see only my surroundings, themselves, or figments of their imagination—indeed, everything and anything except me." *Except me . . . except me.*

Driven on by this steady beat, I strayed from my usual route and turned toward a bridge that crossed a nearby mountain stream. Swollen with the spring run-off, the waters raged their wrathful way down, plunging and foaming violently against this stony path—a path of rage I never dared walk, a bridge I never dared cross. The relentlessness of it all was more than my battered spirit could bear. Gripping the cold, steel handrail, my head filled with the roar of the torrid stream, my stomach felt queasy. I leaned into the spray. My mouth opened, and all of a sudden my silence ended as my voice melded with the roaring waters. "I hate you! I hate you no-account honkies, you goddamn, prick-faced, pasty white oofays, and you good-for-nothin' black motherfuckers, you lowdown, ass-licking cocksuckers." A bitter stream of obscenity

spewed forth. "I hate *all* you bloody motherfuckers. I hate you!"
In that raging release "all you" included myself. On and on
it tumbled out: "I hate you. I hate you. I hate you . . ." Cheeks
ablaze, lungs snatching gulps of air, my jaws released, and with all
restraint gone, I screamed until my voice was too hoarse to scream
any longer. When I finally turned away, I was too weary to run. As
I dragged myself home, the waters still roared, as did the daunting truth—a truth that would demand more than resignation and
couldn't be reasoned away. The Föhn-fed waters were calling me
to befriend my rage, to extend my hand and say, "Gimme five on
the black-hand side."

Stray thoughts and unbidden questions kept intruding as I recon-
nected with old friends and revisited the stages where my youth
had played out. There were reunions with my roommate, Philipp
Hostettler, in Basel, and with Henry and Rhoda Isaacs, my sur-
rogate parents, in Zurich. And since Donna had never been to
Europe, whenever possible we traveled beyond Switzerland to
London, Paris, Venice, and Munich.

In Venice the few narrow entrances into the old Jewish ghetto
where Shakespeare's Shylock lived were at one time locked at night
and guarded. Standing on a small bridge leading into this quarter, I wondered how the word ghetto had emigrated to its current
usage—the poor black inner city. In the United States, the Jews had
moved on but the name, slums, and stigma remained.

Outside Munich sat the concentration camp Dachau. I had to
go. The Second World War had rent the lives of many dear to me.
Edith Geheeb was Jewish and had fled Germany during the early
years of Hitler's Third Reich. The Ecole's office manager, the normally stalwart Frau Varga, who left Germany in 1936 at the age of
16, teared up when she spoke about her family—her mother, two
sisters, and brother had perished in a concentration camp. Henry
Isaacs's family had escaped in 1939 with only their lives. Yet my
friends never brought up the topic, just as my great-grandmother
didn't care to talk about slavery. Perhaps it felt to them that the

pain would devour their souls, perhaps they didn't wish to burden others. Perhaps silence seemed to offer the only possibility of living a life not dominated by the past, so they hid the depth of their despair and fury, and carried on.

My friends' silence, a survivors' silence, mirrors Afro-American despair—more so than the ancient liberation of the Hebrew tribes from bondage. The Jews' liberation from Egyptian captivity celebrated in the Passover meal happened so long ago it has become an instrument of the sacred, the mythic narrative around which Jewish identity was formed. But Afro-Americans have no ritualized way of remembering the past, no ritual to express our thankfulness for our deliverance. No ceremony takes our suffering and mixes it with our triumphs to make a balm to ease our pain. How does one repair the psychic legacy left from being traded as a commodity, managed as a business, kept illiterate by law, and brutalized at will? We have no observance at which we recite our heroic deeds in order to bolster black self-esteem against the effects of this legacy and the ongoing attack of majority attitudes and fears. How do you feel all right about yourself when, in the public imagination, you are a dope pusher, a welfare mother, or an affirmative-action placement? How do you feel a sense of belonging in a society where people eye you nervously and cross the street, or flee the neighborhood when you move in? How do you hold on to your own sense of goodness despite the myriad ways—blatant and subtle—in which black self-esteem is continuously damaged?

To live and prosper in such a world requires a source of strength beyond the individual. It requires an abiding sense that all life is sacred and our existence a miracle—a gift of God. This sacredness is found in our lives and relationships, in our stories, and in our struggles to be free and whole human beings—and in a living ritual that holds up and reaffirms these.

"Because we were slaves unto Pharaoh in Egypt, and the eternal, our God, brought us forth . . ." My Jewish friends recite these words every year during Passover. But my own people have no comparable way of transforming slavery from a scarlet letter to the badge of courage it should be. The slave narrative is missing from the American story. We need a black Haggadah that begins: "We were stolen from Africa and enslaved in America, the land of liberty . . ." And we need a time set aside when families gather for a meal and retell the tale, using a newer, truer narrative. Black history is America's history. Being a slave is as American as George Washington and apple pie. The Civil War, the Emancipation Proclamation, the Great Migration, and the civil rights movement are more central to the American story than the embellished tale of the Pilgrims elevated to an all-American feast day. The Afro-American journey from slavery to freedom is the saga of the unfinished revolution, the unfolding story of America's evolution. This experience is one of the defining characteristics of American culture, and neither exists apart from the other. They are interdependent, and this is what integration means: to bring together the parts to form an authentic whole. If every family in America gathered yearly to celebrate the black struggle, which is the quintessential American struggle to be free, black self-esteem might well flower, and the American psyche might be transformed. For in celebrating that experience all of us would be honestly acknowledging our identity as a people. Afro-American slavery however, like the Holocaust, remains a festering wound—a transgenerational trauma—which the years have yet to change into a redeeming narrative that transforms our slavery from a cause for shame into a source of strength.

My state of mind was turbulent with cascading thoughts as Donna and I approached the Dachau concentration camp. Back came memories of my 1974 visit to Mauthausen, which had been the central camp for all of Austria—a slave labor camp where it was said that each rock "cost the life of a man." Seeing the watchtowers and the gate, and crossing the roll-call ground, I thought of those I knew who escaped and of the many who did not.

It was Sunday when we visited Dachau, and the museum was crowded. A mishmash of languages. I looked around—T-shirts and smiles, baseball caps and cameras hanging from tourists' necks.

"What do they think this is?" I snapped at Donna. Only afterward did I realize why I was so offended: I was attending a memorial service.

The exhibit was made up largely of documents and photographs that traced how an intensified nationalism and anti-Semitism arose in the aftermath of the German defeat in the First World War. Among the displays was an advertisement that, translated, read: "Are you blond? Then you create and safeguard culture!" *Wow! Imagine what it would have been like to be black in Hitler's Germany!* Another advertisement began: "Are you blond? Then you are in danger." *The white supremacists in America must love this. I can see it now: "Are you white? Then you are in danger."*

The displays went on to show how in 1933 Hitler rose to power by offering security in authoritarian rule, pride in racial inheritance, hope for tomorrow in the Third Reich. Germany needed someone besides itself to blame and Hitler, tapping into all that was fearful and hate-filled in the German unconscious, maligned the Jews, these ancient outcasts, and let them serve as the scapegoat—the receptacle for all that the Teutonic race rejected. The Holocaust was the monstrous creation of a gravely wounded and flailing German psyche which sacrificed the Jews—Europe's "blacks"—to its needs.

Halfway through the museum, the theater there played the documentary history of Dachau. People waiting for the next show began crowding around the entrance. When the doors opened, the mob surged forward and I became separated from Donna. Caught in the rush, I imagined passing through the gates of a concentration camp—disheveled, unwashed, hungry, confused, afraid. The other prisoners jostled me, and as we shuffled along, the distance between Donna and me grew and so did my sense of panic. Had it been Auschwitz, we would have been separated right there and then, the men one way, the women another. Those able to work became slave laborers. The sick, the elderly, the pregnant, the children, and the disabled went straight to the gas chamber.

I found Donna, and we sat near the front. The lights went out. Then in even tones the film's narrator recounted Dachau's history. His flat, unemotional voice was enough; anything else would have been too much. Emerging from the dark theater, people looked dazed.

We entered the second part of the exhibit. It documented what camp life was like: the slave labor, the medical experiments, the executions, the exportation of Jews as part of the final solution. I lost interest in the documents; I couldn't even focus on them. Every picture seemed worse than the last—first starving laborers, then executions and then bodies and more bodies, mountains of bodies. I fled. When Donna came looking for me, I asked to return to Munich and we headed across the roll-call ground again. Near the exit stood a barrack. We went in. Again I was reminded of Mauthausen. There were rows of wooden beds, stacked three high, and I imagined the prisoners packed next to each other. Then I saw the slaves.

The floor seemed to heave beneath me. I was at sea on a slave galley filled with African men and women lying below deck on rough wooden planks, not overnight but for weeks and weeks, unable to roll over, unable to sit up, lying in filth, shoulder to shoulder with the dead, stowed like cargo. Millions died, and my ancestors had a hand in it.

The Jews arrived by cattle car, we aboard ship. Those Jews not chosen for slave labor died; those of us who did not die were enslaved. Enslavement rather than extermination, "a place in hell" actor Ossie Davis once said when comparing the fate of the African to the Jew, "but nonetheless a place." The German Nuremberg Laws of 1935 banning intermarriage and disenfranching the Jews echoed America's Jim Crow Laws of the 1890s—draconian racial laws used by Germany and the South, two conquered peoples, to aggrandize themselves, control those they despised, and wring a perverse victory from defeat. Dark skin made yellow stars unnecessary; Negroes sat at the back of the bus, while Jews were completely banned from public transportation. Lynchings were quasi-public events that had a rally-like atmosphere, whereas gas chambers were an efficiently run secret operation aimed not at intimidation but elimination. The end result: Millions of Africans and Jews died, leaving their descendents a legacy of hyper-vigilance that crowds every moment and taints every outsider.

I rested my hand on a table to steady myself, signed my name in the guest registry, and hurried out into the sunlight. By the time I collapsed into the passenger seat of our car, I was gasping for breath. My head throbbed and my jaw ached. The magnitude of such inhumanity overwhelmed my already battered faith in humankind. Hope was slipping away, and I couldn't stop crying. As Donna drove us back toward Munich, tears of anger joined my tears of grief. "Why?" I stammered. "Why?"

No explanation can make the inhumanity of the Holocaust comprehensible, nor can moral resolve, vacillating as it does, provide a basis for hope. Rather, the anguish I felt after our visit to Dachau was soon swept away by the regimen and frenzy of Ecole life, the fun and exhaustion of traveling with Charlotte and Elliot, and our busyness after we returned to Rochester. I simply couldn't deal with it, and didn't.

Only years later, while reading Viktor Frankl's account of his concentration camp experience in the book *Man's Search for Meaning*, did I find part of the answer I sought. Frankl writes:

> [A] very trifling thing can cause the greatest of joys. Take as an example something that happened on our journey from Auschwitz to Dachau. We had all been afraid that our transport was heading for the Mauthausen camp. We became more and more tense as we approached a certain bridge over the Danube which the train would have to cross to reach Mauthausen. Those who have never seen anything similar cannot possibly imagine the dance of joy performed in the carriage by the prisoners when they saw that our transport was not crossing the bridge and was instead heading "only for Dachau."

This passage, which tied together my visits to Dachau and Mauthausen, laid bare the power of hope. At long last, I saw that hope is embedded in the nature of life itself, able to penetrate any moment and make it gracious. Indeed, life would be unbearable if hope did not exist, for sometimes it is all we have.

I'm no longer sure exactly how we became stuck on the face of a cliff, but there we were on a narrow trail looking down a 380-meter drop. I do remember that we went hiking to escape the Ecole. Our Sunday morning hikes helped us get away from the bedlam. Being responsible for fifteen adolescents was a never-ending soap opera. They would pop in and out of our apartment, the door slamming, middle of the night calls to and from California, tears over ended romances, earnest consultations after one was caught out after curfew, and the fretting of our resident hypochondriac.

Our escape from it all brought us to this cliff face, but it wasn't the first time we found ourselves stuck like this. Acrophobic Donna—she had once leapt out of a moving chairlift from eight feet in the air—had a tendency to find herself perched on uncomfortable ledges. Never a tepid spirit, she would commit herself to an idea and charge ahead and I, cautious but never a conformist, would follow. As a result, we led a fairly unconventional life and often found ourselves looking down from the path we had taken, wondering how the hell to manage the rest of the journey.

Similarly, there is no turning back from integration, for it pervades our history, courses through our veins, and is embodied in our culture. Moreover, America's interracial drama is no longer enacted primarily between Afro- and Euro-Americans. Native Americans remind us that it never was, and given America's evolving racial demographic, the black/white divide is becoming increasingly irrelevant as the beige-ing of America accelerates. This blending, as the descendants of the oppressor and the oppressed become one and the same, blurs the color line. New immigrants, with no connection to slavery or Jim Crow, do not even experience it as their past; therefore, the future must head in a different direction. A generation or two from now, Euro-Americans will be stripped of their majority status as interracial marriages increase and the size and influence of the Latino and Asian communities continues to expand. This transformation should not surprise us, for integration has been going on for four hundred years, and the cultural amalgam that is America has proven anything but static. Today it presses forward, as it always has, in unforeseeable directions, uniting and combining and making use of every people and culture available to it. The question we, as a nation, must face is whether to resist or celebrate the inevitable.

As a child, I imagined such a blended world when I came to believe that God—some mixture we couldn't imagine—looked the way all people would look someday. My mother-in-law had a similar intuition; she saw a world in which all people were the same shade of tan and believed that was how universal love would be achieved. She gave up that belief as naïve. But I believe that our childhood intuitions were correct. Children think concretely and would naturally be drawn to color as the answer—it was the best we could do to describe the mysterious, divine unity behind our differences that binds us all together in this experience we share. We call that oneness God—a God who, as a blend of our distinct identities, is capable of giving the all-embracing love my mother-in-law had hoped for.

For Donna and me, stuck at the top of a narrow trail, wondering how we would make it wasn't just a metaphoric problem. It was already mid-afternoon and too late to turn back. Petrified, Donna simply plopped down and refused to budge. She wouldn't even open her eyes. Incapable of worrying about the kids, she, instead, jabbered about Rochester. Donna, who doesn't chatter, chattered, and any topic would have done as long as it kept her mind off the empty space between her and the valley below. Eventually I coaxed her into grabbing hold of my backpack. Then as she stared at my feet we inched our way down. Meanwhile, Charlotte and Elliot traipsed along ahead like little billy goats. Seeing them prancing along took my breath away, but with Donna behind I was in no position to say anything to them. I inhaled and brought my attention back to the trail.

When we reached the bottom, Donna and I collapsed, exhausted, against a chalet-sized boulder. In an instant, Charlotte and Elliot disappeared, and before I could muster the strength to investigate, we heard them. Towering above us atop that huge rock, they were shouting "Look at me! Look at me!" And in their excitement, I heard the future.

On another Sunday, two weeks later, I took a stroll alone and passed the bunkhouse where my college buddy, Art Perkins, had lived. I continued up the road as it arced around a large farmhouse and field where I had helped harvest hay two decades earlier. A trail branched off to the left side in the middle of that arc. Unless you knew it was there, it would be easy to miss. The seldom used, almost tunnel-like path through the woods led past a large rock next to a small garden and a red bench that faced the Wetterhorn. Chiseled into the rock I saw the names Paul Geheeb 1870–1961 and Edith Geheeb 1885–1982. I stopped. The last time I had stood on that spot only Paulus's name was there and Edith was still alive. Her last note to me was dated May 1, 1981:

> My dear Mark:
>
> I am happy that you and yours are living such a meaningful life, and I hope that the future continues to look bright for you. I am doing well, although I spent nine weeks in the hospital after an accident. But now I am back at our beloved school again and hope that my 95 years don't prevent me from accomplishing something good here.
>
> All my love to you.

And she signed in a shaky scribble: *Eure alte Edith* (Your old Edith).

I reached out, stroked the rock's rough crown and felt its coolness, then turned, and sat down on the bench. I breathed in. I have had to learn not to rush but to wait, not to fill my head with chatter but to hold myself open to life's messages.

Sitting there, I looked across an unmowed green meadow speckled with yellow, white, and lavender wildflowers, beyond the pasture woods and, above it all, the serene Wetterhorn. As it had once before, Edith's visage appeared to me. There upon the dark, sheer side of the mountain, I saw her round face with a thousand wrinkles, kind eyes, and short white hair. Then her face dissolved, and before me was my white-haired great-aunt Irene, saying "Oh, my precious child," as she squeezed me to her bosom. In my nose I felt a burning sensation, and a tear formed. Then she too faded and I saw my mother with her brave smile and anxious eyes. And when she too vanished, I felt motherless and bereft and alone. I cupped my head in my hands, shutting out the world. In that darkness, my mind filled with the music of a spiritual: "Sometimes I feel like a motherless child. Sometimes I feel like a motherless child. Sometimes I feel like a motherless child, a long way from home, a long way from home." My body convulsed, and I wept like a child. My chest heaved, lips quivered and nose ran, as "I want my mommy" echoed in my head, and the arms that held me tight were my own.

The more open I have become and more deeply I have felt, the more I have cried. I didn't know what I was seeking that sunlit day when I walked up the road and along the gravel incline toward the memorial. What I found was yearning and grief, and then something else.

One moment tears streamed down my face and in the next I felt at peace—a peace found in being at one with myself. Not timid or fragmented or enraged, not even wounded—just me, right there, right then, in a moment when silence healed rather than hid brokenness. Nor did being at one with myself end with myself; the connections ran deeper. Old Edith, Great-aunt Irene, and my mama were within me and had done as well as they could to teach me what I needed to know: to be true to myself by loving myself as I am, simply because I am. I settled into the silence, breathed deeply, and took in that timeless moment—the vista, the mountain, the sunlight, the beating of my heart, and my own goodness.

I felt whole as I walked down the path and continued up the road to the hotel. It was still early in the day. I stepped in and seeing James's brother-in-law, Peter, I said, "Business looks slow."

"You're crazy," he said. "We've already got too many reservations for dinner. It's Mother's Day and we won't sit down until it's over."

Mother's Day caught me by surprise. Sequestered upon the Hasliberg, I hadn't thought about it for a moment. Yet I must have known. Thinking of Donna, it came to me that I had better get Charlotte and Elliot organized. "See ya later, man," I said and popped out the door. As I headed down the road I felt like skipping. Hardly remembering how, I tried anyway. At first I lopped along, awkwardly scuffing the bottom of my shoes on the asphalt, but then my body seemed to catch the rhythm and my arms swung and my feet bounced and a grin spread across my face.

Epilogue

Dear lovely Death
That taketh all things under wing—
Never to kill—
Only to change
Into some other thing
This suffering flesh,
To make it either more or less,
But not again the same—
Dear lovely Death,
Change is thy other name.

—Langston Hughes,
"Dear Lovely Death"

The substratum of my life is as enduring as the Wetterhorn; the winds of change, however, never cease. In 1989, a year and a half after we returned from Switzerland, Donna and I were called to be the ministers of the First Unitarian Congregation of Toronto, and in 1995, I became a Canadian citizen. My appointment to appear in Citizenship Court was scheduled to take place three days after Quebec's second referendum on separation from the rest of Canada, and I was anxious about the vote's outcome. On November 2, Donna, our kids, and her parents accompanied me to court. Together with immigrants from thirty-four different countries

I rose, and we—a wonderful, colorful jumble of humanity—
mangled "O Canada" with our cacophony. I felt two things that
day: the desire to be Canadian, which bound us together, and a
sense of being a citizen of the world. As usual, I choked up until
I was suddenly brought back to earth and hard political reality.
"It was people like you," the citizenship judge said, wagging his
finger at us, "who kept Quebec in Canada, and if you ever have the
chance, I'm sure you'll know how to vote." I winced at the admonition. It was partisan and tacky and reminded me that immediately
after the vote was announced, Jacques Parizeau, the premier of
Quebec, had blamed the referendum's defeat on "the ethnic vote."

Living in the Great White North is no escape, and with global
warming, balmy winters may well come to the town of Moose Factory before racism ends in Canada or anywhere else in the world. It's
a distinctly Canadian brand of bigotry, but ultimately only a different flavor than I had known in the United States and Switzerland.

Much has changed. My father, a recipient of the National Aero-
nautics and Space Administration (NASA) Exceptional Scientific
Achievement Award in 1978 and the NASA Group Achievement
Award in 1984, retired from Argonne National Laboratory in 1989
and focused his research skills on genealogy.

Philip lives in Ventura, California. He is the president and
owner of Pacific SEATEC, a company that trains and accredits
those who work in the California offshore oil industry; for this
the U.S. Mineral Management Services recognized him with its
Corporate Leadership Award in 2003. As feisty as ever, he is also a
community activist who has served as chair of the Revitalization
Committee for the Ventura Westside Community Council.

My youngest sister, Lauren, is a senior academic preceptor at
UC Santa Cruz, and her son, Jordan, who is half Jamaican, graduated from UC Berkeley in 2006 with a BA in physical geography.
He also speaks fluent Spanish and a smidgen of Farsi and is asking
a question I have asked many times: What next?

But the most wrenching change of all took place in 1998 when a brain tumor claimed the life of our sister Carole. She had been a vice president at Industrial Indemnity Financial Services and Resolution Credit Services, a Xerox affiliate. She is survived by her husband, Stan Sullivan, and their daughter, Michelle, who was just three when her mother died.

Nineteen ninety-five, the year I became a Canadian, was also the year I began my term as president of the Family Service Association of Metropolitan Toronto. The largest such organization in Canada, it serves people in more than twenty-four languages. There, and subsequently on the Canadian Unitarian Council, I was the first Afro-Canadian president.

Considering my family's achievements, I can't help but notice that while each of us, including my mother, succeeded in a different field—science, industry, education, finance, religion, and social work—all of us did so in overwhelmingly Eurocentric environments. Like our ancestors, we have been actors in the American interracial drama. And in these roles each of us not only endured, but tried to make a difference, and in doing so we thrived.

Our children are adults now. The morning after our son's birth in 1982, while Donna slept, I took him to the attic, stood on a chair, and hoisted him above my head, just as I imagine my great-uncle Lloyd did when he whisked my infant father away. Elliot still flashes a cute smile but he is now six-four and a second-degree black belt in Tae Kwon Do. A 2005 graduate of the University of Toronto, he then earned an MA in mechanical engineering from the University of Michigan before joining Bosch GmbH as an associate engineer. His achievements, I suspect, have more to do with high expectations and hard work than the rite I performed, but then again, as Great-uncle Lloyd said, "It worked."

Charlotte, our daughter, who has spent her entire life with a book in her face, now holds a master of publishing degree from Simon Fraser University and, as an editor for Pearson Education Canada, gets paid for her obsession. For her twenty-fifth birthday, eleven of us gathered at a Japanese restaurant in the Greektown neighborhood of Toronto. The last to arrive, I removed my shoes, stepped into the Tatami Room and squatted down next to Donna. Clearly familiar with Japanese cuisine, the kids were arguing over what to order. That done, the conversation turned to the trip three of them were taking to Ecuador and Peru. I looked around at her friends. Besides Donna and Charlotte, there were three other women, all Chinese-Canadian. One was Taiwanese, and another's family hailed from Newfoundland, settling there prior to 1949, the year Newfoundland became part of Canada. Elliot was at the opposite end of the table from me, and so was Chris, my daughter's longtime partner, and another Anglo-Canadian guy. Brian and Shazam were there as well; they looked like their families might have come from the Indian subcontinent, but I couldn't tell where.

Somehow we got onto the topic of having "ashy" skin and our mothers' remedies for it, something the white guys had never heard of and did not have a clue what to do about. We were incredulous. How could it be that we all knew and they didn't? Around and around we went until we came up with an answer: being "white" already, they thought looking like a ghost was normal. Afterward when I asked Charlotte where they came from, she had to think for a moment and wasn't 100 percent sure. Brian was Sri Lankan and Shazam was, maybe, Guyanese. The way she exhaled "Dad" before answering made me want to apologize. You see, I heard what she didn't say: Why are you even asking? It just isn't important.

My children's generation innately navigates the borderlands between races and cultures with an ease I can only hope to know. It is for this I have labored, and still do.

Mark Morrison-Reed
February 2008
Toronto, Ontario

Notes

Slavery Served Us Well

2   *my father's matrilineal ancestors,* In 2004 my father submitted his DNA for a "MatricalnTM Test"; the test traces mitochondrial DNA through the maternal side, and this analysis tied him to the Mende of Sierra Leone.

3   *Old Dick, Old Bess, Old Tom, Old Nelly (Dick's wife), and Johnny,* While African blood flowed through Elizabeth's veins, as one of the wealthiest women in South Carolina, she was listed as a "free white female" head of household in both the Census of 1790 and 1800—a household that included twenty-six and twenty-eight slaves respectively. However, because the Will of Elizabeth Clevland Hardcastle was contested in a drawn out court case and Catherine Clevland did not take possession of Raccoon Hill Plantation until 1825 it is doubtful that she ever received the five slaves. E. Louise gives more details about the Clevland family, a full account of the life of Elizabeth Clevland Hardcastle, and of the legal battle fought over her Last Will and Testament in *Elizabeth Clevland Hardcastle 1741–1808: A Lady of Color in South Carolina Low Country* (Columbia, SC: Phoenix Publishers, 2001).

6   *left for the North at the age of nineteen,* Henry J. Maxwell first went to New York, then Boston, then Portland, Maine, before heading west to Michigan, where he worked to secure the right of the states' Afro-American citizens to vote. Afterwards, bitten by the gold bug, he journeyed to Pike's Peak, prospected, and eventually returned with only twelve cents in his pocket.

9   *Bucknell University Junior College,* In 1947 Bucknell University Junior College, where my Mother attended, chartered as Wilkes College. In 1985 her alma mater bestowed upon her the Eugene S. Farley Memorial Alumni Award.

The Educational Imperative

11   *defending Virginia and the Southern way of life,* Civil War hostilities broke out on April 12, 1861, when the South attacked Fort Sumter in South Carolina. Six weeks later, on May 25, Joseph Rogers Gregory enlisted. His military record reported that he was a POW from February 13, 1863, until March 29, 1863, when he was exchanged, and that he was subsequently detailed on quartermaster duty from November 1, 1863, until discharged on June 1, 1864; it also listed him as illiterate.

Color Conscious

31   *Negroes supplanted working-class whites,* Community organizer Saul Alinsky once called a racially integrated community "a chronological term timed from the entrance of the first black family to the exit of the last white family."

35   *Known as the Chicago Children's Choir,* In 1955–56 Polly McCoo, the first Afro-American to join the First Unitarian Society of Chicago, led the junior choir that would evolve under the leadership of Chris Moore, a Unitarian Universalist minster, into the CCC.

Bon Voyage

40   *through the dating of meteorites,* Through the first accurate dating of meteorites using uranium and helium, Dad provided the earliest confirmation of Clair Patterson's analysis of primordial lead concentrations in terrestrial materials and meteorites. These had indicated that our system was formed 4.55 billion years ago.
      Patterson (1922–1995) was elected to the National Academy of Sciences in 1987 and in 1995 was awarded the Tyler Prize for

Environmental Achievement for his work in exposing the dangers of lead pollution. In *A Short History of Nearly Everything*, (Scarborough, ON: Doubleday Canada, 2003, pp.156–60), Bill Bryson, who clearly admires Patterson, describes this earnest man's achievements.

41   *scientists who had gone to Europe before him,* In 1929 Ernest Everett Just, the acclaimed biologist, had gone to the *Stazione Zoologica* in Naples, Italy, to do research. Over the next decade he would spend most of his time working at the Kaiser Wilhelm Institute in Berlin and later at the Sorbonne; that same year, chemist Percy Lavon Julian began work toward a PhD at the University of Vienna. And Lloyd Henry Newman MD, Dad's uncle, had preceded them all when during the mid-twenties he had done postdoctoral studies in biochemistry at the Sorbonne.

42   *they were completely integrated,* The U.S. Army would not be desegregated until 1948, after President Truman issued Executive Order 9981.

46   *laboring in obscurity,* Vincent O. Carter (1924–1983) was living in Bern before and after my family's 13-month sojourn there. We didn't know him, but I'm sure that if I saw him—and I must have—I rushed home to report the citing of another black person. I assume he must have seen me and I can't help but wonder what he thought of a black adolescent careening about Bern. His reflections on Bern, his life there as an Afro-American, and the vicissitudes of being a writer appear in *The Bern Book: A Record of a Voyage of the Mind* (New York: John Day Company, 1970).

Babes in Switzerland

54   *the first Negro woman to vote in Montross, Virginia,* The Nineteenth Amendment to the Constitution, extending suffrage to women, was ratified on August 18, 1920. Six weeks later, on October 2, Sarah Reed, who was a suffragette, traveled down to the county seat and registered.

58   *the English Speaking School whose quality is poor,* Housed in rented space, including a postage stamp-sized backyard, and

using donated equipment, the English Speaking School of Bern—known today as the International School of Bern—had just entered its second year of existence.

62   *The teachers at the Villa,* Founded in 1903 by a Marianist, the Villa St. Jean International School's most famous alumni include Antoine de Saint-Exupery, author of *The Little Prince,* and Juan Carlos I, the current King of Spain. The school closed in 1970.

67   *the unearned virtue of being white,* "Remember this: Your white skin proves that you are better than all other people on this earth . . . And does it simply because it is white" writes the Anglo-American southern writer and activist Lillian Smith (1897-1966) in *Killers of the Dream* (originally published in 1949; W.W. Norton & Co., 1994, p. 89), her controversial and penetrating exposé of the southern "white" psyche.

Ecole d'Humanité

78   *A dynamite bomb hurled,* This initial report was wrong. Members of the Ku Klux Klan had earlier planted dynamite in the church's basement. The bombing was one of forty-nine dating back to 1947 and there had been thirteen in 1963 alone. During this effort to intimidate Afro-Americans and white civil rights activists, not a single arrest had been made.

94   *a Swiss village as remote as Goldern,* Between 1951 and 1953, on three occasions James Baldwin (1924–1987) stayed in Leukerbad while using the vacation home of a friend. Known for its spa, the village is located in Upper Wallis. The essay "Stranger in the Village," an account of that experience, was first published in *Harper's* magazine in October 1953, and subsequently in Baldwin's *Notes of a Native Son* (New York: Bantam, 1964, p. 137).

The King Is Dead, Long Live the King

122   *or we shall all perish together,* This quotation may come from Camus or my mother may have been confused and the source

was really Martin Luther King Jr., who said, "We must learn to live together as brothers or perish together as fools."

129 *something about the Revolutionary Action Movement,* Ironically, even as we met, the leadership of the Revolutionary Action Movement (RAM) was in jail and the organization in disarray. I had never heard of RAM and didn't know—I doubt whether anyone present did—that RAM and other so-called "communist and black nationalist elements" were being investigated by the infamous House Un-American Activities Committee. Later, members of the Blackstone Rangers would testify that RAM had armed them in preparation for a "national uprising." Others would allege that RAM was involved in "a plot to assassinate all the non-violent civil rights leaders of the country."

I'd Leave Town if I Were You

168 *he'd given me this admonition,* I have come to believe that Dr. Thurman was not making an oblique reference to the demands of ministry but rather to the sacrifice required in choosing ministry. I articulate my understanding of the nature of this sacrifice in "After Running Through the Thistles the Hard Part Begins: the 180th Berry Street Essay." It was published in *Unitarian Universalism 2000: Selected Essays* (UUMA, 2001) and can be found online: www.uuma.org/berrystreet/Essays/BSE.htm.

172 *"a life which belongs to death",* D.H. Lawrence (1885–1930) writes, "There is a life which belongs to death, and there is a life which isn't death. One is tired of the life that belongs to death—our kind of life . . ." *Women in Love* (Cambridge, England: Cambridge University Press, 1987).

Growing Up

176 *Fill your heart with simple joy,* Aurobindo Bose (1893–1977), in addition to *Later Poems of Rabindranath Tagore* (New York: Funk & Wagnalls, 1974), also translated *A Flight of Swans* (London: John Murray, 1955), *The Herald of Spring* (London: John Mur-

ray, 1957), and *Wings of Death: The Last Poems of Rabindranath Tagore* (London: John Murray, 1960).

193   *get the plum pudding,* I found the plum pudding recipe in the back of one of Great-aunt Irene's diaries:

Mama's Recipe: Christmas Plum Pudding
¾ lb. of suet chopped very fine
Mix it while chopping in one tablespoon of flour
¾ lb. of raisins, seeded
¾ lb. of currants
¾ lb. of sugar
¾ lb. of fresh bread crumbs
Grated zest of one lemon
¼ lb. of candied orange peel and citron, cut into thin slices
½ teaspoon each of ground cinnamon, cloves, nutmeg, and allspice

Mix the dry material together thoroughly and then add six eggs one at a time and one half cup of brandy. Add another egg if too stiff and more crumbs if not soft. Wet a strong cloth in cold water, wring it dry, butter it and dredge it well with flour. Turn the mixture into the center and draw the cloth together over the top. Leave room for the pudding to swell a little and tie it firmly giving it a good round shape. Put it into pot of boiling water, having it completely covered. Do not let the water fall below the pudding and in adding more let it be hot so as not to arrest the boiling. Boil four to five hours. After it is removed from the water let it rest in the bag for ten minutes to harden a little, then cut the string and turn it carefully onto a dish. Pour rum or brandy on the dish and light it with a taper. Serve with a brandy sauce. Will serve twelve to fourteen people. It will keep for a long time and may be warmed when used.

The Call

198   *"Black Pioneers in a White Denomination",* Mark Morrison-Reed, *Black Pioneers in a White Denomination,* third edition (Boston: Skinner House, 1994).

Föhn Within

235 **pull the tribe's frenzy back from the edge,** Carl Gustav Jung (1875–1961) recounts this story in his memoir *Memories, Dreams, Reflections* (New York: Vintage Books, 1989, pp. 270–71).

236 **projected onto other people,** "The Negro, for instance, carries the projection of the white man's fear of the dark, spontaneous, instinctual side of himself . . ." Edward C. Whitmont, *The Symbolic Quest: Basic Concepts of Analytic Psychology* (Princeton, NJ: Princeton University Press, 1979, p. 273).

238 **what James Baldwin called a "living wonder",** "In all of this, in which it must be conceded there was certainly no element of intentional unkindness, there was yet no suggestion that I was human: I was simply a living wonder." James Baldwin, "Stranger in the Village," *Notes of a Native Son* (Bantam, 1964, p. 137).

239 **it was entitled "Notes on White Supremacy",** James Hillman, "Notes On White Supremacy: Essaying an Archetypal Account of Historical Events," *Spring* (1986): 29–58.

239 **Hillman's writing was dense,** Hillman begins "Our culture, by which I mean the imagination, beliefs, enactments, and values collectively and unconsciously shared by Northern Europeans and Americans, is white supremacist. . . . [T]he superiority of whiteness is affirmed by our major text and is fundamental to our linguistic roots . . ." This confirmed for me what up until then had been a suspicion—that the "superiority of whiteness" is embedded in the language and beliefs of western civilization: American, Canadian, or Swiss, it made no difference. First, he discusses it in terms of anthropology: "[O]ur concern is only with the placing of white in worldwide survey: that it comes first, is virtually universal, and that it is paired with black." He goes on to explore the "three meanings of whiteness": The Indo-European root of white means "to be bright," and "the first of these [meanings] is the whiteness of heaven." "The second group of meanings connotes innocence." This particular point concurs with what Lillian Smith writes in *Killers of the Dream*: "[W]hiteness is a symbol of purity" and "a badge of Innocence" (p. 89). "The third conven-

tion locates white in the context of the (Jungian) anima. . . . [t]his convention equates white with female, soft, vulnerable beauty."

245   *to be both an American and a Negro,* W.E.B. Du Bois, *The Souls of Black Folk* (originally published 1903; New York: Fawcett Premier, 1961, p. 17).

247   *everything and anything except me,* Ralph Ellison, *Invisible Man* (first published 1947; New York: Vintage Books, 1972, p. 3).

251   *to be black in Hitler's Germany,* Hans J. Massaquoi, whose mother was German and father Liberian, wrote the memoir *Destined to Witness: Growing Up Black in Nazi Germany,* (New York: William Morrow, 1999). Massaquoi was the managing editor of *Ebony* magazine and also a member of the First Unitarian Society of Chicago, where my parents knew him.

253   *was instead heading "only for Dachau",* Victor Frankl, *Man's Search for Meaning: An Introduction to Logotherapy* (New York: Pocket Books, 1971, pp. 70–71).

254   *blurs the color line,* "The problem of the twentieth century is the problem of the color line," wrote W.E.B. Du Bois (*The Souls of Black Folk,* p. 23).

Acknowledgments

Although I didn't realize it, work on this memoir began in 1987. A flyer seeking stories by foreigners about living in Switzerland was passed along to me; did I have a story to tell. The collection when it appeared in 1988 was entitled *Ticking Along With the Swiss* and included a short story by me entitled "Föhn Within." Dianne Dicks was its editor and it was her encouragement that first set me on this path.

Between then and 2005 I led a hectic life as a parish minister. That meant the manuscript got my full attention for two months every summer and every September the effort came to an end except for the stories I tested out as sermons on the two congregations Donna and I served, the First Universalist Church of Rochester, NY, and the First Unitarian Congregation of Toronto. For their goodwill I am thankful.

Over such a span of years the number of people who have read or heard all or part of this manuscript, commented on, edited, contributed stories to, and/or cheered me on is long and includes: Sharon Airhart; Christine Alexiou; Erik Bendix; Dave Ferguson; Jim Chisholm; Jean Hamilton; Kristen Harper; K.C. Hill; Philipp Hostettler; Henry and Rhoda Isaacs; Nancy Kaspar; Stephen Maxwell; Brian Mayo; Karen McCall; Anke Moore McLean; Charlotte and Elliot Morrison-Reed; Katherine Morrison; Jeannie Mott; Julie Parker Amery; Bill Parsons; Art Perkins; Carole, George, and Philip Reed; Ron Rolett; Bruce Schwarzentruber; Leaf Seligman; Janice Tait; Thandeka; Katie Wolff; Larry Wulff; and Karen Yano. Special thanks is also due to Ann Montagnes, my writing teacher; to Mary McDougall Maude and Rosemary Shipton, structural editors who unscrambled it; to Vreni Naess who corrected my German, Swiss German, and Swiss history; to Mary Benard, the senior editor at Skinner House who, with patience and good humor, coaxed from me a manuscript of greater coherence and clarity; and to production editor Marshall Hawkins, who got it done.

The genealogical work and research done about the Naudin/Dibble/ Clevland family by Elsie Goins, about the Newmans by John Kelly Sr., and about the Reeds by my father was invaluable. The narrative details were mined from family correspondence including letters from my uncle

Lloyd H. Reed. They also came from taped interviews with my Great-aunt Irene Hawkins, and Great-uncle Lloyd Newman, as well as my father and my cousin Andrew Maxwell. I also used Great-aunt Irene's diaries, a short autobiography written by my grandmother Eleanor B. Reed, and interviews with my Great-uncles Joe and Harry Reed. Regarding the Reed family history, Darlene Tallent, the research historian at the Westmoreland County Museum and Northern Neck of Virginia Historical Society, was always helpful. Correspondence about my uncle Christopher Maxwell Edwards came courtesy of the Special Collections/University Archives, Ellen Clarke Bertrand Library, Bucknell University.

For background about the Geheebs I relied on Dennis Shirley's *The Politics of Progressive Education: The Odenwaldschule in Nazi Germany* (Harvard University Press, 1992) while background on the Hasliberg came from John Bendix's B.A. thesis: "The Shifting Mountains: Change and Constancy in an Alpine Valley, 1850–1970" (Amherst College, 1978).

I am grateful to my sister Lauren Reed for allowing me to use the materials she collected for her B.A. thesis: "American Studies Senior Thesis, Stepping Back In Time" (University of California, Santa Cruz, 1991). The chapter "The King Is Dead, Long Live the King" couldn't have been written without using the interviews she conducted and her own reflection on that traumatic time. Her research into how South Pacific Islanders arrived in the United States as crewmen was an important piece of the puzzle.

Donna, my wife, has lived with this manuscript as a messy, unreasonable child for twenty of the thirty years of our marriage. For her encouragement, wise counsel, endurance, and love throughout this quixotic project, I am thankful.

I have changed a few names. In a couple of instances, I blended elements from two stories into one and in several places the chronology is altered in the service of the narrative flow. This memoir was a feat of memory aided by my diaries, correspondence, and the reflections of others. The mistakes in all cases are my own.